# THEY SHALL NOT PASS
*The Autobiography of La Pasionaria*

**DOLORES IBARRURI**

# *They Shall Not Pass*

## THE AUTOBIOGRAPHY OF

## LA PASIONARIA

**INTERNATIONAL PUBLISHERS**

Translated from Dolores Ibarruri, *El único camino*

Copyright © by INTERNATIONAL PUBLISHERS CO., INC., 1966

First Edition

Library of Congress Catalog Card Number: 66–25065
Manufactured in the United States of America

# Author's Preface

On the occasion of the publication of this book in English, I send my warmest and deepest fraternal greetings of friendship to the democratic movements of the English-speaking world, especially the heroic fighters of the Abraham Lincoln, British, and MacKenzie-Papineau Battalions, who volunteered to defend Spanish democracy in the arduous years of 1936 to 1939.

When I was writing this book I did not have in mind merely to publish some brief memoirs, which I considered secondary. I wished, rather, to offer written testimony to the traditions of struggle of the Spanish people, and to set forth the truth about our war in answer to the lies of reactionary propaganda of yesterday and today.

Above all and very especially I wished to show the unwavering heroism of the Republican fighters; the abnegation, grandeur and spirit of sacrifice of the fighters of the International Brigades of which you were a part, my dear esteemed friends, you in whom our people saw the fraternal representatives of peoples so far from Spain yet so near in our affection and in our hearts.

Days and years have passed. The old hatreds have abated, and time has closed the wounds which the war opened in the bodies and consciences of millions of men.

New generations now step into the arena of struggle. And there are those who, not having been in war or lived through war, raise anew the banner of democracy, of liberty and justice, for which the most heroic fighters of our war of liberation gave their blood and their lives.

And when again, in the streets of our cities, young people devote themselves to the future democracy of our country, proclaim their desire to make Spain a free country open to progress, in which civil liberties for all Spaniards and freedom of action of all political groups will be possible, we think that our struggle was not in vain. After the long fascist night, the dawn of a new day now rises over Spain. The fruits of the sacrifice of our people are beginning to mature—fruits whose seed was watered by the tears of our women, with the blood of our best men, with the sweat of all who fought for a Spain of peace, liberty and democracy.

Thanks friends of North America, Great Britain and the Commonwealth nations for your struggle of yesterday, and for your constant friendship for the Spanish people!

*June 1966.*                                 DOLORES IBARRURI

# Contents

# PART ONE

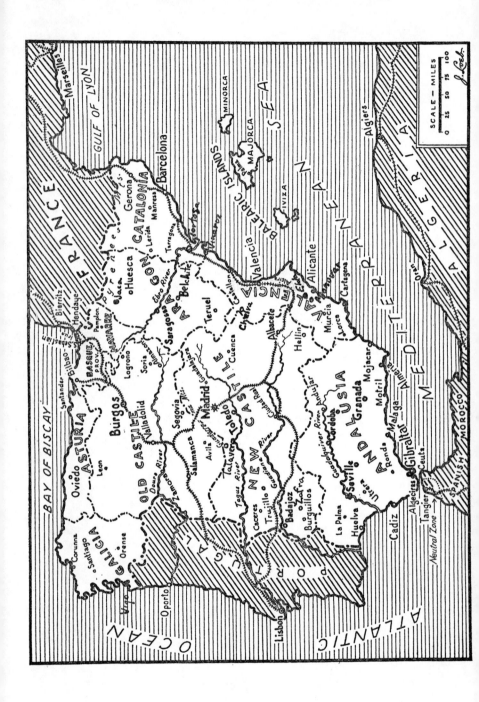

# 1

# In the Beginning There Was Mineral . . .

> *Whenever I go to you to find myself,*
> *Bilbao, scene of my childhood, beloved cor-*
> *ner where I first anxiously tried my wings,*
> *my early years rise to the surface of my soul*
> *and prophetically sing to me with memories*
> *charged with hope and consolation.*
>
> —MIGUEL DE UNAMUNO

Of the three provinces which constitute what is today called Euzcadi and was formerly known as Euzkalerría, Vizcaya is the most famous. This province is so well known that it has given its name to the entire Basque Country.

Vizcaya, it must be admitted, does not have those things which give tone and character to other regions of Spain. It has no mosques, no Gothic cathedrals, no Roman aqueducts or walls, no barren plains such as those which maddened Don Quixote.

Vizcaya's fame is derived from its people, whose date of origin and genealogy is unknown. And from its men, hard-working and long-suffering, forged in a permanent struggle with the hard earth, so hard that it could not be cultivated with the wooden plowshare, but only with the iron spade; and in the struggle with the untamed, stormy sea, whose damp breath covers the mountains and valleys of the ancient Basque Country with rain and mist.

When Greeks and Romans were writing history and Spain was a Roman province, the fame of the Basques reached to the limits of the known world, along with myths and legends concerning their character and customs and the wealth which lay hidden in their mountains.

The interest of historians was particularly aroused by tales of a fantastic mountain composed entirely of iron, and whose steep slopes sank into the storm-lashed Bay of Biscay. And the legends of the iron mountain were not simply products of the imagination. An extremely rich deposit of iron ore extended, almost without interrup-

11

tion and practically on the surface of the earth, from the province of Santander to the west of Bilbao, more than 20 miles, giving the mountains through which it passed their own characteristic color. For centuries only a very small part of that immense mineral wealth was tapped. It was only toward the middle of the last century, when the Industrial Revolution had already occurred in several European countries, that blast furnaces and great steel mills replaced the rudimentary ironworks, thus making the Basque Country the center of Spanish heavy industry.

The richness of Basque minerals was extraordinary. While the best foreign ores had a metallic yield of 48 per cent, the ores of Vizcaya reached a yield of 56 per cent and more of iron. Appreciating the importance of the Basque ore for the national economy, a famous Spanish playwright of the 16th century, Tirso de Molina, wrote: "Thanks to Vizcaya's iron / Spain can conserve her gold . . ." Unfortunately, this was an optimistic assumption on the part of the poet. The indolence and ineptitude of the Spanish ruling classes had placed in foreign hands not only what was left of the gold in the almost exhausted coffers of the Spanish state but also the iron which could have saved the Spanish treasury.

The ruling classes, lacking concern for the national welfare and satisfied with the crumbs they received from foreign exploiters of Spanish mineral wealth, turned over to these interests the abundant copper, lead, zinc, tin, silver and mercury existing in the Spanish soil and subsoil. Thus Spain was deprived of the resources which constituted the basis for her industrial development and economic and political independence.

No great obstacles were encountered by irresponsible rulers when they virtually gave away the copper of Río Tinto, the mercury of Almadén, the lead of Linares or the zinc of Santander. But the iron ore of the Basque Country had been protected up to a certain point by the existence of local laws and customs which were recognized and respected even before the formation of the Spanish state. The disputes about the succession to the throne after the death of Fernando VII in 1833, the alleged cause of the first Carlist War,*

* First Carlist War, 1834–39, between the conservative Church and northern regionalists on the one hand, and the liberal Army on the other. The latter was victorious in this partly religious, partly successionist conflict.—Ed.

were skillfully used by those who behind the scenes were inciting
the two sides to fight in order to gain for themselves access to the
mineral deposits in the north of Spain.

Using as a pretext the fact that the Basque Country supported the
Carlists during the war, the Madrid government arbitrarily and un-
justly revoked the centuries-old Basque privileges.

This was a crude political maneuver to cover the plans which had
been hatched in foreign chancellories by those interested in exploiting the mineral wealth of the Basque Country. While it is true that
the Basque villages, deluded by the Church and the most tradition-
bound, reactionary groups in the region, saw in the Carlists the defenders of their religion and their privileges, it is no less true that
the cities, nerve centers of the commercial, economic and political
life of the country, remained on the side of the government.

What the people lost in national liberties the native and foreign
bourgeosie gained in exceptional opportunities for enrichment. For
here, as everywhere, capitalism advanced by destroying without hesitation what the people held most sacred: Freedom, independence,
national customs and traditions, social and family relationships.

Under the protection of the royal laws and under the impetus of
the forces that manipulated the strings of Spanish politics at that
period, the exploitation of the mineral wealth of the Basque Country
was begun on a large scale. Individual exploitation of the deposits
to which all native Basques previously had the right was ended.
Conditions and laws came into being which regulated mining for
the benefit of a few. The regular supply of ore for the old ironworks
came to an end. The English, French and Belgian blast furnaces required tens of millions of tons of Basque ore and they got it free.
The traditional privileges which might possibly have slowed down
the plundering of our national resources, utilizing them more rationally, were no longer in effect. But because of the resistance of
the Basques, who clung desperately to a past which would never
return, the complete and open exploitation of the mines of Vizcaya
really got under way only after the revolution of 1868* or perhaps

* Following 30 years of coups and counter-coups with alternating liberal
and conservative generals, Queen Isabella II herself was expelled by the
liberal General Prim. When her successor Amedeo I abdicated after a
year, the first Spanish Republic was proclaimed.—Ed.

even later, when the last illusions of the traditionalists crumbled under the thunder of the cannons defending Bilbao in the fourth and last civil war of the 19th century.

When peace came after the Carlist defeat, the bitterness of the fratricidal struggle was revealed in the bloody devastation of Viscaya's countryside. Long, broken lines of earth marked the trenches of the opposing armies and now served as a common tomb for the thousands of soldiers of both sides—irreconcilable adversaries in battle, now united in death.

In the towns and villages women clad in black took over the management of their homes to replace their dead husbands. Families forever deprived of the love and support of those who had fallen in the war, could not understand why it was that their sons, husbands, brothers and fathers had been sacrificed in an absurd and criminal conflict, which had sown in every town and village, and at times in the same family, the seeds of hatred and vengeance.

The tears for the fallen had not yet dried, prayers were still being said and candles burned "for those who are no longer with us," when the valleys and mountains of the Basques rang with the voices of foreigners, and it became easier to grasp the reason for the scourge which the war had visited on thousands of families.

Strangers to the country were avidly examining the mountains and hills, fields and pastures, rises and ravines, their hobnailed boots walking over the freshly covered graves. They measured and marked the land as if it were their own. They surveyed, made maps, drove in stakes, stacked stones as boundary markers and spoke an outlandish jargon that no one could understand: "Incorporated companies, ownership, concessions, forced expropriations, importing capital, cheap labor, exporting ore, industrialization."

Public law was changing because property relationships were changing. Yesterday, this plot of land was held communally, that plot belonged to a family, and the one over there to another family. Today, everything was strange.

The shepherds could no longer graze their flocks on communal land nor could the people cut firewood in the municipal forests. It was forbidden. The road home was no longer a road; it fell within a concession and was shut off by barbed wire. The land, which still bore the marks of their grandparents' and their parents' labor, was placed in litigation by the new owners. A law had been passed that legitimized the rights of the outsiders and deprived the people of rights which had been established and maintained for centuries by usage and custom.

Strange names appeared on signposts. Here, Luchana Mining; there, the Orconera mine; farther on, the Franco-Belgian, Rothschild and Galdames mines; in Posadero and Covarón, the MacLennan and other smaller mines.

The heavy oxcarts which carried the ore from the veins to the old ironworks and to the barges in the Galindo and Somorrostro rivers were being displaced by mining railways that joined the most remote corners of the mining region to the ports and to the steel manufacturing zone, which was experiencing a parallel development.

The geography of the country was transformed. Mountains disappeared, slopes were destroyed, fields and meadows were covered with rubbish. The hills were leveled off to the valleys and the bottoms of ravines were elevated.

Inclined planes were constructed, trenches were opened, bridges built. The ore cars on their high wooden trestles passed over workers' huts, over chestnut and oak trees.

The explosions of dynamite, the screeching of cable and railway cars, the panting of locomotives and the incessant ringing of picks and drills broke the silence of the valleys, and a new life filled with new desires, worries and alarms seethed where once there were peaceful mountains and placid villages.

Around the village there sprang up a working-class neighborhood —squalid, jammed, depersonalized.

The remote village sleeping in the peace of the countryside had been rudely awakened, and it grew rapidly into an industrial or commercial center.

The zortzicos and other Basque songs that sang nostalgically of wars, legendary heroes and freedom were no longer heard. The Echecojuana no longer appeared, as in the song of Altabiscar, at the door of the ancestral home, to summon the Basques with his war horn to defend their land against foreigners. Now the foreigners were invited into Basque homes, and seated around the massive oak tables next to the fireplaces, while they ate roasted codfish and drank sweet cider or sour chacoli. Chestnuts roasted in the embers, while they argued with their hosts about the payment of concessions, the price of mining stocks and the market quotations on railway and shipping company stocks.

# 2

# Proletariat

Vizcaya was being industrialized at a feverish rate. Along with the intensive exploitation of the mines, great factories, blast furnaces, dry docks for shipbuilding and mills of all kinds were rising up from Portugalete to Sorossa, from Lamiaco to Deusto.

The Nervión River was enclosed in a channel of stone and steel. And ships of all nationalities came up the rivers in search of ore, lifting a forest of multicolored flags in the rains and mist of gray Bilbao.

Life began to flow through new channels. Peace triumphed over war, and with peace, came industry and commerce. Immense productive forces were released. Vizcaya became a magnet for men and capital.

The hatreds of the old factions, which had bloodied the country repeatedly, were diminished. A fever of production and enrichment interposed a barrier between the recent past and the future in process of being born. This was the modern age of business transactions, commerce, industrialization, and the wage labor of thousands of workers subjected to the most inhuman exploitation.

A heterogeneous working population, which had arrived from the farming regions and from the slums of the large cities, crowded into the filthy shanties erected near the mines by mining companies, or into the rooms of mining families who had taken up permanent residence.

The mines were worked in a simple, cheap fashion. There was hardly any need to remove refuse. Neither deep shafts nor expensive galleries were needed. The mineral was right there, on the surface of the earth, everywhere showing the pale or purplish tints that give the mining zone its characteristic range of color.

The exploitation of the mines was characterized not only by the greedy way in which the country was plundered of its principal wealth but also by the brutal treatment of the men who worked in them. The miners worked from dawn to dark with no set hours. They left home before it was light and did not return until well after nightfall. The bunkhouses that the mining companies offered as shelter to those who came from other regions resembled the lairs of wild beasts rather than human dwellings.

At night, when the miners went to bed, the interior of their bunkhouses looked like a scene from Dante. The air was filled with the smoke of the harsh tobacco they smoked and illuminated by the flickering light of an oil lamp hung in the center of the room. The blurred figures of half-naked men could be seen moving among the cots or seated on their bedrolls in a foul atmosphere compounded of sweat, fermented food, and the odors of the latrine, which was located in a small compartment opening onto the main room in each shack.

The men slept on sacks stuffed with cornshucks placed on top of narrow wooden benches. They covered themselves with their own *tapabocas*, a kind of coarse wool blanket which they wore to protect themselves from the cold and the rain, and which, except in the summer, were almost always damp or wet.

The miner's clothes, soaked with sweat and mud, were hung from a nail at the head of his bed in the cheerful company of sardines, herring and codfish, pieces of rancid bacon and jerked beef—not to speak of strings of garlic, onions and peppers—each contributing its own peculiar odor and flavor.

If one of the men contracted smallpox or typhus, endemic diseases of the period for which the bunkhouses were permanent sources of infection, he was removed from his cot and taken to a hut where the sick were housed. If he died, his bunk was sprinkled with lime water, and his cot was immediately occupied by someone else. The temporary laborers, most of whom were of peasant origin, were, because of the unhygienic conditions, carriers of mortal illnesses and epidemics which spread without control from Vizcaya to Castile and from Castile to Vizcaya.

In those human beehives, peopled by men from every region of Spain, language, customs, beliefs and superstitions were amalgamated, melted down and remolded in the crucible of their common life. Working and suffering together, they evolved a system of ideas and ethics of their own in which religious faith was intermingled and confused with blind confidence in the practices of witchcraft. They feared witches, ghosts and apparitions, and trusted in the power of the Gospel or of Saint Peter Zariquete, patron saint of sorcery, against the evil eye. They believed in the miraculous powers of the rope belts of Saint Blase or Saint Anthony or in laurel blessed on Palm Sunday to cure the illnesses of men or cattle, to drive away thunderstorms and to protect their homes or flocks from lightning.

But under the hard shell of religion and heresy, of ignorance and superstition, which led to docile submission and fatalistic resignation, there still lived in the souls of those men, like a live coal under the ashes, a fierce feeling of human dignity and rebelliousness which nothing could extinguish. At times, when unbearable injustices or suffering overflowed the dikes of respect and resignation, the embers burst forth into an uncontrolled blaze.

Because of the conditions under which the mines were worked, cave-ins were frequent, and there were numerous fatal accidents that claimed dozens of victims. One such disaster occurred in the San Miguel mine in the 80's, where what the miners called "the hat" fell in and buried a large group of workers who, aware of the risk, had been forced to work under the threatening cornice. And there they remained.

The mine owners felt, and the authorities agreed with them, that it would involve useless expense and effort to remove the miners from that tomb. "After all," they said, "what difference does it make if they're buried here or in the cemetery!"

Miners were paid at the end of the month and were forced to buy their food and clothes in special stores owned by the mine owners or by high company officials. And many, many times when, after four long weeks of unending work, sweat and privation, they approached the pay window to receive their wages, they found there was nothing to collect. Their expenses, according to the accounts kept by the manager of the company store, were in excess of the wages for a month of backbreaking labor. And there was no way out. The debt, inflated and sometimes invented to cover the thefts of the clerks or manager of the store, tied them to the mine. The mine owners exchanged lists of debtors as well as blacklists of the more rebellious workers. When a worker was in debt to the owner or manager of a mine, he was not admitted into another until the debt had been paid. It did no good to protest. The law was on the side of the boss, and with the law came the rifles of the Civil Guards and the jails and kennels in the towns, or the knives and clubs of the mine managers' goon squads.

The owners of the mines, despite the burden of their weighty business affairs, did not neglect the spiritual health of the miners, however. On Sundays and religious holidays they generously offered them one hour, so that they could attend services at the church nearest the mine. This was obligatory.

To take care of other necessities of a less spiritual nature they allowed unscrupulous people to recruit prostitutes of the lowest kind from the provincial capital, taking them to towns in the mining region on paydays. The more fortunate miners were relieved of their pennies; their less fortunate brothers were left with terrible diseases for the rest of their days.

The fact that the men who came to work in the mines were from so many different regions of Spain gave the management the criminal idea of fomenting regional rivalries and prejudices by dividing the workers into crews on the basis of their provinces or regions. Thus, one work crew would be composed entirely of men from Navarre, another of Castilians, and so forth. Two things were accomplished by dividing the workers into regional groups: It increased the amount of ore mined without additional cost, and it prevented the workers from acquiring a feeling of comradeship that might unite them in opposition to those who exploited them.

Each morning the manager went to one of the crews. On Monday he talked to the workers from Navarre, on Tuesday to those from Aragón. The procedure was always the same, and the result identical.

"Today," he told the men from Aragón, "the fellows from Navarre have said they're going to fill so many wagons."

The workers listened, gritting their teeth and looking at him angrily. The manager's words irritated them like the bites of a horse-fly, but their regional and manly pride would not allow them to be outdistanced by others. After a brief discussion they accepted the challenge.

"We'll load more wagons."

"How many?"

"Navarre won't beat Aragón."

Afterwards the manager moved on to incite another crew with the goad of regional rivalry. Work began at a feverish, exhausting rate. If a worker stopped for a moment to wipe off the sweat or simply to catch his breath, his comrades scolded and insulted him. A blind animal hatred burned in the members of each crew even against each other. The young men felt it against the older men who could not work as fast as they, and the older men against the young men who were setting a killing pace. The workday ended and Aragón won. The men from that region still had enough breath left to taunt their rivals with a biting song:

> Little Navarrese
> Don't be such a braggart
> For the coins of Navarre
> Are no good in Aragón.

Another day the Navarrese were the victors in the brutal contest with another crew, and braggadocio raised to the level of a national virtue inspired another swaggering song:

> No one can break the chains
> In Navarre's coat of mail
> Because they're made of iron
> That comes from the mines of Vizcaya.

These artificially provoked rivalries did not always vent themselves in song. Sometimes the disputes were settled with guns or knives and ended with some in the hospital or the cemetery and others in jail.


[3]

## The Word Socialist

The Socialist movement in the Basque Country had its origin in the first organizations of the International Workingmen's Association, founded in Spain after the revolution in September 1868.

Bilbao, the capital of the Basque Country, was one of the places where the first workers' organizations, affiliated to the First International, the International of Marx and Engels, were established.

Bakuninism* had no roots in this region, in which the mining and metallurgical industries were beginning to create large proletarian concentrations.

The weekly newspaper, *The Worker's Voice*, published by those societies, was the organizing and unifying force among the small groups of workers who had formed resistance associations to defend their class interests.

These nascent working-class organizations which sprang up sporadically under the impetus of industry, especially in the mines, were to be crushed under the first harsh blows of repression. But the seeds of Socialism had been sown and would grow in time.

After the Spanish sections of the International Workingmen's Association had been split by the divisive activities of the Bakuninists, and the Socialist Party had been formed in 1879 and, ten years later, the General Workers' Union (UGT), the Socialist labor movement began to grow in organization and numbers in the Basque Country, especially in the capital.

The first Basque Socialists extended the workers' organizations into the manufacturing and mining zones by tenacious and patient efforts, and they made such progress that in the last decade of the 19th century and the first years of the 20th the mining zone already constituted the basis of the Socialist labor organization in the Basque Country.

It was not easy at the turn of the century to reach the workers in the mines. The towns in the mining region were the private preserves of the foreign companies and were jealously protected from revolutionary infection by the Civil Guard and the company goons. Nevertheless, in a relatively brief period of time Vizcaya had become a bulwark of the Socialist workers' movement.

One of the main tasks of the Socialist propagandists of the initial period, and even afterwards in the first years of the 20th century, was to end the regional rivalries and to awaken the spirit of solidarity, of union and comradeship among the miners, so that they could defend their common interests against those who exploited them all.

---

* Named for Michael Bakunin (1814–76), a Russian revolutionary and a founder of anarchism, whose disputes with Marx led to the split in the International Workingmen's Association at the Hague Congress in 1872.—Ed.

Until the Socialist seeds began to take root in their consciousness, showing them their strength, the workers could not believe that they had rights and that they could alter their conditions. They were not happy, but what could they do? A minority protested at times. Others bit their lips and clenched their fists in the face of injustice but they felt helpless before their exploiters.

The workers did not yet know the strength of their class. They were only aware of their numbers. And at times they turned their desperation and anger against those who came to work in the mines, just as they had before, not regarding the new arrivals as companions in misfortune and members of the same class but as competitors who were going to challenge their places in the mine or the bunkhouse by offering to work for a few cents less than they did.

Up to 1890 there had been only isolated protests in the mines, protests which always ended with the defeat of the workers and resulted in even greater pessimism in that mass of unorganized laborers, whose class consciousness was just beginning to awaken. They reacted instinctively against injustice, oppression or abuses, and often solved disputes with foremen or managers with their fists or their knives.

Now they were beginning to speak and act in a different way. The work of the Socialist propagandists was beginning to bear fruit. At mealtime in the various mine shafts a new language could be heard among the workers. They were talking in low voices of strikes, protests and demands.

Toward the end of the summer of 1890, the situation was so tense in the mining region that everyone expected something very serious to occur. The workers were not hiding their hostility toward those who exploited them. They protested against the bunkhouses and company stores and talked openly about the blacklists. They denounced thefts and abuses committed by the foremen and managers. Their protests were crystallizing and taking shape.

The same phenomenon was taking place in the steel mills, and the miners and mill workers were growing more and more closely united.

The English company Orconera, the most powerful of the foreign concerns exploiting the Vizcaya mines, which was used to its word being considered law, fired five of the most militant workers in mine Concha 3 on May 13, 1890.

The miners' response was immediate. The fellow crew members

of those who had been fired left work in solidarity with their comrades. The same day the entire mine was paralyzed. The next day none of the workers in Orconera's mines went to work, and to show their solidarity with them, all of the miners in the entire mining zone went on strike.

This first big strike, with which the miners daringly erupted onto the social scene like an advance guard of the militant proletariat, shook the capitalist social structure of Vizcaya to its foundations. And with good reason! The mill, construction and railroad workers all went on strike in sympathy with the miners. The industrial life of Vizcaya was at a standstill to the angry surprise of a bourgeoisie which refused to believe that it was not all-powerful and that it could not continue to exploit the workers in the mines as it had been doing.

The government declared a state of war in order to exert pressure on the strikers. Armed forces from all over Spain were sent against the miners; their meetings and demonstrations were broken up with bullets. There were dozens of dead and wounded in the savage onslaught.

But the owners and the authorities had miscalculated. The guns of the forces of law and order could not diminish the thirst for justice of these men who faced death every day in the mines. Once committed to the struggle, they were determined to carry it to the end, no matter what it might cost. The workers answered violence with violence. They burned the bunkhouses, assaulted the company stores, throwing their contents into the streets, and destroyed the mine installations. Releasing brakes and cables, they sent the ore cars hurtling down the steeply inclined planes, to be smashed below. They blew up rails and locomotives with dynamite. They burned the trestles over which the ore cars passed and threw the tools into the calcining furnaces. They advanced like an avalanche, leaping over obstacles and smashing barriers, destroying everything they found in their path.

In the course of the struggle the workers became conscious of their own strength and learned that their will also counted, that without them there would be no shipping of ore, no dividends, no palaces, no elegant carriages, no fortunes, no checking accounts in the banks. In a few days the strike made tens of thousands of workers aware of their own existence. They would never again be mere workhorses, a victimized mass condemned to live and die like outcasts.

The government, alarmed at the workers' firmness, had to intervene. It sent the military governor of Guipúzcoa, General Loma, as a mediator. When the general became aware of the living conditions of the miners and of the justice of their demands, he threatened the mine owners with the withdrawal of the army if they did not negotiate with the workers.

The strike ended with a victory for the miners. According to General Loma's proclamation, the owners agreed to the following conditions: First, to eliminate the bunkhouses and allow the workers to live where they pleased; second, to allow the workers to make purchases in stores other than those operated by the company; and third, to shorten the work day to an average of ten hours for the whole year, divided in the following fashion: In January, February and December, nine hours; in March, April, September and October, ten hours; and in May, June, July and August, eleven hours.

After this struggle and this first victory, the mining region of Vizcaya ceased to be a bulwark of reaction. It became a stronghold of rebellion against the Vizcaya of the *nouveaux riches*, of the reactionary capitalists. The strike of 1890 stands out in the history of the Basque working-class movement like a guide post marking the dividing line between two epochs.

The strikes and protests that occurred between 1890 and 1906, among which there were four general strikes, 17 partial strikes and numerous protests in the various mines, showed how far the workers had travelled in the struggle to improve their living and working conditions, and in the development of their class consciousness.

As the labor movement developed in the course of unceasing struggles, one of its basic requirements was for adequate meeting places. These were difficult to obtain because landlords who were willing to rent them to the labor movement were threatened with boycott by the local bourgeosie. In spite of this, modest halls could be found by paying twice the rent anyone else did.

As the movement grew, it became easier to find suitable meeting places, and the workers in Gallarta were able to rent, at first, two apartments in a tenement and afterwards, the first floor in a large house. Gallarta was the main mining center, but similar things happened in the other towns of the mining zone.

The workers prepared the hall for meetings and festivals. The executive boards of various labor organizations met there, heard the workers' demands and complaints and gave them advice.

A mutual aid society was founded, using the union local as its headquarters. The hall's administrative committee, in response to the workers' requests, organized a modest library, which, for a nominal charge, provided the workers with books that their own meager resources could not have afforded.

The red flags, which belonged to each one of the unions affiliated with the union hall, were kept in glass cases along the walls. After the Socialist International proclaimed May First as a day for workers all over the world to show their unity and solidarity, these flags were carried in every May Day march.

The mine union was divided into sections in a manner reminiscent of the old guilds. Drillers, helpers, carpenters, locomotive engineers, stokers—each group formulated its own demands, organized partial strikes and had its own organizational structure and flag.

In the May First demonstrations the sections marched under their respective flags. There was a harmless rivalry over who had the best flags, some of which were marvelous works of craftsmanship, with embroidery and intricate carving on their staffs. They were regarded by the workers with profound pride.

The meetings in the union local were stimulating, more because of the vitality and warmth engendered by the active participation of the miners and their families than because of the oratory—even though some of the speakers were outstanding agitators. If it was a meeting to discuss the conflicts which had arisen in this or that mine, there was a passionate expression of conviction and determination. If they were listening to a speech, they listened in utter absorption, especially when the speaker showed insight into their own problems, and when they recognized that others were concerned with the workers' problems and sorrows. But it was especially on the eve of strikes that the hall became a forge in which the miners' fighting spirit was brought to its highest pitch.

The union halls gradually weaned the workers away from the taverns and filthy cafés, opening up perspectives of a new life. Small theatrical groups and choral societies were organized. The choral groups gave performances outside of the hall, and their songs spread into the mines and working-class neighborhoods. They became a

part of the people's culture and were an effective means of agitation
and organization, especially among the youth.

Every workers' struggle or celebration, every revolutionary anniversary had its song which had first been sung in the union hall
and was then sung by tens of thousands of men and women, young
and old. Who could remain indifferent when he heard a group from
the choral society go through the workers' neighborhoods at dawn
on May First, singing:

> Arise, fellow-workers,
> For the day has dawned
> It's the First of May.
> When the general strike is called,
> You'll see how quickly,
> We workers will come forth
> Telling the big shots,
> "You'll exploit us no longer."
> Let's sing together
> Of the glory of labor
> For having thrown off
> The yoke of slavery.
> Down with capitalism
> That lives on injustice.
> Long live the workers
> United in brotherhood!

On March 18 of every year, the anniversary of the Paris Commune,
a solemn meeting was held in which songs were sung celebrating the
epic struggle of the Paris workers, and speeches were made recalling
the meaning of the Commune and the heroism of those who fought
for it. This is one of the songs about the Commune:

> Let us sing to the memory
> Of those who raised the red flag
> Of the heroic Communards
> Who were the glory of their nation.
> Brave workers of France
> Gave proof of their valor
> To the gold-sated killers
> Who are born without pity.

> Beloved Commune, we revere you,
> And when another Commune arises,
> Your defenders will be avenged.
> We promise this
> And it will come to pass.

In the election campaigns when the masses were mobilized against the outrages of the bourgeoisie, who trampled on their right to vote and who won the elections through bribery, fraud and stuffing the ballot boxes, the workers sang this song to influence those who had been exposed to propaganda urging them to boycott the polls:

> To the polls, comrades,
> The victory must be ours.
> We must never stop fighting
> Until we triumph.
> Our candidates who stand for equality
> Will win,
> And the owning class with all its wealth
> Will be defeated.
> The faithless worker
> Who sells his vote to the bosses
> Only deserves our scorn
> For his duplicity.
> To the polls now, don't hold back,
> Let's defeat the enemies
> Of our freedom.

They also sang during strikes, and the vigorous language of the songs served as a warning to those who, against their true interests, gave aid to the bourgeoisie in its efforts to break the workers' resistance. One of the songs went this way:

> The scab is a social derelict
> Who helps the boss steal from the workers
> The right to a better life.
> Traitor!
> The worker who betrays a strike
> Will get what he deserves
> Before very long.
> He will see his children scorned,

Despised and shut out
Because of him.
Some day he'll realize
The dirty work he's done
Against his own interests.

When the Socialist youth organization was founded in the first years of the century by Tomás Meabe, the "Song of Youth" was like a cry of hope that signaled youth's growing consciousness of its own identity and the future of its class:

Young workers, new proletarians,
Come to us, come without fear . . .
We are the partisans of a noble cause,
We are the advance guard of a better world.
Come, swell our ranks,
Lend us a hand, be ready,
For our fight is the cause of humanity
And will be long and hard to win.
Socialism is our red banner,
We will never let it fall,
We will give our lives to hold it high,
We will carry it to triumph.
Our red flag will remain
The faithful symbol of its sacred mission:
To lead the oppressed
To their liberation.

The Spanish proletariat expressed its solidarity with the 1905 Revolution in Russia, and a song was composed at that time which I learned as a child from the miners in my region:

Don't lose heart, Russian people,
Go on fighting, do not weaken,
For the International supports
Your revolution.
We, too, demand revenge upon
The autocratic rabble.
Let the blood of the oppressor
Run through the streets like a river.

On the days when the workers would hang the red flags of their organizations in the windows of the union hall, the whole neighborhood came alive. Even to those who were not affiliated with the union, the red flags said something which they could not put into words but which nevertheless stirred them to the core.

The union locals reflected the advance and to a certain extent the victories of the labor movement and the development of the workers' class consciousness. The union organizations helped to educate the people in the struggle against brutal exploitation, to raise their standard of living, and to make them conscious of their strength and their role in society.


[4]

## Unsanctified Burial


Great steps forward had been taken in the organization of the working class, even though this process was still intermittent and insecure. The task of the Socialist propagandists and organizers in Vizcaya at the turn of the century was beset with problems and challenges.

In addition to persecution by employers and authorities, they had to cope with the bigotry of the Church, which maintained a climate of hostility toward any new idea among the people. The Church clung desperately to positions it had occupied for centuries of uncontested power, and now it could no longer light the fires of the auto da fé in city plazas to burn the Socialist heresy alive.

This state of livid anti-Socialism was heightened after certain events that occurred in Bilbao in October 1903 during a large Carlist Catholic celebration. The élite of the Carlists who remained in the capital of the Basque Country were brought together as a challenge to all liberal and democratic forces and especially to the workers and Socialists.

The participants in that celebration clashed with a group attending a Socialist meeting, and the Carlists demonstrated their Christian fervor by attacking the workers with fists and clubs. Outraged by this attack, the workers hurled Carlist banners, standards, saints and lanterns into the river, where, after floating for a brief time, they disappeared in the turbulent waters of the Nervión. Many workers were wounded by the Carlists and the police; reprisals were carried out against others in their places of employment for the crime of having attended a Socialist meeting.

This vigorous response to the Carlists, which showed them that they were still unable to conquer Bilbao, made the ecclesiastical authorities and their faithful followers even more intransigent. Ruthless acts of fanatical intolerance were perpetrated in every town and village.

A simple and human tragedy had occurred in the mining zone, which stirred up the fires of religious fanaticism. It resulted in a shameful outcome which was eventually to recoil on the instigators.

The 15-year-old daughter of a minor office clerk, known for his progressive ideas in Gallarta, was gravely ill with tuberculosis. The sickness had advanced into the final stages and the girl's death seemed near. Her parents, who adored their daughter, tried to encourage her and to conceal the gravity of her condition from her by making plans with her for the future.

The girl's condition was known all over town, where everyone knew everyone else. Certain fanatical women, self-appointed guardians of public morality, put pressure on the parents in a thousand different ways to invite the priest to visit the girl. The father firmly refused to allow a priest to enter his house and enjoined his wife not to permit either the priest or any of the sanctimonious women to approach their daughter on any pretext whatsoever.

The father's decision to bury his daughter without benefit of the Church was also widely known, and this prospect so affected the good ladies of the town that one would have thought that the salvation of their own souls depended on preventing it. "What is going to happen?" they asked each other. "If we tolerate a civil burial in the town, it will open the door to all types of impiety. And once the barriers have broken down, God knows where these devils will take us. No matter what it costs, we must not allow a burial to take place outside the Church."

They laid their battle plans. They established a permanent watch over the home of the sick girl, inquiring about her condition, harassing her relatives and neighbors, not caring in the least how much pain their unwelcome persistence caused the girl's parents and relatives.

She died in the first days of autumn. Her father decided that the burial would be civil, and his decision, though expected, caused a tremendous sensation. The news travelled rapidly through the town despite the defection of the women who usually went from door to door (for a small sum) to announce a death, and the hour of the funeral. They refused to announce this burial, for fear of reprisals by the wealthy ladies of the town.

Heated arguments took place everywhere. The workers were on the side of the grieving family, and in many mines they decided to leave work an hour ahead of time in order to attend the funeral procession.

The authorities, puppets of the mine owners, were placed in a serious dilemma. The Church was considered to have exclusive jurisdiction over the cemetery, and a person whose funeral was not carried out in accord with the Catholic canons could not be buried without the special authorization of the ecclesiastical authorities.

The ladies, who had gathered in the sacristy of the church, thought that the battle had been won. "Since there is no civil cemetery," they said, "where are they going to bury her? You can only enter the cemetery behind the priest's cross."

But the dead girl's father remained firm. He would not give in no matter how great the pressure. "My daughter will have a civil burial. There is no civil cemetery? That's not my fault. The cemetery is not the private property of the Church. It belongs to the municipality, to the people, to the religious and the nonreligious alike. If the priests don't want the 'grace' of their blessings to fall on the ground that is going to cover my daughter's body, then let them limit their blessings to individuals who want them and not to the cemetery as a whole. The cemetery is municipal property, and my daughter will be buried there."

Feelings were so stirred up that the governor of the province felt it necessary to send a number of Civil Guards to maintain order.

The local authorities notified the bereaved family that if it insisted on having a civil burial, it could not accompany the coffin to the cemetery by the usual route. They would have to carry it over narrow, out-of-the-way paths without a procession, as if they were carrying a victim of the plague. They were absolutely forbidden to pass through the center of town.

"My daughter will be carried along the usual route," the father replied to the constable who had communicated the authorities' decision to him.

At the appointed hour for the funeral a large number of workers bearing the flags from the union hall had gathered in front of the family's house. Among them there was a small group of women who, in spite of the reactionaries' threats, wanted to accompany the body and show their sympathy for the grief of the family.

Four workers lifted the coffin onto their shoulders and the procession moved silently forward. Behind the body walked the father, alone; and a few steps behind him, under the red banners of the workers' organizations, hundreds of men and women who, united with him in his grief and determination, were fighting for a right which bigots were trying to deny them.

As the sad procession left the house, a solemn voice began to sing a funeral march, which was immediately taken up by the entire group:

> Listen, poor mortals
> To the funeral hymns
> Sung by the workers
> To the body of our dead ...
> Soldier for the idea
> Of love and progress
> He always fought bravely
> Against the forces of reaction ...

In the tense atmosphere of the street, the simple, ingenuous verses of the funeral march sung by men who faced death every day in the mines acquired an impressive grandeur and solemnity. The procession was so moving that women kneeled in the street, weeping, and men took off their hats and bowed their heads respectfully.

The road that led to the cemetery, which was the main street of the town, passed in front of the church. As the procession approached this point, the center of town, the Civil Guards appeared in the side streets while the ladies of the town waited in front of the church. There could be no doubt as to their intentions.

A group of the most determined moved forward to cut off the

procession and force it toward the church. Then they tried to seize the coffin. The father and some of his companions beat off the furies. Then, as if at a signal, buckets of boiling water and stones were hurled at the procession from the balconies and windows of nearby houses, wounding several workers, while the boldest of the ladies again flung themselves onto the coffin. And again the workers cleared them out of the way with little ceremony.

Then the Civil Guards intervened to help the attacking women, and at the same time tried to tear the flags away from the workers, who stood their ground and defended themselves from the Guards' rifle butts. They arrested the father and the men who were carrying the coffin. The hysterical ladies were at last able to seize the corpse and carry it to the cemetery, escorted by the Civil Guards. The priest was waiting there for the victorious faithful who arrived laboriously dragging the white coffin along like a battle trophy.

But they were not able to enjoy their victory for long. From the day the funeral had been violated, workers began to send affidavits to the committee of the Workers' Society expressing their desire to have a civil burial, no matter what the circumstances of their death might be. The authorities were forced to set aside part of the cemetery to serve as a civil cemetery.

And it was not only civil burials that the religious authorities and zealous ladies had to accept. The most advanced workers refused to baptize their children, and marriages which were not confirmed by the Church ceased to be a scandalous novelty.

Although the small-town fanatics were extremely preoccupied with religious practices, they paid very little attention to the crying need for sanitary services and doctors for the growing population of the mining region.

Illnesses and deaths were wrought by divine will and had to be accepted with resignation. The deaths of children, which filled their mothers with sorrow, had to be celebrated. "They are angels who are returning to heaven. Why mourn them?"

But no one was resigned to death and illness, and that was why the practice of magic was habitual with families who lacked the money for adequate medical aid and yearned to find a cure for their suffering.

There were people with "the hand of a saint," gifted with "grace," who could snap a dislocated shoulder blade back into place for a small sum of money; these were those who possessed antidotes against the bite of mad dogs; there were diviners and those who could ascertain whether the evil eye had been cast on someone.

Their methods of cure were varied, from the most ingenuous to the most monstrous. The simplest were cobwebs for wounds and hemorrhages and, for infected sores, an ointment made by the priest's housekeeper or a salve made from snakes by the medicine man. There were horrible remedies for tuberculosis. A bag containing certain herbs was hung around the neck for hemorrhoids. For pneumonia and colds, there were mustard plasters and brandy.

The most picturesque of all the treatments was that used to cure hernia. It was an almost sacred rite. One had to wait for the night of the summer solstice, which corresponds to the eve of the festival of Saint John, June 23. During that day a tree was selected near the village. It was sawed down the middle without completely splitting it, and a large wedge kept the two halves separated without breaking them until nightfall.

A few minutes before midnight the patient was taken before the tree and stripped nude. When the clock in the town hall began to strike, he passed between the two halves of the tree while his parents, relatives or friends chanted the following litany:

> Take him, Peter.
> Give him to me, John.
> So that our Lord, Saint John, will cure him.
> Take him, Peter.
> Give him to me, John.
> So that our Lord, Saint John, will cure him.

Then the two parts of the tree were brought together, plastered with manure and tied tightly with wires. If the tree did not dry up, it was assumed that the patient would be cured. At times the tree did not die, but the hernia continued to torture the poor victim until it was either held in with a truss or, in serious cases, operated upon.

If someone wanted to obtain some impossible possession, he prayed to Saint Rita, while if he had a toothache, to Saint Philomena. If the impossible request was not fulfilled or if the pain did not go away insults were poured on the poor saints and their mothers and fathers and all their ancestors without the slightest compunction.

Almost everyone in the Basque Country had bad teeth. It was

attributed to the hardness of the water, but the fact was that the people did not brush their teeth. That simple method of preserving one's teeth and avoiding cavities was unknown to them.

Praying to Saint Philomena or breathing the smoke of henbane was a standard cure for toothaches, for one only put oneself in the hands of the medicine man as a last resort. There were no dentists for the miners; instead, there were the official tooth extractors, in my town a medicine man called Cárcamo.

Cárcamo sold medicinal herbs, cured every kind of sore, pulled teeth, mediated disputes, wrote petitions, and administered enemas and plasters to a person suffering from ileus as well as to a glutted calf or to a mule with gripes. On Sundays and holidays after high mass Cárcamo set up his stand with herbs, elixirs and salves on one side of the plaza. There he carried on his many and varied business affairs. He had a helper who ran around in the mountains and ravines like a monkey, searching for precious herbs and hunting down lizards and snakes.

Anyone who went to Cárcamo to have a tooth pulled was either a hero or a madman. He seated the patient in a chair, while his assistant forced his head back and shoved a wooden plug into his mouth so that he could not close it. Then Cárcamo seized the tooth that the patient had pointed out with a pair of pliers and tugged until it came out. The victim roared and raged and tried to get up and escape from the torture. Impossible. The assistant held him in a headlock, and he ran the risk of breaking his back if he resisted too much.

Sometimes Cárcamo made a mistake and pulled the wrong tooth. That brought the house down on him. Salves and herbs flew through the air, and poor Cárcamo had to be saved from the irate patient by the merciful intervention of the onlookers or by the police.

To cure burros, goats, cows, pigs or sheep of "melancholia" and "unknown" ailments, he hung a rope belt of Saint Blase or a scapulary of Saint Anthony around their necks and gave them a piece of mouldy bread to eat. The bread had been blessed on the day of one of those saints and was kept in every home as an infallible cure-all.

Once, the cow of a neighbor of ours, an old Basque who believed firmly in the evil eye, was sick. He called the woman who understood such spells, and she confirmed his suspicions. The cow was bewitched.

The house was filled with lamentations and steps were taken to exorcize the spirits which had entered the animal's body.

Laurel that had been preserved from Palm Sunday was burned in the stable, where the cow lay suffocating. They sprinkled the floor and the walls with holy water taken from the church font on the Saturday before Easter, and hung a scapulary of Saint Anthony around the beast's neck. In a corner on top of an empty box they placed an image of Saint Peter Zariquete, with two candles burning in front of it. However, in spite of all these sacred rites, the animal was obviously dying.

A woman advised them to read the Rule of Monks of Saint Benedict to the cow. Finally a neighbor intervened with the prudent suggestion that the owner of the cow call the veterinarian before it was too late. The owner shrugged his shoulders hopelessly:

"Our cow is bewitched. What can the veterinarian do against that?" he replied sadly.

"Don't be stupid; call the veterinarian. You're going to be left without a cow."

He thought and thought and finally decided to go for the veterinarian. The latter was a man who had come to the town full of good intentions, anxious to help the peasants. His intentions had run up against the wall of superstition and quackery, but he had held out, and now he was beginning to break down resistance to his ideas.

When he entered the stable and saw the sick cow in the midst of such sanctity, he stopped short and said, in a tone that brooked no argument:

"Either Saint Anthony goes or I do. Choose. I know your tricks. If the cow gets well, you'll say that the saint did it. If it dies, you'll blame the veterinarian."

Turning on his heel, he walked resolutely toward the door. The owners of the cow were stunned. They didn't know what to say, and they didn't even dare to move. They looked at each other indecisively, each waiting for the other to act. But who dared to make the first move in such a crucial decision? It was no small thing to offend the patron saint of all animals.

The man nervously crumpled his beret in his hands, while his wife, with her eyes full of tears, was, like her husband, thinking: "What if the cow dies?"

The woman's sister cut the Gordian knot. She pulled the scapulary from around the animal's neck, blew out the candles, kicked the saint into the rubbish and said in a strong voice: "To hell with the blessings! Cure the cow."

The old farmer gasped in horror, but when he saw that no thunderbolt had descended, he recovered rapidly. He felt as though a great weight had been removed from him. "In any case," he thought, "I'm not the one who threw the saint out of the house. And my sister-in-law doesn't own any cattle."

The veterinarian cured the animal, and a few weeks later the Basque and his wife were knocking at his door. They had come to pay his fee and to ask to be admitted into the arrangement he had made with others to care for their cattle whenever they were sick. And to show their gratitude for having saved the cow, which was their greatest treasure, they also had brought him a couple of chickens and a basket of apples.

[5]

## Soldiers in the Streets

The year 1903 emerges clearly from my hazy memories of the past like a sharply defined mountain peak which neither time nor subsequent events have been able to dim or distort.

My childhood memories are dated from this year on, and it could almost be said that it marked the beginning of my conscious life, awakened by certain events which I witnessed in fearful astonishment when I was not yet eight years old.

A new general strike had been called in the spring of 1903 by the miners in our region. The center of action and leadership was in the town where I was born, and in the district where I lived with my parents and where the union hall was located.

This was the third general strike, and it was equal in importance to the one in 1890. It was in its second month, and there was no prospect of solution because of the intransigence of the mine owners. Despite the fact that the workers' demands were extremely moderate, blood had already been shed in several clashes between the strikers and the armed forces. Barricades had been built in several places.

The solidarity of the Spanish working class was being demonstrated by the aid which the miners received. Some help even came from people in the middle class who were outraged by the fierce and unreasonable attitude of the owners.

Families of workers in the manufacturing zone, office employees and small businessmen took the miners' children into their homes for the duration of the strike. The miners were reluctant to send their children away, but they did so to spare them the privations of the prolonged strike, which they were prepared to continue until their demands were satisfied.

The summer was slipping by and with it the most favorable season for shipping ore. Some signs of yielding began to appear in the owners' association, but the most obdurate decided to play a final card in an effort to end the conflict in time to take advantage of the remaining weeks of good weather for the export of ore.

First, they tried to break the miners' resistance by making the office workers, who were better paid than the strikers, run the trains which carried the ore to the ports. This attempt failed because the workers' wives threw themselves on the tracks in front of the locomotives, with their children in their arms, and stopped the trains.

The longer the strike lasted, the more violent were the clashes which occurred. Workers all over Spain followed the struggle of the Vizcaya miners with great anxiety because the strike was not just a matter of economic demands, such as establishing a weekly salary and ending the company stores (which continued to exist, despite General Loma). The principal issue was the right of the workers to have their own organizations and to have these organizations recognized by the owners. The struggle was decisive for the immediate future of the unions, and that explained the resistance which the mine owners and contractors were putting up.

One day the rumor spread that the companies had sent agents to Castile and León to recruit laborers who were promised a salary twice as big as the miners earned. In the beginning people refused to believe it, but then the rumor began to acquire a more concrete character. Someone revealed the date and route of arrival of the scabs and at the same time the provincial authorities declared that they were ready to "energetically defend the right to work."

The miners, on the other hand, were determined to win the strike no matter what it might cost. They organized the necessary vigilance and other measures to defeat the new maneuver. Thus they knew the exact moment when a group of outsiders, who looked unmistakably like peasants, were brought into town and herded together in a bowling alley until the time came for them to go to work. Both sides began to prepare for a tough battle.

Strikebreakers were not the only new arrivals in the mining zone. A regiment of infantry pulled in during the early morning hours so that their sudden appearance in the streets might make the maximum impact. They had been sent by the government to "guarantee the right to work." That night it was known in the mining zone that the troops would be used against the strikers.

The next morning the roll of drums threw the whole town into a commotion. An officer was going through the principal working-class districts with a squad of soldiers, reading a proclamation by the military governor establishing a state of war in the province. The decree was posted at several points. It forbade meetings and stated that any attempt to interfere with the "right to work" would be punished severely. It also said that groups of more than three persons would be fired on without warning.

The workers clenched their fists in rage when they learned of the government measures. "Bastards! Just like 1890!" they commented. "So they're showing their teeth? We'll see who has sharper ones!"

That night the men who were the most active Socialist workers did not sleep at home. This was a precaution, in case the police decided to round them up. The women also were laying plans. They had no intention of letting their men down. If strikebreakers were going to be used, there would be some broken heads before they reached the mine.

Some groups of miners placed themselves on the slopes above the mines, hidden in the rough terrain, ready to go into action.

The mining families were used to getting up at dawn. That day everyone was up before it was light, but when they looked at the streets their hearts sank. The soldiers were there, and they were not just any soldiers, not like those they had seen coming back from the war in Cuba, sick and black from the sun, wearing clothes of striped cotton and straw hats. These were professional soldiers, like the ones you saw in pictures, wearing blue uniforms with red stripes down the outer edge of their pants and oilcloth shakos on their heads with straps under the chin.

The children were the first to break the spell. We ran into the streets and looked the soldiers over, up and down and from all sides. They were motionless, leaning on their rifles with expressionless faces. What could they be thinking?

Then from the bridge that joined our district with the mine, we went to see what was happening and the sight was terrifying. Soldiers and Civil Guards and other armed guards were everywhere. The soldiers had strict orders not to let anyone pass through the streets.

The plans the women had made the night before, when they thought they would only have to deal with strikebreakers or Civil Guards, were upset when they found the streets guarded by soldiers. For a moment they hesitated. They did not hate soldiers as they did the Civil Guard.

"The Civil Guards join their corps voluntarily," they said, "knowing that they will have to kill. But the soldiers. . . ." This had created a very serious problem, because the people did not want to fight the army. Besides, what would the soldiers do? For a time the miners' wives were confused and undecided, until finally one of the most determined spoke.

"Listen. Let's leave the soldiers alone. Don't bother them. But God help the scabs! We'll take them apart!"

The women agreed. Then each one, according to plan, took up her post behind the closed windows and balconies. It was almost time. Then the children began to shout, "They're coming, they're coming!"

When the first group of strikebreakers entered the neighborhood, the windows and balconies opened violently and insults were hurled at them as, with heads lowered, they walked toward the mine escorted by Civil Guards.

"Scabs! Blacklegs! Cowards!"

One of the strikebreakers, younger and more daring than the others, made a defiant gesture toward the women. He didn't have a chance to repeat it. Stones rained down on him and his companions.

The Civil Guards raised their rifles, and the women withdrew from the balconies and ran out into the street. Pale and motionless, the soldiers looked at them. They seemed to be made out of stone. Women appeared from everywhere with babies in their arms.

"You're our sons," they said to the soldiers. "You can't fire on us. We're just defending our bread! Look how we live."

The soldiers didn't fire and the women broke through the cordon. The army withdrew its units rapidly because everywhere they were fraternizing with the people.

The bell calling the men to work tolled insistently, and the women watched the mine with worried looks. That was where the fate of the strike would be decided. Everyone was thinking the same thing: "Would they dare?"

They did. A small group of men wearing white shirts, a color which the miners didn't wear and which made the strikebreakers stand out from a great distance, was advancing toward the mine. The Civil Guards, with their rifles at the ready, watched the heights above them. They had good reason to suspect that the miners were up there.

In spite of their escort the scabs didn't reach the mine. The strikers hidden in the rocks set off some charges of dynamite, raising a cloud of rocks and dirt and making a tremendous noise which terrified the men who had come to take their jobs.

The strikebreakers never forgot the lesson. They had never heard dynamite explode before, and they ran back the way they had come as fast as they could, shouting to the others to return home.

Without moving the Civil Guards fired at an invisible but active enemy. Their bullets bounced harmlessly off the rocks, but the Guards didn't dare to advance. They were afraid of getting the same reception as the scabs.

For all practical purposes, the strike was won. There was a nation-wide clamor demanding an end to the owners' refusal to negotiate. A special delegation from the Institute for Social Reforms in Madrid investigated the workers' demands and found them justified. And the commander of the armed forces, General Zapico—like General Loma in 1890—offered to arbitrate between the owners and the miners.

On October 31, 1903, after several months of struggle, the workers won their demands. The Minister of Government presented a bill in Parliament which would require the mine owners to pay the workers in cash and not force them to trade in the company stores.

The miners returned to work victoriously. However, the end of the strike did not mean the end of conflicts in the mines. The owners followed their traditional tactics of yielding when they were forced to, only to attack the workers again at the first opportunity, always making them pay for losses suffered during the periodic depressions or drops in exports.

[6]

# Miners' Children

My parents lived and endured privation in this region of the Basque Country, cradle of rebels, of daily struggles, of the most extreme reactionaries, of medieval fanaticism and superstition, in these jagged, rich-veined mountains, in this mining basin which lifts its scarred face before the Cantabrian Sea.

I was born in Gallarta on a December day in 1895. I was the eighth of the 11 children of Antonio the Gunner, as my father was called because of his job in the mines.

All of my relatives, Castilians and Basques, were miners. My paternal grandfather died in a mine, crushed by a block of ore. My mother worked in the mines until she was married, and my father was a miner from the time he left the Carlist army at 18, at the end of the last civil war, until he died at the age of 67. My brothers were miners and my husband a miner.

I come, then, from mining stock, the granddaughter, daughter, wife and sister of miners. Nothing in the life of mining people is strange to me, neither their sorrows nor their desires nor their language nor their roughness.

The miners' work was hard even when they were in the prime of life, and it became unbearable and inhuman when they were old. This was not so much because they weren't as strong as when they were younger as because of the jobs they were given to do—if they were lucky enough not to be thrown out of the mines.

I've not forgotten anything. Among the painful memories of a sad childhood and an adolescence that was not relieved by hope, I see my father, an old man, cleaning up the wastes washed down the embankments by the rain or by the water from the ore tanks.

He worked with a small group of old miners like himself, who stood in a sea of mud with their pants rolled up above their knees, shovelling the mire, which contained small pieces of ore, onto screens.

When they came out of the water they could hardly put their shoes on. They were livid, trembling with cold, exhausted. But they couldn't give up that painful job. As old men they had no alternative. It was either that inhuman, killing labor, or begging, and begging was even more horrible, humiliating, dehumanizing. It meant picking up a piece of bread thrown to them like dogs, or a couple of pennies, or just a "God help you." It meant becoming a heavy burden to one's children and entering a new social category, pauperism. It was better to die than do that. Better to meet death with dignity, working until the end.

That was the life of our parents, and that was our life. It was like a deep pit without horizons, where the light of the sun never reached, illuminated at times only by the bloody glare of the struggles that burst out in flames of violence when the capacity to bear brutal treatment had reached the limits of human endurance.

During my adolescence I was filled with a bitter, instinctive resentment which made me lash out against everything and everybody (at home I was considered incorrigible), a feeling of rebellion which later became a conscious indignation.

But the transformation of an ordinary small-town woman into a revolutionary fighter, into a Communist, did not occur in a simple fashion and merely as a natural reaction against the subhuman conditions in which the mining families lived. It was a process upon which the negative influence of the religious education I received at school, at church and at home acted as a brake.

As soon as we knew how to talk and walk we were taken to the kindergarten through which several generations of miners' children had passed.

In that school, and for the modest sum of one peseta a day, the teacher freed our mothers from the need to care for their small children during the greater part of the day.

The school, which was located in a large old house, was dark, cold and damp, with virtually nothing attractive about it. Our first school

had the following educational materials: Two ancient posters showing the alphabet in capitals and small letters and riddled with holes
from years of being poked at with pointers; a blackboard, and a map
of Spain, which was never taken down to show us the towns and
cities of our native land.

The "kennel" or town jail was located on the floor under our
school, thus giving it a macabre touch. We could look through the
holes in the old, rotten wood and see the men whom the law considered dangerous but who were almost always rebellious miners
jailed on orders from their bosses, or men who had been caught in
Sunday brawls, or beggars.

That incongruous relationship between the jail and the school,
which was our first step in the acquisition of a social consciousness,
made us cruel and tended to distort our natural feelings. Anyone
who acted contrary to the established order of things was a criminal
who had to be punished—that was how our teacher explained the
arrests of the prisoners we saw. This impelled us to do our bit to help
the forces of justice.

When the teacher was not paying attention, the older boys urinated
through the cracks in the floor or poured water through the holes
from the water jug. The infuriated prisoners below shouted and
sometimes threw their shoes against the ceiling to the immense
pleasure of the children who knew then that they had hit their target.

When the children were seven years old, they were supposed to
enter the elementary school, although sometimes they stayed in
kindergarten until they were eight or nine, because there were no
places vacant.

At school we learned to read and write, but our real university was
the streets. When we left school in the afternoon, it was there that
we settled our childish arguments and quarrels and discussed local
events, which almost always had to do with the tragic accidents that
occurred in the mines almost every day.

Our interests and inclinations were born and developed under the
influence of the atmosphere in which we lived. In the midst of the
painful ordeals of the mining families, it was moving to see the
mothers' desire to give their children at least a minimal education.
The mothers were afraid that later they might not be able to provide
for their education, and this fear was based on a deeper fear, that

of an accident. The basic insecurity of the miners' lives was due to this ever-present threat.

"At least our children should know how to read and write," they said. It was a common sight to see the mothers taking their children to the school every morning or afternoon, the mothers almost dragging them along by the hand and the children crying at the top of their lungs.

The towns in the mining zone of Vizcaya were depressing and dirty, with the exception of Somorrostro, which is located in a marvellous valley. There the mines were located outside of town, which was not true of other mining towns.

These towns had no forests nor parks nor gardens nor wide streets nor places for children to play. Instead there were embankments, tunnels, refuse dumps, drains, steep slopes, bridges, sinks, galleries, inclined planes, elevated railways, cars and locomotives. All of this, even though it was so incongruous with childhood, nevertheless formed part of our lives because we played our games and spent our days in these surroundings.

There was no one who did not know by the time he was ten years old, about the destructive power of dynamite and how to prepare cartridges so that they would be even more powerful. This knowledge, acquired too soon, produced frequent accidents which were difficult to avoid under the conditions of life in the mining region.

An average of 120 girls attended the elementary school for girls, and as many boys went to their school. Class lasted from eight-thirty in the morning to noon, and from one-thirty to five in the afternoon. As for our teachers, they had to have truly encyclopedic knowledge for their task, and the truth is that some of them did. To their credit it must be said that they endeavored with apostolic zeal— between slaps and pinches—to combat our ignorance and polish up our intelligence.

Even though the children loved their teachers (I remember my teacher with real devotion, Doña Antonia Izar de la Fuente, who, old and retired, was killed in the bombing of Guernica), and even though the school was not ugly, with its large windows and its walls decorated with colored plates representing religious scenes from the Fall down to the Crucifixion, it did not appeal to us.

This was because of the routine teaching, the monotony of the classes and the application by our teachers of the Latin maxim,

"Letters enter with blood." Many times we felt their pointers descend on our shoulders for some prank or when we didn't know the lesson. However, we were lucky in our town, compared to Somorrostro where the teacher, Don Domingo, was famous for his brutality.

It was said that in that town the children's ears grew well above their foreheads because they had been stretched when he lifted them up by the ears. The students in that school were so terrified by Don Domingo that when he slowly rose from his seat in front of the class and picked up his pointer, peering at the pupils over his glasses, they all adopted defensive positions until they could see where he was going. When it was clear which part of the classroom he was approaching, the children in that spot scrambled out of their seats and leaped over the desks to get out of the way of the dreaded pointer, amid roars of laughter from the others. Then the teacher, seeing the culprits escape and irritated by the laughter, rained blows on those closest at hand. This produced a general stampede, with everyone trying to get out of the door at once.

At school we studied, sang and prayed. But we were the children of miners, of those miners who shook Vizcaya with their strikes and protests, and although they forced us to sing at school of our love of God, in the streets we sang the songs from the union hall. These appealed to us even more because they were forbidden at school, so we sang:

> Emperors and popes, kings and bishops,
> And all reactionary ministers,
> Say they are poor while they swim in wealth—
> May their heads roll in the Revolution!

At school we sang songs which glorified the slave labor of the mines, like the following:

> The mountains of Vizcaya
> Are pure iron and nothing more . . .
> And her sons mine the ore
> In utter joy and contentment.

But in the street we sang, to the displeasure of "respectable" people, a stanza from the song which was considered the most revolutionary of all:

> Come, workers, let us abandon
> Fields, factories and mines,
> Abandon the labors that enrich the idle
> And get on with the Revolution.

When we entered elementary school we really came into contact with science. "Who made the world? How many days did the creation take the maker? What did he make on the first day and the second and the third, up to the sixth, because, on the seventh, he couldn't do any more and rested?" This gigantic task of creating suns and constellations, millions of stars, larger and smaller than our planet, and every kind of plant and animal, from man and woman down to insects, batrachia, microbes and viruses, was disposed of in a few brief questions and answers, repeated over a period of several years until they became an inseparable part of us.

The short and simple summing-up of the most complicated problems of astronomy, natural science and world history which I assimilated during my school years from 1899 to 1910 was to be repeated to me 20 years later, in the sacramental words of the same text, when my daughter Amaya returned from her first day in school.

The lessons in sacred history were followed by the class in religious doctrine. Our teachers and priests put us into contact with the presence and omnipotence of the Creator and made us aware of His immutable laws and inescapable justice. But even though this tended to create a feeling of fatalism and resignation, at the same time it soon led to skepticism and doubt, because, in spite of everything, we too possessed the "powers of the soul" and "memory, understanding and will."

They made us pray to get souls out of purgatory, for example. And in the midst of the monotony of the *miserere* or the *ora pro nobis,* a skeptical thought would suddenly illuminate the mind with a logical question: "If God's judgments are immutable and he condemned these souls to a hundred years in purgatory, then why are we praying?"

In the church in my town, the "grave" where we prayed to the dead of my family was near the altar of the Passion, and on the altar there was a glass box in a niche with a bony Christ lying inside, the terrifying sight softened with a tulle-and-lace veil. Above the mortuary niche Saint John and the sorrowful Virgin watched from their re-

spective recesses over the eternal sleep of Christ, while their pain
was depicted with more or less artistry in their sad, pale faces.

My faith was concentrated on that altar. The sorrowful mother
and her dead son moved me to tears. In that simple figure I wor-
shipped the living image of the Virgin Mother, whose heart, pierced
with seven daggers, shone on the black velvet dress. At times, when
the reflection of the candle flames danced in the glass tears incrusted
in the Virgin's face, it seemed to me that she was really crying. This
made a profound impression on me.

I never stopped to think about what that image was made of, or
for what purpose it had been made. I was used to seeing it just as it
appeared on the altar, and if anyone had asked me, I wouldn't have
hesitated to reply that it was made of rare substances and animated
with the divine breath . . .

. . . Until one day, when my faith suffered a deep shock. The
teacher in my school was curator of the sisterhood of the Heart of
Jesus, and it was her responsibility to arrange the altar every week.
She usually took the older girls along with her to the church to help
her, and I went with her several days without anything out of the ordinary happening. But one day, following her instructions, I climbed
onto the altar table to dust one of the niches. When I got down—
without turning my back on the images, which was considered a sinful breach of reverence—I looked over my shoulder to keep from
stepping on the altar slab and saw a sight that froze me in my tracks.
Two Sisters of Charity were handling a kind of manikin without the
slightest ceremony. Where there should have been legs there were
two triangles made of strips of wood. The dummy stood on the bases
of the triangles. Big wires ending in very white hands came out of
the sides of the sack of sawdust, and on top—merciful heavens!—on
top was the Virgin's head. Her hair with its blond curls undone fell
over her face and shoulders as though she had just gotten out of bed.

My Virgin was like one of those scarecrows the peasants put in
the wheat fields to frighten off the sparrows!

I watched them dress the manikin as though I were hypnotized.
First a batiste chemise, then her petticoats and her dress, then they
curled her hair and finally they put on her black robe with silver
embroidery, her crown of stars and her heart with the seven daggers.

I shivered and my teacher asked if I felt ill. I stammered out an excuse. We finished arranging the altar and left. I didn't look at the Virgin.

That night I dreamed of thousands of scarecrows dressed in black or purple velvet scattered all over the world, making people cry.

At times my younger brothers and sisters and I had edifying conversations at home with our mother. One of us would ask her:

"Is it true that we are all children of God?"

"That's right."

"And we are all brothers?"

"Everyone!"

"Then if x and y are our brothers—and we named the richest people in town—why does our father have to go to work every day even if it rains, and their father doesn't do any work at all, and yet they live better than we do?"

Here our mother's knowledge of theology ended, and, not knowing what to say, she said angrily:

"Be quiet now! Children ought not to ask such questions."

Our poor mother! How could she explain to us what was in reality a painful enigma to her, an enigma she confronted each day with an unanswered "why?" on her lips, a "why?" whose answer she could not so much as guess or imagine.

Our happiest times were vacations. Our mothers left us completely to our own devices. We would go to the far end of the town, wandering through the byways; we would make excursions to the nearby mountains, climbing the Serantes, the Montaño or the Punta Lucero, from which we could catch sight of the Bay of Biscay in the distance. And we would dream, dream. . . .

We dreamed of Argentina and of Mexico, of fabulous Eldorado; we recalled the names of navigators and discoverers . . . Christopher Columbus! Juan Sebastián Blanco! Magellan, Pizzarro, Hernán Cortés, Vasco de Gama! We loved the immensity of the sea, whose extent we considered to be infinite.

We climbed the hills to pick wild berries and madrona apples in summer and to gather chestnuts in autumn. Accustomed to a hard life, we were not afraid to take risks. We—both boys and girls— raced through the mine sites; we leapt onto moving freight cars; we slid down the steepest slopes; we hung from aerial tramcar cables; we crawled through tunnels; we explored the mine drifts and the

railroad trestles. We possessed no toys, but any of us could have
written an anthology of childrens' songs and games.

The terror-inspiring beliefs and superstitions that the Church tolerated and even encouraged were transmitted from father to son;
many of these were concerned with exorcizing evil spirits from persons thought to be bewitched or possessed by the devil. From the day
we were born our mothers sewed onto our belts or blouses little bags
sold by the Little Sisters of the Triano Hospital and containing
images of the Evangelists or of Saint Peter Zariquete, patron saint
of sorcery.

In order not to give encouragement to malicious tongues, nor to
scandalize the pious, I shall not relate in detail how, at the age of
ten, I was taken to a church in the town of Duesto, where San
Felícismo was venerated, to be "de-bewitched!" I shall not tell the
whole story lest it stir up a suspicion that the demons were never
really exorcized from my body!

The fear of ghosts was widespread among both children and adults.
Just as in earlier epochs characterized by "witches' sabbaths," miracles
and burnings at the stake, the villagers claimed they saw "souls in
purgatory," souls whose former possessors had sailed away in Charon's
ferry, leaving a promise to a saint unfulfilled. The sole mission of
these disembodied spirits was to ask the deceased's former friends or
relatives to pay for masses or novenas which had been promised during his lifetime, since heaven made exacting demands, and no one
could enter heaven in a state of indebtedness. It would seem as if
Saint Peter's office received, along with the souls of the dead, the
blacklists of debtors! And the gatekeeper of Paradise apparently
proceeded in the same way as any Vizcayan mine overseer or manager:
"So you're in debt? Well, no Paradise for you." And the poor soul
would wander in search of shelter, until he might meet with an
archangel not averse to a bribe!

During the summer evenings we sat on our doorsteps and told
stories; more often than not they were tales of the supernatural, and
our voices would tremble with fear. Then the silence of the street
would be shattered by the shouted commands of our mothers ordering us in to bed; terror-stricken by our own stories, we dared not
move for fear of stumbling over a ghost in the darkness. Then our
mothers or older sisters would come looking for us, herd us along

home with slaps and buffets vigorous enough to put the entire heavenly host to flight!

The staircases of the miners' houses were pitch-dark; so were the streets at night, barely lit as they were by small oil street-lamps—until later, when electric wires were strung. The darkness was our accomplice in the pranks we enjoyed playing on more timorous women and children. We would pull up pumpkins from the gardens or pilfer them from the shed where they were piled for feeding to the hogs; first, we would hollow them out, then we would cut out holes for eyes, nose and mouth, transforming the pumpkin into a skull like the real ones we had often seen at the charnel house in the cemetery! We then covered the openings with the skin of a red onion and put a lighted candle inside; in the dark the effect was eerie.

We placed the pumpkin-skull on the point of a stick in the darkest corner of our chosen stairway and waited at the door for results. Success was almost always ours; the cries of the frightened victims and the curses of their families filled the house with commotion; meanwhile, we exploded with laughter, not unmixed with nervousness, because we had scared ourselves, too.

Once our trick ended in fiasco; after that we never repeated it. There was in our neighborhood an office worker's family, whose members included a pampered boy who never wanted to play with us. Accustomed to having his parents clear his path of all obstacles, he was incapable of so much as leaping a mud puddle on his own. He was, furthermore, a talebearer. Since we knew him to be the soul of pusillanimity, we prepared not only the pumpkin-skull but also a real, live "ghost," whose job it was to lend more realism to the scene.

One of our group volunteered to be the "ghost." We drew some lines on his undershirt to simulate ribs; these were drawn with phosphorescent match tips, so that the "ribs" would glow in the dark with a faint greenish light. We prepared the palms of his hands in the same way, so that they shone like giant glow-worms.

We placed the pumpkin in a dark corner as usual and nearby stood our "skeleton," his glowing hands moving in stiff gestures. Then came the climax. Our victim, who had gone on an errand for his father, entered the vestibule; we followed silently, holding our breath and nudging each other. He climbed the steps apprehensively, not making a sound—so as not to be frightened by the echo of his own footsteps. Suddenly there was a loud crash, followed by the tinkling of broken glass—the boy was carrying a bottle of wine for his father—and a shriek of horror. "Fa-a-ther! Fa-a-ther!" Our skeleton, undaunted, continued to wave his phosphorescent hands.

Then the door opened and on the threshold, holding an oil lamp, was the boy's father. He surveyed the scene, and his rage knew no limits. Surprise immobilized our skeleton who wished the earth would open and swallow him up. He tried to turn away, to conceal his phosphorescent ribs; he wanted to run but stood there frozen.

The indignant father seized him by the collar and gave him a phenomenal clout, then picked up the pumpkin and hurled it down the steps, where it smashed with a deafening sound. Thunderstruck, we waited for our chastised ghost to appear; when we saw him coming down the steps, laughing and crying all at once, cursing the father and the son, we breathed more freely. He showed us his scars of battle, and swore that he would knock the teeth out of the chicken-hearted brat who had to call his father for protection.

The regional rivalry fostered by the mine owners found its expression in aggressive competition among workers' districts and villages; even the children participated.

In order to reach the Concha mine with our fathers' or brothers' lunch or dinner, we were obliged to pass through the village of La Concha. The children of La Concha were our sworn enemies, and every day there were scuffles and fracases. Lunchboxes and hampers sailed through the air or rolled down the slopes, while the contenders, rolling on the ground, exchanged punches and scratches. Stones wrapped in napkins were converted into weapons. Any boy from La Concha who ventured into Gallarta, our "territory," risked the same treatment.

Whenever we carried lunch to the mines we passed through "enemy territory" in tight little clusters, our flanks guarded by the most courageous among us: the "Concheros" pursued the same policy when passing through Gallarta. Thus, what might have been a fight between two boys became a pitched battle among many, with stones as the principal weapons, either hurled directly or by slingshot. Some of the boys were phenomenal marksmen; wherever they aimed, the stone was sure to land. The role of the smaller children was to carry out a rear-guard action.

The Concheros had a leader whom we called "Cananas" (cartridge belt) because he wore an old hunter's belt with large cartridge pouches, which he kept filled with stones. Cananas was brave and daring, which did not alter the fact that he was also the victim of many stonings—a fact attested to by the scars on his face and hairy body. He was always the last to leave the battlefield, even if he were covered with blood.

These barbarous practices went on for many years, keeping alive the hostility between one village and another, between one workers' district and another. Little by little, hostility diminished; it finally disappeared alogether, along with the growth of labor organization and stronger sentiments of unity, solidarity and class consciousness. As far as the children were concerned, there was the added fact that they no longer had the arduous task of taking meals to the fathers —in cold weather or hot, in rainstorm or windstorm—after the working day was shortened.

[7]

# Destiny

Not all the families in Gallarta were "lucky" enough to have a child who could work in the mines at the age of ten or eleven. A child's labor added a small supplement to the family budget. A boy who might be our playmate one day would suddenly no longer be one of us; he would become a wage earner, with a role to play in his family and in society. But so many of them never reached manhood! Among the many young miners who, barely beyond childhood, lost their lives in mine accidents, I remember a boy from my district who was much loved by everyone for his sweet nature. He went to work at the age of 11, and at 15 was already a skilled worker, qualified to work in adult crews even though—as was customary— he earned a child's wages until he was nineteen.

The spirit and character of the boy, Bonifacio González, were put to the test by a strike which was called in the mine where he worked. The miners had demanded a 50-céntimo increase; management refused; a strike was called. A foreman called Bonifacio and his father aside and told them, "If you both stay on the job we'll give Bonifacio an adult's wages, and we'll give you a two-real raise. If you strike, you'll both be fired."

The father, vacillating, looked imploringly at his son. "That means almost two pesetas a day more, between the two of us . . . this is a serious matter, being fired, . . . the black list . . . hunger and suffering for my children, my wife." Bonifacio refused to acknowledge his father's supplicating look. He merely asked: "Will the other workers also be given a two-real increase?"

"No; the others, no."

"Then, you want us to work as scabs?"

The foreman shrugged contemptuously. "Call it anything you like."

"Father, let's go home. We may starve but at least we won't be scabs."

In spite of his youth, when Bonifacio had first begun to work he became a member of the workers' organization, and every night he could be found in the library of the *Centro Obrero*, the union hall, absorbed in books that were to open up to him a new world of justice and fraternity. When the Catholic ladies found out that Bonifacio was spending much of his spare time at the *Centro* and that he was discussing with his fellow workers what he had read, they were alarmed and went to visit his mother.

The ladies belonged to the Saint Vincent de Paul Charity Society, which occasionally gave the families of sick miners a card that they could exchange in a local store for a quarter of a pound of bacon or a little cooking oil. Thus piety and docility were guaranteed.

Bonifacio's mother, confused and ill at ease, received the visitors. In past times of great need, they had never visited her; she assumed that at last they had been apprised of her needs and had come to offer her their charity. Her doubts and her illusions were both soon dissipated. She asked them to come into the kitchen, and invited them to sit down on some wooden benches made by her son, which she always polished and cared for with care and affection. They were as shining and clean as the Eucharist plate. The ladies seated themselves, their scrutinizing glances observing every detail.

"You don't live so badly," one of them said. "Everything is very clean."

"It takes hard work to keep things clean," the woman answered mildly. "As you know, to be poor does not mean to be dirty; and we prefer a clean house to a pigsty."

"Oh, yes, of course. But to do this kind of house cleaning you need soap and lye, and they cost money."

"Yes, you're right; and muscles and willpower, too. But it's better to eat a little less, if necessary, and buy a little more soap, so that our children can live in clean houses."

"Are you educating your children to be princes?"

"No, I'm educating them to be men—even though all mothers feel that their sons have the right to live as princes are said to live."

"You're very ambitious."

"No, I'm merely a mother."

One of the ladies noticed a lithograph on the wall; its subject was a worker being crushed under a cannon; on the cannon was a bag of gold and seated on the bag was a fat monk and the caricatured figure of a merchant. The lady's anger knew no bounds; she leapt to her feet and pointed at the picture: "How can you have this object hanging on your wall? Is this how you educate your sons? And you expect the Lord to help you? If you live in mortal sin, how can God's grace protect your home?"

For a moment the mother was taken aback by the lady's irate words. But then she remembered the pleasure with which her son had made the carved frame for the lithograph, and she answered in a quiet, firm voice: "Look, my son brought 'this object' home. And, inasmuch as my son is a good boy—anyone in the neighborhood will tell you the same—I don't think the picture can be very bad. What my son likes, I like."

"Are you out of your mind? Don't you know such pictures are made by atheists, by Socialists who don't believe in God, by those hoodlums who keep the village in an uproar with their demonstrations and strikes?"

"I don't know who made the picture. All I can say is that if the people who make such pictures are like my Bonifacio, then they can't be bad. They don't believe in God? That's between them and their conscience. I answer only for mine."

"No, señora, you're mistaken. You answer to God not only for

your own conscience; you answer to Him for your children's conscience too. For example, what have you done to stop your son from
going to the *Centro Obrero* and reading those disgraceful books
which are poisoning him and all of you?"

"What have I done? Absolutely nothing. He said to me: 'Mother,
I'm going to the *Centro;* the best miners go there. There are books
at the *Centro,* and I want to learn about things I don't know and
understand other things that aren't clear to me.' I answered: 'Go,
my son and learn; wisdom is better than rubies.' And he went. That's
all there is to it."

"That's all there is to it! All! You yourself are pushing your son
toward damnation! God will punish you!"

"God punish me? Even more? In my house there's one illness
after another! My husband and my son work like burros and they
earn a pittance! You think that's not enough punishment? Look,
I'll tell you . . . at times even *I* begin to doubt God's existence.
I've never before said this to anyone; I tell it to you now so that
you'll know that it's poverty that turns us into unbelievers. God?
Where is he when we're dying of hunger, when we don't have a crust
of bread to put in our mouths? If God exists, he's blind and deaf
to the poor. You think that talking like this is a sin? The devil with
sin! When our men come home from the mines covered with mud,
wet to the bone, dog-tired, and there's only a pot of garlic soup made
with a lot of water and a little bread, and the house is dark and
cold—then we curse heaven and earth, and we feel that hell itself
can't be worse than our lives on earth."

"Hush! That's blasphemy!" one of the ladies said, covering her
ears. "Let's get out of here, this is monstrous. These people are beyond salvation. If the mothers—the mothers!—speak like this, imagine what the children say!"

"The children? They're saints, like my Bonifacio."

The ladies took their leave, bursting with indignation. Before long
their visit was the talk of the neighborhood. Opinions were divided;
a few women who hoped to receive the quarter pound of bacon
commented with uneasy disapproval, as they stood in a store doorway. The store owner nodded his approval.

"Have you ever heard of such a thing?" said one, addressing her
question to the storekeeper? "What nerve! Who would believe that
that no-good mother of Bonifacio would dare to offend the ladies!

If we don't treat them with respect, they won't help us. And the worst of it is that, because of her, the rest of us will lose."

"That's a lot of rot," cut in the clear, loud voice of a young woman sitting on the balcony of the house next door and nursing her baby. She pulled the baby away from her breast, rose to her feet and leaned over the railing: "Bootlickers! Pigs! Why can't you leave decent people alone! Bonifacio's mother was right to answer the ladies as they deserved to be answered. If they came to my house I'd throw them down the stairs. Now you can go and report to them what I've just said; maybe they'll reward you with a fine-tooth comb to help you get rid of your lice! And you, you bleary-eyed reptile, crawl back into your hole!"

Several months passed. One day several dynamite charges were detonated in the mine where Bonifacio worked. Some of them failed to go off and work could not continue until they were deactivated. Bonifacio was assigned to this dangerous job. It was the lunch break and, as his father left to join his friends for lunch, he warned Bonifacio to be careful. "Don't worry, father; I know what to do."

Bonifacio easily deactivated the first charge; there were problems with the second, since it had no deactivating mechanism. He realized the risks involved in using a drill but, confident of his skill, he decided to risk it. He had barely begun when the dynamite exploded with a thunderous din, hurling Bonifacio into the air, along with tons of rock and earth. The sudden explosion struck terror into the miners. A hoarse cry came from the depths of the father's heart, and he ran toward the mine. There was his son, covered with blood, crushed under a pile of stones. He fell on his knees next to the broken body and tried to revive the lifeless body—unwilling to accept the terrible truth.

"My son! My son!" he murmured, supporting the battered head in his arms. A lacerating anguish tore at his heart. His son dead? No, impossible. A deep sob shook his body. Tears, burning like fire, rolled down his pale, emaciated face. "My son, my son! Why couldn't I have died in your place? Why, why?"

"Come, Dionisio," said one of the other miners. "There's nothing you can do. You must resign yourself. It's the end that awaits all of us. Today it was your boy, tomorrow it may be me, or my son."

With a shudder of rage and anguish, the grieving father lifted his head abruptly. "No," he said, in a stifled voice, "we can't resign ourselves. We can't accept the destiny of animals. No, and again no! That's not the way it should be . . . this will have to change."

The sad news spread rapidly through the neighborhood. The women ran to the dead boy's house to comfort his anguished mother. The father entered the house, crushed, broken in spirit. "We no longer have a son," he murmured to his wife, pulling her to him. She was inconsolable. In her infinite pain, the threatening words she had heard from the charity ladies a few months ago—within these very walls—came back to her, hammering at her brain: "God will punish you! God will punish you!" The tortured woman fought against the obsessive memory, which merged with the nightmarish vision of her son, mutilated and destroyed by the explosion.

"God? There is no God!" she shouted. "My beloved son, where are you, what has happened to you? Where are you, my heart, where?"

The violence of her pain was succeeded by a crushing lethargy of spirit. It was as if the mainspring of her life had broken, as if her heart had left her breast. She wept no more; she thought no more. She seemed to live in a kind of monstrous nightmare, beyond the world, beyond life.

The neighbors closed the windows and surrounded her bed, so that she should not hear the street noises, nor be aware that the coffin bearing her son, who a few hours earlier had joked with her and kissed her, was being carried past the house on the shoulders of his fellow-workers to the cemetery. Behind them walked the other miners with heads bowed; they had left work in protest. Behind the miners came the children of the neighborhood, weeping. Grief-stricken, we wept for the friend whom we would never see again.

Compounding the grief suffered by Bonifacio's family, whose life was forever darkened, was the knowledge that because of an unjust piece of legislation the mine owners would benefit by his death. Bonifacio had been doing the work of an adult, producing even more than most since he was young and strong. But he was only 17 when he died, and this meant that his father was not legally entitled to death benefits, which covered only workers over the age of 19. Child labor was a bonanza for the mine owners; they incurred no responsibility whatsoever.

# From Childhood to Maturity

At 15 I finished school. I was in poor health and not able to go to work. This meant an added burden for my family, which I was reluctant to impose on them. Since my good grades qualified me for further academic training, I decided to take the one-year preparatory course for the Teachers' Normal School and then the two-year teacher-training course. After completing the first two years, my adolescent dreams faded, in the face of hard economic realities; books, food, clothes were all expenses my parents simply could not continue to meet. So I transferred to a dressmaking academy for two years. After this apprenticeship, I worked as a domestic for three years in the homes of local business men. At 20, seeking liberation from drudgery in other people's homes, I married a miner whom I had met during my first job as a domestic.

My mission in life was "fulfilled." I could not, ought not, aspire to more. Woman's goal, her only aspiration, had to be matrimony and the continuation of the joyless, dismal, pain-ridden thralldom that was our mothers' lot; we were supposed to dedicate ourselves wholly to giving birth, to raising our children and to serving our husbands who, for the most part, treated us with complete disregard.

My mother used to say, "She who hits the bull's-eye in her choice of a husband, cannot err in anything." To hit the bull's-eye was as difficult as finding a pea that weighed a pound. I did not find such a pea. May the happy wives forgive me; but each of us judges the market by the good values we find there.

Although I had no tendency to be nostalgic about the past, I used to long for the time when women worked in the mines. However brutish the work, it offered an outlet no longer available to women in the mining valley; in addition to wages, it had added a social dimension to women.

When the demand for ore fell off and there was an excess of manpower, women workers were no longer hired. This discriminatory act was carried out under the hypocritical cloak of solicitude for the mother, the woman, the family and the home. Women were freed from brutalizing mine work only to be converted into domestic slaves, deprived of all rights. In the mine, the woman was a worker and, as such, she could protest exploitation together with other workers. In the home, she was stripped of her social identity; she was committed to sacrifice, to privation, to all manner of service by which her husband's and her children's lives were made more bearable. Thus her own needs were negligible; her own personality was nullified; in time she became "the old lady" who "doesn't understand," who was in the way, whose role eventually became that of a servant to her household and a nursemaid to her grandchildren. This was the tradition of generations.

When my first child (a girl) was born, I had already suffered a year of such bitterness that only love for my baby kept me alive. I was terrified, not only by the odious present but also by the dismal, pain-filled future that loomed before me, as day by day I observed the lives of the miners' wives. Nevertheless, like other young people, I built castles in the air. And, full of illusions, I closed my eyes to my surroundings and built my dream house on the shifting sand of "contigo pan y cebolla" ("with you, bread and an onion"), believing that mutual attraction and fondness would compensate for and surmount the difficulties of privation. I forgot that where bread is lacking, mutual recrimination is more likely to enter; and sometimes, even with bread, it still creeps in.

Raw, stark reality struck at me, as at other women, with merciless fists. A few fleeting days of illusion and then. . . . Afterwards, the icy, wounding, pitiless prose of existence. Out of my own experience I learned the hard truth of the popular saying "Madre, ¿qué cosa es casar? Hija, hilar, parir y llorar." ("Mother, what is marriage? Daughter, marriage is weaving, giving birth, weeping.") Weeping, weeping over our hurts and our impotence; weeping for our innocent children, to whom we could offer nothing but tear-stained caresses; weeping for our dismal lives, without horizons, without hope; bitter weeping, with a curse in our hearts and on our lips. A woman's curse? A mother's curse? What is so surprising about that, since our lives were worse than that of the most accursed?

Was life worth living? My companions in misery and I often asked this question as we discussed our situation, our wretchedness. They spoke with resignation; after all, what could we women do? I rebelled against the idea of the inevitability of such lives as ours; I rebelled against the idea that we were condemned to drag the shackles of poverty and submission through the centuries like beasts of burden—slapped, beaten, ground down by the men chosen to be our life companions.

I was then 21 and my daughter Esther was still an infant. When my husband's wretched wages were not enough to pay the rent; when, instead of meat we ate a few potatoes cooked with red peppers to give them color; when we had to mend our *alpargatas* (rope-soled canvas shoes) with wire; when I had to patch the patches on my husband's work clothes; when, for lack of food, I hadn't enough milk to nurse my baby, I confronted my husband with a desperate question: "Do you think we can go on living like this?"

The answer was disheartening: "How do you think the others live?"

"The same as we. But I can't resign myself to living worse than animals. Let's go away; let's go somewhere else where life isn't so hard, where we can at least feed our children."

"Somewhere else? Wherever the ox goes he will be harnessed to the plow."

It was true. Where could the worker go where he would not be cruelly exploited?

The intimate daily contact with harsh reality began to fray the fabric of my religious convictions. And everyday I moved a little further from religious superstitions, prejudices and traditional fears of the supernatural. I was beginning to learn that our poverty—the lack of the most basic human necessities—was not caused or altered by the will of any deity. The source of our misery was not in heaven but on earth. It arose from institutions established by men which could be altered or destroyed by other men.

I began to read Marxist literature and for me it was a window opening on life. My ideas and sentiments began to change and take concrete form, although there was much I did not yet understand. My former Catholic beliefs began to dwindle, although not without resistance, as if they were determined to leave a shadow, a fear, a doubt in the depths of my consciousness. The struggle for a Socialist society—even though it was clearly not imminent—began to give content and substance to my life; it was the force that sustained me under the oppressive conditions of our pariah-like existence. The more I learned about Socialism, the more reconciled I was to life, which I no longer saw as a swamp but as a battlefield on which an immense army of workers was gaining daily victories, advancing even through its defeats.

My new faith was more reasonable and more solid than my religious faith had been. Now I expected nothing from the mercy of an unknown and unknowable god; my expectations were anchored in the strength of mankind—our own strength, our own struggle. I was not willing to leave the world as we had inherited it. I would struggle to change it, to make it a better world, to open a path for our children that would lead to a society without oppression and without poverty.

In my eagerness to learn, I read every book in the library of the Somorrostro *Casa del Pueblo*. And I must acknowledge that, accustomed as I was to Catholic literature of the *Quo Vadis* type, I found Socialist prose as rough as sandpaper. Out of sheer boredom I would let the "labor press" fall from my hands. (This still sometimes happens now.)

I read Marx and Engels, who more than compensated for the mediocre Socialist literature I had been reading. After virtually memorizing the *Communist Manifesto*, I boldly plunged into an abridged edition of *Capital*; although the selections were perhaps not the best, they nonetheless helped me to understand, if only on the simplest level, the cause of our poverty and the origin of our exploiters' wealth.

However, the study of Marxism was difficult for me, since there was no one to help or advise me; at that time there were no courses, no political schools in the vicinity. The study and understanding of Marxism was difficult for others as well. The secretary of the Miners' Union, a well-known Socialist, asked me one day, after I had begun to work on the publication *El Minero Vizcaíno* (The Vizcayan Miner), how much I knew about socialism; he asked me what works I had read. I told him, and also mentioned that I was studying *Capital*; he looked at me pityingly and asked, not without sarcasm: "And have you understood any of it?"

"Not much," I answered, "but enough to learn the origin of our capitalists' fortunes. I've learned how surplus value is created. This helps me to understand many things which, until recently, I thought had a divine origin; today I see them in a different light."

He smiled ironically and concluded the conversation with: "How are you going to understand these concepts if I, who have studied them for ten years, don't understand them too well?"

[9]

# 1917: A Decisive Year

> *In order to have a happy life it is necessary to have a firm conviction. And in order to die fearlessly it is equally necessary to have a firm conviction.*
> —PETER USAKOV, 18th century Russian revolutionary democrat.

1917 was a year of important struggles in Spain. In addition to domestic problems, of which there was an abundance, our country reflected the international instability; there were, in particular, repercussions of the revolutionary movement in Russia which had led to the downfall of Tsarism and the establishment of the provisional government. The monarchy in Spain was crumbling. The workers and peasants were the most militant groups, and it was their struggles that impelled the bourgeois democratic forces to take a stand. In Catalonia the regionalist movement was in full swing, creating problems for the central government. The army was totally undisciplined, as a result of the favoritism shown in high circles toward a group of "palace officers" who made up Alfonso XIII's African military command.

Discontented officers everywhere organized defense juntas, out of a patriotic desire to correct the situation, even though such actions were in violation of military rules and statutes. Morocco fought against Spanish colonialism; left-wing deputies, along with Catalonian deputies of the upper industrial bourgeoisie, walked out of the Cortes (parliament) to convene elsewhere.

The Socialist Party, together with bourgeois opposition groups, was making plans, although they had no intention of carrying the struggle against the monarchy to its ultimate conclusion. Socialist propaganda, deliberately ambiguous, gave the working class the impression that the revolution was in preparation. To deepen this impression, small firearms were distributed in several regions—especially in Asturias and the Basque provinces—to metalworkers and miners, with the advice that they should be prepared for any contingency.

While waiting for instructions, a group of miners from my district decided, on their own, to prepare for coming events by making bombs; in this undertaking, I was an eager participant. We made the bombs from the dynamite stored in the company powder magazines, to which the miners had access. We set up our workshop in a nearby cave and began to store bombs while we waited for the uprising order to be given. The bombs were completely primitive, made with tin cans of dynamite, nails and pieces of metal, sealed with cement, and with an inch-long wick which had to be ignited. We tested them and they were perfect, above all from the psychological point of view —the din they produced was bloodcurdling!

The political temperature was rising. We went without sleep, waiting for the call to action at any moment. Time passed, and there was a risk that our revolutionary ardor would subside. The workers were impatient and began to whisper about the leadership, which had hinted at such momentous events to come.

Ignoring postponements and delays, which boded no good, the railroad workers, tired of waiting for a revolution that didn't come off, struck against the railroad companies on August 10, 1917, forcing the Socialist leaders into involvement against their will in a strike movement of national scope and revolutionary character.

In Asturias (especially among the miners) and in the Basque provinces the struggle acquired an insurrectionary character. The army was sent against the strikers, the commanding general declaring that he was ready to exterminate the strikers as if they were vermin. The strike cost the working class hundreds of dead; thousands of other workers were jailed throughout Spain. Among those arrested was the (Socialist) strike committee.

The news of the strike's failure spread rapidly. What were we to do? The first thing was to get rid of our arsenal. Some of us, in the dead of night, and in the greatest of secrecy, threw our bombs into a muddy stream, where the dampness would render them useless. I breathed easier; even if someone were to denounce us, as did in fact happen, a denunciation without evidence would carry no weight.

After we had cleared the cave, my husband took refuge in a shepherd's hut. At dawn, several members of the Civil Guard came to our house, looking for my husband. When they found neither the "culprit," nor bombs nor arms of any kind, they threatened to arrest me unless I revealed his whereabouts. I refused. They left, warning me that they would give me no peace until my husband gave himself up.

Meanwhile my husband had gone to look for one of the Socialist leaders who could advise him; he was told to give himself up to the Civil Guard, which he did, and he was, of course, immediately put under arrest. He was taken to the Larrínaga de Bilbao prison, along with Rufino Castaños—a Socialist doctor, who joined the Communist Party when it was later organized—and Merodio, a well-known Republican and small industrialist. Large numbers of arrested strikers were pouring into the jail.

The defeat of the August revolutionary movement was a great lesson for the workers. Just as after all defeats, the hindsight strategists appeared, who claimed that the strike should not have been called; that "conditions were not ripe"; that "it would have been better to wait"; that "mistakes were made."

I was alone with little Esther; those of my husband's old friends and fellow workers who were able to escape had gone to Santander or Galacia or León. I was furious with my husband for having given himself up. It seemed absurd to me that workers, above all, Socialist workers, should voluntarily report to the authorities, under the illusion that they faced no reprisals. As long as they were free, there was always something they could do; in jail, there was very little.

I didn't know what to do, to whom I should turn. I couldn't expect any help from my family. And in a town where mining was the only activity, it was impossible for me to find work.

Since we had planted potatoes in the spring, I knew that at least we would not starve. I sold part of the crop and kept the rest for our own consumption. A neighbor who kept sheep provided us with a pint of milk daily; in exchange for it I mended her children's clothes. One day I received a money order for 50 pesetas, sent to me by a group of miners, friends of my husband, who were working in the

León mines. Only those who have been in circumstances like mine can imagine how welcome it was. This windfall eased my situation somewhat, and I resolved to move from the hovel we'd been living in, which was hardly fit for animals—without light, without water, freezing in winter, roasting in summer, afloat on a sea of mud.

In order to visit my husband in prison I had to take a mountainous and dangerous road along the cliffs—carrying my infant on one arm, a lunch basket and clothing on the other. I could have gone the last three-and-a-half miles of the journey by train, but I chose to save the price of the ticket by walking the entire distance.

I moved to Gallarta, renting a room there from an old couple. It was shabbily furnished, but there was electricity, and the town itself was fairly modern.

I was on the verge of selling my sewing machine since there was no indication that my husband would be released soon and I was running short of money again, but my mother urged me not to take this step (during this period she had begun to be a little less censorious toward me). Out of pride I complained to no one about my situation. It was touch-and-go for a while, but we managed to survive until my husband was freed.

One stormy November day—the sky was crackling with thunder and lightning, a fitting background for a world-shaking event!—our local newspaper vendor electrified our street as he shouted out the sensational news: "Revolution in Russia!"

My heart turned over and I ran to the street to buy a paper. The vendor wouldn't let me pay him because he knew my husband was in jail. "Here, take one," he said, "and rejoice. The Socialist Revolution has broken out in Russia."

I glanced down at the paper and a banner headline leapt up at me: "Bolsheviks Take Power in Russia. Leningrad Workers, Soldiers Storm Winter Palace; Provisional Government Arrested, Soviets Established."

One name stood out in the report: Lenin. I didn't, at the moment, grasp the immense revolutionary significance of the event, nor did I realize how it was going to affect my life, the lives of millions of men, the life of all humanity; but instinctively I knew that something immeasurably great had taken place. And my thoughts focussed on that far-off country, which, from that moment on, was to be so close to us. Two names were fixed in my consciousness, hammering at my heart and my brain, Russia and Lenin.

My former sadness vanished; I no longer felt alone. Our revolution, the revolution which even yesterday we considered to be remote and beyond reach was now a reality for one-sixth of the world.

As I rocked my baby to sleep I sang—not the old lullabies I had learned from my mother, but revolutionary songs which I had learned in my village and which had lain dormant in my memory. They were awakened by the echoes of the October Revolution.

On my first visit to the prison after the victory of the revolution, I found the prisoners so elated that even a death sentence would hardly have dampened their exuberance.

With the October Revolution, the revolutionary temper in Spain mounted; it spread to various social levels; from the industrial regions it extended to and took hold in farming districts, prompting large-scale struggles of the peasants, particularly on the huge latifundia of Andalusia and Estremadura.

It was now that the Basque nationalist movement began to flourish as never before. The old movement, of which the *fuero* (privilege or exemption granted to a province) was the rallying point, now based itself on a more generalized nationalism; its goal was to play a leading political role in the Basque provinces. Competing with it for this role was the Socialist Party, which did not grasp the importance of nationalism. In the face of the threat to it by the nationalists it fought fiercely to maintain the political influence it had enjoyed in Vizcaya.

The 1918 elections, in which Indalecio Prieto was elected deputy, were won with fists and pistols. I don't record this as an a *posteriori* recrimination, for I, too, wholeheartedly welcomed our candidate's triumph, and I, like all of working-class Vizcaya, hailed him at the victory meeting. Even though I had gone along with the idea that one does not defeat the enemy by smiles and legal niceties, I did not relish taking men from the mining district to win the elections in Bilbao and, if necessary, to crack the heads of the nationalists. Because I wanted our Socialist candidate to win, I kept silent, not taking exception to the electoral chicanery of Paulino Gómez and his cohorts. (Today they function in the Basque government in the role of dedicated nationalists, having carefully glossed over their antinationalist past.)

The violence resorted to by the Socialist Party in its struggle against Basque nationalism set a pattern which subsequently led to bloody clashes between Socialists and Communists, the more unfortunate because they created antagonisms within the working class.

In addition to Prieto, the Socialist Party elected Pablo Iglesias and the Strike Committee to the Cortes; the government had been forced to free them from jail, along with all the others taken prisoner during the August strike.

For many years there had been clashes among factions within the Socialist Party. The creation of the Third International, in March 1919, contributed greatly to clarifying the differences among them. The struggle around affiliation with the Communist International—which represented and embodied Marxist Socialism, and which brought to the international labor movement the experience of the Socialist triumph in the largest country in Europe—lasted for many months. This was due in large part to the unwillingness of certain Socialist leaders to affiliate, and also to the lack of courage and decision on the part of others who were willing to change the reformist orientation of the party.

What might be called the "class-struggle" period of the Spanish Socialist Party ended in 1917, when the party's policies began to lean toward collaborationism; and the old workers' party was transformed into a kind of republican party.

Men of high prestige, such as García Quejido, founder of the Socialist Party and the *Unión General de Trabajadores* (UGT), Acevedo, Perezagua, Virginia González, and many others left the Socialist Party and, together with Socialist Youth groups, founded the Communist Party of Spain.

The Somorrostro Socialist group, to which we belonged, joined very early, along with the National Committee of Supporters of the Communist International, set up in 1919. When the Communist Party was organized in April 1920, the Somorrostro group became one of the most active units in Vizcaya. In 1920 I was elected to the first Provincial Committee of the Basque Communist Party, and later I was a delegate to the first congress of the party.

During the summer of 1921 the national leadership of the party decided to organize an armed insurrection. (This episode has never before been mentioned publicly.) It was to start in Bilbao, and we Communists in Bilbao and the mining district were to be its shock forces. In our revolutionary infantilism we thought everything was possible, and so we devoted all our efforts to organizing the insurrection. At meetings where we discussed the coming insurrection, only one voice (and a sensible voice it was) spoke out against it—that of an old miner, José Sánchez Rey. With a keen grasp of the political issues involved, he made us see that conditions for an insurrection did not exist, nor did we have sufficient influence to lead the workers to an uprising.

"If we go through with it," he said, "it will mean collective suicide for the Basque Communists, and neither the party nor the working class will gain by it. I don't say this out of cowardice—I am willing to be the first in the struggle if the party resolves to go ahead with it—but because I am convinced that it would be madness."

Caught up as we were in a kind of revolutionary fever, possessed by sectarianism, we listened to his words with icy resentment. And if we did not react violently against him it was only because we held him in deep esteem, which he had earned by his long years of struggle and his fidelity to Socialism. We nonetheless were sure that he was mistaken, attributing his "mistake" to the influence of Social-Democratic reformism.

We were visited for a second time by a party leader, Eduardo Ugarte, who had earlier given us instructions for preparing the insurrection; this time he rekindled our revolutionary spirit with the assurance that orders for the uprising would arrive any day. But, as in Zorrilla's famous ballad, "one day passed and then another; one month passed and then another." And what finally arrived was the order to shelve all insurrectionary plans, rid ourselves promptly of all the explosives we had collected, and stow away our arms until circumstances required their use.

We were criticized for "anarchist tendencies." In actual fact we were not the guilty ones, but rather those in the party leadership who had invoked party discipline to involve us in insurrectionary preparations; the very leaders who had infected the party with revolutionary infantilism and narrow sectarianism. Our party might well have served as the model for the kind of errors Lenin described in "Left-wing" Communism, an Infantile Disorder, the errors of Communist Parties which, isolated from the masses, were not able to work out strategy and tactics that took into account their countries' specific situations.

If there ever was a party capable of making any sacrifice, it was our party. But in spite of its capacity for struggle and sacrifice, its sectarianism rendered its good qualities sterile and ineffectual, isolated it from the masses and reduced its influence to the most militant groups of the working class. Meanwhile, the bulk of the working class continued under Anarchist and Socialist influence.

As the party developed, a question of prime importance arose: How to win the unions, which were the bulwark of the Socialist Party. In spite of long-established Socialist influence, in the early stages this was not as difficult in Vizcaya as it was in other regions, because of the sharpness of the daily struggle between the workers and their exploiters.

For example, in the Covarón lead mines in Somorrostro—owned by the English MacLenan company—the miners were treated in the same way as the company treated its colonial workers. The company had a policy of shutting down the mines at the onset of winter and the rainy season, leaving the workers unemployed and destitute. When spring came, hiring would begin, but their policy was to hire only young men—no one over 45—even if he had worked in the mine for 30 years or more. The MacLenan company liked the energy and strength of young flesh, nerve and muscle—assets that were soon depleted in the mine drifts, where the walls oozed damp-ness from the Bay of Biscay, into which the mine abutted. But what did it matter to the company, as long as women continued to produce mine fodder to replace those whose strength was sapped by days of grinding labor. The Socialist leadership of the Mine Workers' Union had long tolerated this situation, but not the workers themselves. Every year when rehiring began there were struggles and protests.

During the spring of 1921 the company once more attempted to pursue its usual tactics and impose its usual conditions. But there was a new element in the picture; there were now Communists in the union who were not disposed to tolerate the management's maneuvers. The company urgently needed to begin operations; they had in their pockets large contracts for lead that was already at the docks, and within a few months they would be able to dispose of all their accumulated stock. After that the mine would close— sounding the knell for hunger and desperation in the miners' house-holds.

The miners, led by the Communist leaders of the union local, refused to work. They demanded the hiring of workers without regard to age; the establishment of a home for those workers who were dismissed because of advanced age; a wage increase for all workers; the allocation of 25,000 pesetas for the establishment of a consumers' cooperative. There was nothing farfetched about these demands; they were all well within the realm of the possible.

The company director howled with rage; the workers held firm. Time passed; every morning the mine bell clanged its call to work and every morning the workers remained deaf to it. The company exerted pressures but the workers wouldn't retreat. They met at the *Casa del Pueblo* and reaffirmed their intention to hold out until their demands were met. The company appealed to the Executive Committee of the union (Socialist-led). The committee sent a delegation to meet with the miners and convince them to modify their demands. "You must be sensible," the committee spokesman told them. "Your obstinacy will make you lose the chance of future concessions from the bosses. Right now you have the bull by the tail; if you refuse to modify your demands, don't complain later if the bosses, when *they* have the bull by the tail, refuse to make compromises."

This suggestion met with a deafening roar of indignation. The miners tore up their union cards and threw them in the faces of their representative. And they didn't give in. Eventually the company was forced to meet most of the workers' demands.

A few months later the workers in the Hoyo mine, owned by the Marquis de Urquijo, struck for better working conditions; the mine drifts were frequently full of water and were therefore in constant danger of caving in. They demanded improved safety measures and wage increases. The contractor flatly refused to meet their demands. He had learned about "the bull's tail" from the gentlemen in the union's leadership and he showed a suicidal obstinacy, declaring that he would "make the workers eat dirt."

At the start of the strike the workers assumed that their demands would be met with no great delay and so they had left the mine pumps fully manned, to avoid flooding. In the face of the contractor's bullheadedness, the workers decided to call the pump workers out on strike. The mine drifts immediately began to flood; by the end of the first day the deepest level was already impassable and the water level was rising. The situation had reached a critical stage and, with the support of the authorities, the boss decided to bring it to a head. He recruited strikebreakers. We, the miners' wives, battled them in an attempt to throw them out of the mine, but we were driven out by company guards under a rain of blows from their gun butts.

On the very day when the company thought it had vanquished the strikers, the contractor was shot by the miners. Reprisals began at once. Dozens of miners, certain of them known to be Communists, were arrested; roped together in twos, they were led off to the Larrínaga jail.

There was a series of such struggles both in the mines and the foundries in which the Socialist leadership either did not participate or failed to defend the workers' interests until the last stages of the struggle. The workers came to realize the necessity of putting into the leadership those who had at all times fought alongside them, and proven themselves to be firm defenders of the people's rights. The Mine Workers' Union, most of the *Casas del Pueblo* and other important groups in Bilbao and the mine district came under the leadership of the Communist Party, but not without desperate opposition on the part of Socialist leaders.

In 1922 the employers' association attempted to cut wages—already pitifully low—in the mines and foundries. The metalworkers answered with a threat to call a paralyzing all-industry strike, which forced the bosses to retreat. The Communist leadership of the Mine Workers' Union—whose secretary was José Bullejos, respected by the workers for his militancy—exhorted the workers to resist management's onslaught against wages; at the same time the Socialists were advancing the familiar slogan "Let's all share the poverty," in support of the false theory that struggle during periods of crisis is impossible.

We organized a meeting in Gallarta, where the party explained its position, pointing out the injustice of management's attack on wages and the fallacies of the Socialist stand. After the meeting, as the speakers were walking to the railroad station, a group of Socialists emerged from an alley; their belligerent intentions were all too evident. There was a fight in which three Communists—among them José Bullejos—and one Socialist were killed; another, seriously wounded, died the following day in the Triano miners' hospital. I had a narrow escape. Originally I had planned to go to the station with the others, but I had stayed behind to visit my parents.

# The Missionaries

One fine day after the Hoyo strike, while my husband was still in jail, a group of "missionaries" appeared on my doorstep; they were led by Doña Sebastiana Ugarte, the wife of one of the richest mine owners in Vizcaya.

We lived on the second floor of a modest village dwelling; a dark, sagging staircase led to our rooms. Busy with my cooking and with looking after Rubén, my infant son, I hadn't noticed that a big, imposing-looking car had parked outside. When I realized there were people on the stairway I thought it must be the police, as so often had been the case recently. I waited for their insolent faces to appear at my doorway. My surprise knew no bounds when, instead, I saw Doña Sebastiana and some companions. I had known her by sight since childhood, and her daughters and I had gone to school together, until they were sent to a French private school to rub off their provincial airs and manners. Doña Sebastiana and I had never spoken to each other. I was the daughter of a miner; she was the wife of a mine owner; and the distance between us was unbridgeable.

When I was a simple village girl, I meant no more to Doña Sebastiana than one of her dogs or cats. But when the village girl is transformed into a Communist woman who engages in struggle, who denounces the shameful exploitation of the miners, whose voice is heard, the señora is overcome with sudden fright. And she no longer minds lowering herself by coming to our squalid rooms, rattling the coins in her purse in the face of our misery.

I greeted her, not concealing my perplexity at her visit. I led her and her group into the living room and asked them to be seated. "What a surprise, Doña Sebastiana?"

"Why should you be surprised, Dolores! We drove over to Somorrostro to visit some friends and we've taken advantage of the opportunity to say hello to you, to see how you live and find out if we can be of any assistance."

73

"Assistance? . . . to me? I don't see how. As far as the way we live is concerned, I don't have to tell you anything; you can see for yourselves. This is our palace—windowless bedrooms; dark, damp kitchen; bare cupboard; empty bread-box; empty wardrobe; my husband in jail; and I alone with my baby, doing a little sewing to earn a few cents for his milk. Not a pretty picture, is it? No, it isn't; and, unfortunately, it's not a unique picture either. Many others live just as I do; this is our life. Three months ago my little girl Esther died; I had to borrow money for the coffin. And before that, I had borrowed money to buy her medicines. Do you understand, Doña Sebastiana, why I am a Communist? Do you understand the pain, the bitterness, the desperation we mothers have in our hearts when we cannot feed our children or cure their sickness, when they die before our eyes because we have no money for doctors or medicine?"

"I understand your grief; our children die too. Do you remember Genoveva?" (I had gone to school with Genoveva, who had later died of tuberculosis.)

"Yes, I remember her; and I was sorry to hear of her death; she was a sweet, kind girl. But what a difference between your Genoveva and the little girl you saw sitting downstairs, resting her head on her arms, lacking the strength to hold it up. She has tuberculosis, too. Any day now she will die, perhaps in the street where she spends her waking hours because there is at least more air in the street. What can her parents do to keep her from dying? Nothing. Her mother is out of her mind with sorrow; she can no longer shed a tear. It's horrible to see your children die and not be able to stop it, or even to ease their suffering."

"Life is a vale of tears and there's no such thing as absolute happiness in this world," remarked one of the ladies who had been silent until now.

"A vale of tears, you say? Indeed it is a vale of tears for us, the workers, who possess nothing but our hands and our strength. For the others, those who live by exploiting our strength, it's an Eden, a Paradise. And since we're not resigned to living in a vale of tears forever, we are struggling for a better life for all of us."

"But until this better life for all becomes possible," Doña Sebastiana interjected, "'at least the problems of many individuals can be solved. For example, wouldn't you like to have a comfortable house, a piece of land, some cattle, a good job for your husband?"

"Of course I would. But it's so unlikely that we don't even dream of such things."

"I could transform the unlikely into reality for you."

"In exchange for what, Doña Sebastiana? You wouldn't make such an offer unless there were conditions attached."

"In exchange for what? Your own salvation. Abandon the path you have chosen; return to your religion, and I'll help you to be as happy as anyone can be in this world."

"I'm grateful for your good intentions; but you misunderstand me and you offend me with your offer. If you want to play the role of missionary, go to the house next door. A family with seven children lives there; they are dying of malnutrition. Offer them what you have offered me and, believe me, they will be profoundly grateful."

"That's not possible, Dolores. I want to help you because I know you, I know your parents; you and my daughters were friends. But I can't solve everyone's problems."

"I understand, and indeed it's impossible to misunderstand. I don't know what life holds for me, but I do know that the road of struggle for socialism, the road which I have chosen, is the only road for us."

"How they've poisoned you!"

Doña Sebastiana and the ladies stood up. "Before we leave I want to make a plea; visit me in Gallarta and we'll continue our talk."

"I'm sorry, but I can't promise what I can't do. I shan't visit you in Gallarta because there is nothing more we can say to each other."

"We shall pray for you."

"As you like."

The missionary ladies made their exit. I don't know whether they prayed for me. If they prayed, the evidence would seem to indicate that God did not respond to their entreaties!

For me 1923 was not only the year of the establishment of the Primo de Rivera dictatorship* and the unleashing of brutal attacks

---

* General Miguel Primo de Rivera (1870–1930), formerly Captain-General of Catalonia, took power and established his dictatorship in 1923, following the Morroccan wars. Referred to by King Alfonso III as "my Mussolini," Primo de Rivera fell from power in January 1930, and died a few months later in Paris. The King was deposed within a year, ushering in the Republic.—Ed.

against Communists, it was also the year in which my triplet daughters—Amaya, Amagoya and Azucena—were born. Triplets born in the family of a striking miner! The strike had already lasted so long that we had spent our last cent. The only food in the house was bread—because the baker gave us credit—and potatoes.

Clothing for the newborn babies was of course a problem. I made a few little shirts and diapers out of threadbare bedsheets, and there were a few things that had belonged to my two eldest. In previous deliveries a neighbor had helped me, but because of birth complications I needed medical attention. Although we were unable to pay the doctor, he offered to look after me and expressed his willingness to wait for his fee until my husband was working again.

I spent 18 days in bed, cared for by my neighbors, each of whom, poor as they were, would every day bring me something nourishing; a bowl of soup, some eggs, apples, a jug of milk.

Citores, an old miner who could no longer find work, had no alternative but to become a beggar. With what he collected, he bought me one day two yards of diaper cloth and a half-pound of chocolate. I couldn't refuse his gift, even though I knew how needy he was himself; not to accept it would have been to offend him deeply. How generous the mine community was to me! Encarnación Inoriza, Rosario Orueta, Rosario Berastegui, friends and comrades of those trying days, I have not forgotten you!

As for my family, only my eldest sister Teresa had any affection for me. The others. . . ? I was a Communist and they were literally afraid to acknowledge me as a member of their family.

My little Amagoya died soon after birth. A neighbor made a little coffin out of a crate, which my husband carried on his shoulder to the cemetery. (And at that very moment rumors were circulating that Communists received gold from Moscow!)

Two years later Azucena died, and only Amaya and Rubén remained. In 1928 Eva was born; she lived only two months, and is buried at the side of Amagoya, Azucena and Esther. Every day, when I took lunch to my husband at the mine, I had to pass the cemetery where they were buried; each time my heart was torn with anguish. As I write these lines I weep, remembering the sufferings that filled our lives. It is difficult to measure the amount of grief a mother's heart can contain; it is equally difficult to measure the capacity for resistance to suffering that such hearts can acquire.

Life went on, and so did the struggle. Bitter hostility to Communists created a bond that united the bosses, the government authorities and the Church—and even the Socialists, whose collaboration with the dictatorship had destroyed in them any vestige of class solidarity.

There was a priest in our town who showed his animosity to us in every conceivable way. Although he had grown up in the town, he pretended not to know any of us. I was the special victim of his unconcealed loathing, until one day. . . .

In our quarter there was a widow who lived on the earnings of her daughters, who had gone to Bilbao to work as domestics; she grew potatoes and beans on a small piece of communal land, which helped see her through the hard winter months. One of her daughters fell seriously ill, and her employers, without a moment's hesitation, fired her. She returned to the village and consulted the local doctor. His diagnosis was quick and easy: "A hopeless case—it's galloping consumption."

The mother was beside herself; how could it be? Several other doctors confirmed the diagnosis. There was nothing to do but resign herself and care for the sick girl until the inevitable came to pass. But care for her with what?

The mother assumed that since she was Catholic, and since her meekness had led her to side at all times with the rich, charity would be forthcoming. But charity was deaf and blind when there was no political motivation like an election, when mattresses, milk and layettes were given away, recommendations for factory jobs distributed, and largesse dispensed lavishly—all for the purpose of winning votes.

Because there was scant good will toward the mother of the sick girl, and because of the contagious nature of the illness, none of the neighbors visited them. One day the mother and I happened to meet at the public laundry. When I inquired about her daughter she burst into tears. "God in heaven! What misery to be poor! No one thinks of us, we're left to die like dogs, no one holds out a helping hand," she sobbed. The reproaches she had earned for her servility were on the tip of my tongue. But I didn't want to add to her misery; she was a villager, and if we other villagers didn't come to her aid, no one would.

That night after putting my children to bed I went to her house.

"I've come to sit up with Rosa so that you can get some rest," I said.

"Do you know that my daughter has consumption?"

"Yes, I know."

"And you're not afraid of catching it?"

"No, I'm not afraid. In what worker's house hasn't there been a case of tuberculosis?"

Convinced that I really was willing to stay, she told me what needed to be done for Rosa during the night, and she went to bed. At dawn I went home to prepare breakfast for my family. I slept a little in the afternoon and in the evening I went back to stay with Rosa, whose death was clearly imminent.

Since there are no secrets in small towns, the fact that I had been looking after Rosa at night spread rapidly. Since she was a Catholic, to whom the last rites had already been administered, this caused a scandal in local "good society." "Are we going to put up with such a thing—that Pasionaria* should be the only person to sit up with Rosa during her last hours on earth?" they asked. So they drew up a plan.

On my third night of my vigil with Rosa, the parish priest appeared in the room. I answered his somewhat curt greeting and sat in my chair, not moving. He sat down facing me, and thus we passed the night, without uttering a word; if Rosa groaned or asked for something we both rose to attend to her needs. At dawn we left the house together, I, to go home and he, to church, where he would say early mass. It was clear to see that what I had done as a simple gesture of neighborliness toward a family in distress had been interpreted as a political gesture. But I continued to sit up with Rosa every night, resolving to do so until the end came. One night the priest arrived to find me already sitting at Rosa's bedside. He was more cordial, his stiffness had vanished. He greeted me affably and, sitting down, opened a friendly conversation—about the weather, about crops. The ice was broken.

And thus we continued every night until Rosa died. Afterward, something changed in the attitude toward Communists. The priest no longer crossed the street to avoid meeting a Communist, and no

* Literally, "The Passion Flower."—*Ed.*

matter how reluctant "respectable society" was to acknowledge it outright, we had risen in their estimation.

The priest's fanaticism was not altogether absolute, but, as it happened, his rigid ideas of morality were indirectly the cause of his premature death. He seemed to believe that any departure from monastic behavior patterns was sinful; he feared that he might appear to be like other men. He loved to swim, but rather than go to a public beach, he chose to swim on an isolated part of the coast near the mines. One morning, as he was about to dive into the water, he slipped and fell among some jagged boulders; his leg was broken and he lay there, unable to move; the tide was coming in and he was in danger of drowning.

Later in the day a passing miner heard a man moaning softly; he approached and realized that it was the parish priest. Since it was impossible for one person to extricate him, the miner ran for help; with the aid of several other miners, the priest was rescued from his stony prison and carried to the nearest hospital; his condition worsened rapidly, and he died of gangrene a few days after.

Some time later I received an "In Memoriam" card from his family, bearing his photograph and a few lines written by one of his sisters, in which she expressed the hope that I would not refuse to accept the card. I did not refuse. Eventually I put it away in a drawer. Several months later my husband and a group of comrades were arrested at a meeting of the Provincial Committee in Bilbao, and when night fell a squad of political police came to search our house. The only "compromising" document they found was the "In Memoriam" card, clearly and unmistakably addressed to me.

Official consternation! "How is it possible?" they asked. "This 'In Memoriam' card was sent to you?"

"I don't owe you any explanations."

"It's understandable," said their sergeant. "Extremes meet. Priests and Communists."

"That's a lie," I answered.

"If you don't shut up," one of the policemen moved toward me, "we'll have to lock you up with your friends."

"Lock me up if you like; after all, that's your job."

He glared at me threateningly. Disregarding the lot of them, I began to tidy up the house. Such simpletons as these—how could they possibly have understood how I, a Communist, came to have an "In Memoriam" card, commemorating the death of a priest?

My husband had just gone back to work after his release from jail, when he was arrested once more. I was furious and desperate; we were just beginning to lift our heads above water when once again the privations were going to begin, the black days. During his detention I was responsible for the house and family as well as for a variety of political undertakings. I attended local and provincial party meetings and attempted to carry out the tasks assigned to me, tasks which were not always easy and were almost always risky, due to our "infantile" revolutionary activities—transporting arms or dynamite, distributing illegal propaganda, hiding comrades wanted by the police.

Sometimes I had to take my children to meetings, because there was no one to leave them with; sometimes I would put them to bed and slip out of the house quietly, hoping they wouldn't wake up and realize I was gone.

One night we were holding a meeting at the *Casa del Pueblo*. It had been closed by the authorities, but I had a set of keys. I took Rubén, then about two, with me. We were to meet in a room off the stage, and I left Rubén in the auditorium, which was dimly lighted. For a while I could hear him wandering around the room; then there was silence and I assumed that he had fallen asleep on a bench. After the meeting I went to the auditorium to take him home but he wasn't there. It occurred to me that he might have slipped out and run home alone. I felt a deep uneasiness because the road home crossed a brook swollen by rain. In a panic I ran to our house; no Rubén. I was terror-stricken. It was past midnight—where to begin looking for him? I tried all the neighbor's houses; no one had seen him. My close friends among them dressed and came out to join the search. We shouted his name in the fields and on the roads—no answer.

Someone suggested that we return to the *Casa del Pueblo*; perhaps he had fallen through the stage trapdoor, perhaps he had fallen asleep in some hidden nook. A thorough search of the building proved fruitless.

At each side of the building's entrance there were tiers of seats, erected for outdoor meetings and fiestas. One of the search party climbed up to the top tier. A sudden exclamation broke the tension that enveloped all of us—me, above all.

"There he is!" he shouted joyfully.

There was Rubén in the recess between two tiers, sound asleep. I snatched him up; my joy made him seem as light as air. But my strength was deceptive. After the anxieties I had suffered, I could barely stand. A comrade took Rubén from my arms and carried him on his shoulders to our house. It was late and we walked fast, since the comrades had to go to work early and day was dawning.

During much of the time between 1917 and 1931 I was alone with my children; my husband was often picked up in police raids and jailed, along with some of the other comrades, whose wives suffered as I did. In 1927, on a visit to the Larrínaga prison, where our husbands were incarcerated, we wives and relatives met together and decided that if the prisoners were not released within a week we would hold a protest demonstration on the following Sunday. We planned to lie down on the streetcar tracks, in order to bring our plight to the attention of the public and apprise them of the legal abuses to which our husbands were subjected—such as being held without trial for an indefinite period, until the governor of Vizcaya might deign to release them.

All the wives and other relatives had supported the plan to demonstrate, but only a few appeared on Sunday. There were Ramona Arrarás and her children, Esther Arrieta and her children, Comrade Casado's aged mother, and I, with my Rubén and Amaya. Although few in number, we were willing to throw ourselves onto the streetcar tracks as planned.

Our children—Esther's and mine were about four and seven, Ramona's slightly older—knew of our plans. They were very solemn, each holding his mother's hand, resolved to imitate our actions, even though—as they confessed to us later—they were terrified at the thought of being run down by a streetcar.

As we walked toward the site chosen for the protest, a group of Communist youths approached us with a message from the Provincial Committee, urging us not to go through with our plan. We then decided to visit the governor and demand liberty for the jailed members of our families. A large group of Communist women joined us, and we all walked into the headquarters of the provincial government, much to the surprise of the building guards, who were completely at a loss as to what they should do. By the time they had emerged from their state of consternation, we women, with our children, our lunch-baskets and bundles, were already in the governor's waiting room.

On hearing our voices, a secretary approached us. Justice demands that I acknowledge here that he treated us with the utmost respect, in fact, with kindness. He asked us to be seated and requested that we choose a small delegation, which would be received by the governor.

The women elected Ramona Arrarás, Esther Arrieta and me. I counseled firmness and no whining; we were, after all, not asking for charity or favors. A few minutes later we were presented to the governor. He stood rather peevishly, throughout the entire interview, and we took this to be a sign that the interview would be a short one. He asked the purpose of our visit.

"The purpose is simple. Our husbands have been locked up for a long time and held without trial. They have committed no crime; we ask you to release them."

"You have a most unique method of addressing your petitions to the authorities. You ask no one's permission for an interview and you even bring your children along."

"We need no one's permission to ask for justice. We gave ourselves permission. And if you don't choose to listen to us, the people in the street will listen."

The governor, dumbstruck, looked at us as if we were freaks. At last he spoke, asserting that our husbands had been arrested at an illegal meeting where subversive literature had been found. He went on to say that they were being held under the orders of the Security Headquarters, to which authority we should address our petition.

I objected. "What about your authority? An order from you is enough to authorize an arrest, but yet you say that the authorization to release the prisoners must come from Security. Who is the supreme authority in the province, anyway, you or they?"

"You women are very insolent."

"Insolent? If you lived as we do, you'd be insolent too."

Then he tried to convince us of the evils of Communism, claiming that the people lived badly in the Soviet Union. His assertions were so stupid that it took no effort at all to refute them.

We returned to the subject of our interview. "Concretely, Señor Governor, what can we expect from you?"

"I repeat, I can do nothing. I will transmit your demands to Security and they will decide."

"Let's go," I said to my companions. "You all know what we'll have to do next; we'll shout our protest until the very stones hear us. We'll soon see if the governor can or can't take action."

The next day the governor happened to meet a friend of ours, to whom he said: "Heaven protect me! What a predicament I'm in! Those miners' wives came to see me yesterday and they were terrifying. If the wives are so fierce, imagine what their husbands are like!"

[11]

## End of the Dictatorship

Events throughout Spain gave proof that the end of the dictatorship of General Primo de Rivera was imminent, in spite of the support given it by the Socialist Party. Opposition began to crystallize in political organizations and in the army. Students, too, were very active in the struggle. On the initiative of Professors Marti Jara and Don José Giral, Republican groups organized the *Alianza Republicana* (Republican Alliance), which many intellectuals joined. After the monarchy was overthrown, some of them occupied high posts in the national government. Among those who worked for the overthrow of the dictatorship were Generals Aguilera, Romanones, Melquiades Alvarez, Lerroux. The *Confederación Nacional de Trabajo* (National Confederation of Labor, CNT) offered its collaboration.

When the dictatorship convoked the Consultative Assembly in 1927, the Communist Party called a general strike in Vizcaya. Virtually all the miners and other workers in the mine district responded to the strike call with enthusiasm, but the task was not so easy in Bilbao, where the Socialists, who had commitments to the dictatorship, were opposed to the strike.

I left my children in the house of an old comrade and took a train to Bilbao. A group of Communist women, I among them, went to all the factories and workshops, urging the workers to strike. In many cases our exhortations met with success, in spite of the fact that we had the police at our heels constantly, and in spite of the attacks and insults of the Socialists.

In 1930 the Communist Party called the Conference of Pamplona (held, in spite of its title, in Bilbao) under conditions of utmost secrecy. I was a delegate from the Provincial Committee of Vizcaya. We discussed tactics for the forthcoming period, which was clearly going to be a stormy one, and a plan was drawn up. The party leadership was strengthened with new comrades, and I was among those elected to the Central Committee. In the course of the conference the divisive activities of a group of Catalans was discussed and condemned. This group later organized the Trotskyist-oriented *Bloque Obrero y Campesino* (Workers' and Peasants' Bloc).

It was during the election campaign in 1931, which culminated in the overthrow of the monarchy, that I first began to speak at public meetings—not without a certain reluctance. It seemed to me that speaking to the masses was enormously difficult and carried with it a heavy responsibility.

Ever since my childhood I had liked attending public meetings, and, since the miners' struggle was then very intense, political life was correspondingly active. There were frequent meetings and conferences among all groups in the political spectrum, and we village children flocked to them, especially to those held in the town square or in the sports arena. I never missed a meeting. I drank in what the orators said, whether Socialist or Carlist, even though I did not understand their political goals. But the musical sound of their language, the sonorous phrase, the impassioned attack, the sarcastic word, the blistering jibe, filled me with enthusiasm. Afterwards, at home I would reconstruct the speeches that had impressed me most. As time passed, as I heard those reputed to be great orators, many impressed me unfavorably because of demagoguery or histrionics or lack of simplicity and stimulating content. Now it was I, a Communist, who was to stand on the platform.

On April 14, 1931, the king and the royal family were obliged to abandon the country, and the Republic was proclaimed. These events came about as the result of elections on April 12, when a majority of Spaniards voted the monarchy out. Its downfall pried loose the hold of an oligarchy composed of aristocracy and finance capital on the political leadership of the nation. This group, which had dominated Spain since the restoration of the monarchy in 1874, was now replaced by a Republican-Socialist regime.

It appeared that Spain was on the threshold of a new epoch of progress and democratic development. But the illusions of those early days of Republican-Socialist euphoria were rapidly dispelled by the cold wind of conservatism emanating from the new governing forces. We Communists were especially able to judge only too soon how little difference there was between the old regime and the new.

In 1931, we organized a meeting in the Campos Elíseos Theater in Bilbao to celebrate May Day. Our plans were to hold a street demonstration at the close of the meeting. On emerging from the theater, we found all the surrounding streets blocked off by squads of security police. When we attempted to walk past them, they threw themselves upon us, raining blows with their sabers and trampling us with their horses. Many workers were wounded. We fought back with stones and bricks. I picked up a flag and, followed by a group of comrades, marched through the streets of Bilbao, protesting the disgraceful outrages perpetrated by the security police, and the violence with which the Republican-Socialist government was inaugurating its accession to power. Ours was a small, local incident, but it was nonetheless significant as a foreshadowing of what the people, especially the working class, could expect from the new regime.

Nonetheless, the restoration of the Republic opened up new paths for the development of democracy. It is possible that without the collaboration of Socialists in Republican governments more progress in this direction might have been made. Had the Socialist Party not joined the government, had it formed an alliance with the Communist Party and the CNT, it might have played a definitive role in rallying the workers for the formation of a united Marxist party of the working class. But the Socialist Party, under the Republic, acted not as a spur to revolutionary advance but as a brake upon it. Its collaborationist policy, which day by day diminished its role as a party of the working class, made it an adjunct of the government. As such, it shared the responsibility for the unpopular policies which destroyed mass support for the Republic. And although one of the principal political objectives of the Republicans and Socialists in power was to gain the adherence of the big bourgeoisie, not even this goal of theirs was achieved.

In the Republic's early days of popular enthusiasm and ardor, of revolutionary impetus among the masses, of cowardice and fear among the classes that had formerly controlled Spain's destiny, all democratic reforms seemed within the realm of the possible. But the men who formed the provisional government, and those who later constituted the successive Republican-Socialist governments, were not capable of instituting the reforms that Spain needed. Never before in Spain's history was there a more propitious moment for the people to bridge the gap that separated them from more advanced countries. Never had the popular consciousness known such vitality. Never had the determination to liquidate the subjugation of the past surged with such elan in the masses. Their will was like a live coal, burning with desire to end poverty, backwardness, ignorance. But the men who guided Spain's destiny, who were carried to power by the unanimous decision of the populace, turned their backs on it and governed for the benefit of the privileged classes.

The most urgent task of the democratic Spanish revolution was to change the system of land ownership, which was based on the latifundia; to wrest from the aristocracy the lands they left uncultivated for the purpose of transforming them from a source of income into a source of labor; to put an end to the land hunger of the peasants; to put an end to their age-old poverty, with its concomitant backwardness; to incorporate them into the struggle for the creation of a new Spain. All this would have resulted in winning millions of people for democracy and progress, people who had traditionally lived under the degrading influence of the aristocracy and the local cacique [political boss]. Spain was, after all, not the servile, adulatory bureaucracy that bowed and scraped before the new Republican political leaders; Spain was primarily the workers, peasants, intellectuals, and middle class. Spain's roots were in the factory and the field, in the thousands of peasant villages clustered around the church towers, dominated and oppressed by the priest and the cacique, who were at the beck and call of the large landholders. All these facts were ignored, and the roots of the old regime were left intact, to proliferate throughout the nation.

The days passed, and the months and the years. In this people's republic, Deputy Margarita Nelken charged in the Cortes, "The workers go hungry; in many towns of Andalusia and Estremadura peasants are eating wild roots and berries." Land ownership continued to be based on the latifundia. A handful of rich landowners, owning tens of thousands of acres of land—only part of it in cultivation; millions of peasants, victims of centuries of hunger and destitution, some of them landless, others owning a parcel so tiny that its cultivation could not so much as provide food for its owners.

Cristóbal de Castro, in his book *Al servicio de los campesinos* (At the Service of the Peasants), published in 1931, presents statistics which reflect vividly the tragic situation of Spanish agriculture. The book quotes a report published in 1930 by the *Dirección General de Propiedades* (Property Office), based on data collected in 1928. The following figures refer to the amount of cultivated and uncultivated land in hectares (one hectare = 2.471 acres):

|  | Cultivated | Uncultivated |
| --- | --- | --- |
| Province of Ciudad Real | 894,000 | 1,022,000 |
| Granada | 588,000 | 605,000 |
| Valencia (touted as a model of cultivation) | 172,000 | 327,000 |
| Spain as a whole | 31,000,000 | 19,000,000 |

Christóbal de Castro concludes: "Ours is the only remaining European nation whose agricultural economy is based on the latifundium. Ours is the only European nation to maintain this inhuman system of ownership. Ours is the only European country that tolerates large expanses of uncultivated land. Only Spain offers the tragic spectacle of vast feudal domains, each under the domination of a feudal lord, each populated by migrant, homeless villagers dispossessed by the latifundist."

There were still, according to Castro: "Millions of human beings who live in huts and hovels, in caves and barns with their animals; they eat contaminated food and drink polluted water and they are unacquainted with hygiene, culture, hospitals, railroads, books, newspapers and theaters."

There were peasants who lived, even before and after the Republic was proclaimed, in precisely the same conditions as serfs in the Middle Ages. A case mentioned by Castro is typical and tragic, characteristic of feudal Spain: "About ten miles from Saragossa there is a feudal village, Sobradiel, which belongs lock, stock and barrel, to a count of the same name. We are told by local peasants that this village—even now, in the 20th century—is a fief where life is made intolerable for the wretched slaves of the land, who suffer the most implacable tyranny."

To read certain of the rental statutes is to confirm Castro's description. They are so inhuman, so cruel, that one might be reading the pages of Paul Louis Courier* on medieval feudalism. Besides the steep rent demanded for each parcel of land, the unfortunate tenants pay a minimum of 800 pesetas per year for their miserable hovels. They are, furthermore, made to pay maintenance costs for their houses, even though the rent paid is higher than that paid in Saragossa for equivalent dwellings.

Item: field weeds will be considered the property of the landlord, and beet tops will be classified as weeds.

Item: the tenant will pay for removal of leaves from, and cleaning of, water pipes.

Item: the tenant may not sublet.

Item: the tenant may not establish cafés, stores or any other business.

Item: the tenant may not keep rabbits nor breed cattle, without permission of the señor.

Item: the landlord may dismiss the tenant for reasons of public or private morality, for lack of piety, for insubordination or lack or respect.

Such was the feudal and latifundist Spain inherited by the Republic, which it made no attempt to transform; such was the Spain that continued unchanged until the Civil War.

During the first months of the Republic there were some attempts at agrarian reform. The government's first plan, limited though it was, was rejected as being too radical. Neither then nor during later attempts at reform was there a real effort to advance the democratic revolution; on the contrary, the men in power tried to retard it. Instead of radically changing existing land ownership patterns,

---

* Paul Louis Courier, 1772–1825, French polemicist who was jailed for his pamphleteering; died at the hands of an assassin.—Ed.

y endeavored to divert the attention of the peasants from such
ıdamental questions.

Agrarian reform was not merely the concern of one or another
ion or province; it was the very essence of the democratic revolu-
n. This was a fact which the leaders of the Republic were ob-
rately unwilling to face.

Manuel Azaña, chief of state under the Republic, was interviewed
a correspondent of the *London General and Economic Press*
rtly after the Republic was proclaimed. On the subject of the
arian problem and the eagerness of the peasants to own their own
d, his words must surely have calmed the fears of the large land-
lders. He advised the landless peasants not to entertain the illu-
n that they would be granted land. He declared this to be an
possibility in *la República de Trabajadores de todas clases* (The
public of Workers of All Classes)—the title bestowed on the
public by the Constitution—just as it was impossible to provide
rk or to put an end to the hunger and misery which was their only
ritage.

There was no way out. The Republican and Socialist leaders, speak-
; through Azaña, were telling millions of landless peasants that they
re not to pin their hopes on the Republic. Once again the experience
Spanish history was making crystal clear the fact that the bourgeoisie
uld never carry out its own revolution—the democratic revolution
—and that only the working class was capable of bringing it to fruition.
was the inability of the Republican-Socialist regimes to find a solu-
n to the problems of the bourgeois revolution that lay at the root of
eir historic responsibility for the war unleashed in 1936 by the
cists and reactionaries against the Republic and the people.

# PART TWO

PART TWO

# 12

# First Arrest

3y 1931, at the outset of the electoral campaign which resulted in
 overthrow of the monarchy, the situation within the Communist
ty was grave and its ranks were depleted. The wave of repression
 passed, leaving in its wake broken wills and low spirits. But it
 not only repression that had weakened the party. Equally im-
tant was the role played by the incorrect policies of the leadership
 by a sectarianism that had not been eliminated before the ad-
t of the dictatorship. However, the party soon began to recuperate,
king new gains among workers all over Spain and in the Basque
untry in particular.

oward the end of September 1931, the party leadership decided
transfer me to Madrid to work as an editor of *Mundo Obrero*
'orkers' World), which was to be the party's central organ. I was
 to be in charge of women's activities in the Politburo. But
an proposes, God disposes," though in this case it was not God
 decided but the police. It happened like this:

everal weeks before my transfer to Madrid, there had been a
uor clash between Socialists and Communists. The incident had
en provoked by the bullying taunts of the Socialist Civil Guards
one of the most popular camp grounds in the Basque Country.
is would have been forgotten had it not been for the irresponsible
ion of a leader of sorts in the party youth group, who later that
ht provoked another incident. This time the consequences were
ody; two Socialists and one Communist were killed; several Com-
inists were seriously wounded.

n the mining area where I was living we knew nothing of what
l happened until we received the newspaper on the following day.
 were dismayed by the news. That night, those of us who were
charge of the party's organizing work in Somorrostro met at my
use to decide what measures to take. We still had no details of
at had happened; but we were deeply worried. When we were

93

about to leave, there was a knock on the door. At first we thou
it was the police; we were quite used to this, for whenever a st
was being planned or whenever there was any sort of political acti
afoot, police raids and investigations became as common as our d.
bread.

The comrades left through the back of the house which led t
garbage dump, and I opened the door. It was not the police l
several of the comrades who had been wounded in the fight. T
came to my house, always open to those in need, in search of shel
and a place to hide. Among the comrades was Ambrosio Arra
who, with a bullet in his stomach, could stand up only with the
of the two other comrades whose wounds were less serious.

I told them to come in. One had been shot in the leg and
other in the arm. I took care of the less serious cases with whate
simple remedies were available. But I did not dare touch Arra.
One of our group went to a town a few miles away to get t
doctor, who was a friend of ours. He came and after examin
Arraras told us that his condition was critical, that peritonitis v
imminent, and that this would mean almost certain death.

We decided to send those who could walk to a little town
Santander province, where some friends of ours would take care
them. Arraras, whose fever was slowly subsiding, stayed in my hou
When his condition improved, we took him first to another vill
in the mining district and then to Santander province. And this v
his bad luck and mine.

The village was holding one of its well-known public outings,
tended not only by people from the mountains but also by ma
from Vizcaya. Among them were a group of Socialist Civil Guar
As luck would have it, they bumped into Arraras, who had reckles
decided to go out and have some fun. The chase began. Travel
over little-known roads and mountain passes, Arraras arrived at
house late at night, on the eve of my departure for Madrid. V
pointed out to him the imprudence of his actions, which not o
broke all rules of underground work but also endangered the co
rades who had helped him.

I told him that I had to leave the following day, under orders
the party, and that therefore he could stay only for a couple of d
—the time needed for my mother, who had come to help us, to p
things in order. He understood, and I said good-bye to him the f

wing morning. With my children Rubén and Amaya I went to the
ilroad station to take the train to Bilbao.

Instead of taking the main road I decided to take a shortcut. As
reached the top of a hill, I saw a man who was gesturing for us
stop.

"It's Mariano," said Rubén.

Mariano was an old worker who, because of his rebelliousness, was
vays being persecuted. Nobody would give him a job, and his family
d to go through a hell of poverty and suffering. When he caught
with us, he spoke nervously and rapidly: "A truck full of Civil
uards and two police cars are on their way to your house right
w."

Without hesitating a second, I sent my ten-year-old Rubén home
tell Arraras that the police were after him. Rubén ran fast and
t home just ahead of the police. He barred the door and showed
raras to a window through which he could escape unnoticed.
raras left at once, while Rubén went to open the door for the
lice, who were furiously threatening to break their way in. They
rmed in, and when they did not find what they were after they
ned everything upside down, all the while loudly threatening
ry one of us.

Arraras did not manage to escape, for while the police searched
r house, the Civil Guards surrounded the hills where he was hiding
l closed all the roads and paths; and just as he thought the road
s clear, he was caught.

Since I was afraid of being arrested, I asked the comrades in the
vincial Committee whether they thought it was wise to go on to
drid. They thought I ought to leave, because, in any case, the
ice were more likely to arrest my husband than me. However, it
n't turn out that way.

One afternoon, as I was leaving the editorial offices of *Mundo
rero*, I was arrested and taken to the General Bureau of Security.
as classified as a common criminal and put into a cell together
h prostitutes and other women of ill repute to await further de-
ons from the authorities.

Nobody asked me for a statement, nobody informed me, in spite
my repeated requests, as to the reasons for my arrest. Close to
night on the third day of my arrest, a security guard opened the
r of the cell and shouted: "Everybody to the paddy wagon."

"Me too?" I asked.

"You too!"

It was ridiculous to protest and, in any case, useless. There was order to transfer all of us to the prison, and the guards followed t order impersonally—they were only doing their job.

Going into the women's prison was really something! My ce mates were fortnightly guests of the "Quiñones Street Hotel," as th called it, and they were well known by the warden and the nu who ran the prison. They went in quite casually, and were even ceived with a certain sympathy.

But I was an outsider, a prisoner who was in jail for no specifi reason and who was being held for a Bilbao court. The nun in char ordered me to undress. I refused.

"Why should I undress when I've already gone through the Ge eral Bureau of Security where they took note of every bit of clothi I have on me?"

"We just want to know if you are sick, if you have any weapons tobacco," said the nun.

"If you want to know whether I'm sick, call a doctor. I have weapons because I'm no criminal nor do I have tobacco because don't smoke. I have been arrested for political reasons, and you ha no right to inspect me or treat me any worse than the other p oners."

"Maybe you don't smoke, but your clothes smell of tobacco."

"I don't doubt it. For almost three days I have been locked up a cell at the General Bureau with women who never stopped sm ing."

The nun didn't quite know what to do; then she nodded to l assistant and said between her teeth: "Let's go!"

The women with whom I came in had already been sent to th quarters, a large room on the ground floor facing a small courtya where they spent most of their time. Most of them were in jail having practiced their profession before the hour set by police regu tions.

They took me to the second floor, where the common crimir were kept. An enormous door, like that of a stable or a garage, clo the entrance to this section. The "top deck," as it was called in pri jargon, had no windows to the outside. The nun showed me t cot where I could lie down.

The top deck was silent and dark, and the thick acrid smell of urine crept into one's nose and throat, causing an unpleasant irritation. The latrines were in the same room, which made the air almost unbreathable.

As soon as the nun had locked the door, the women began to whisper to each other. It sounded like a beehive. From a corner, a hoarse voice complained insultingly: "Night is for sleeping! You could've come earlier!"

I remembered reading years before, in a book dealing with prison life and customs, about the importance of making other prisoners respect you. I went to prison determined to make them respect the fact that I was a Communist and also determined to tolerate no insult or affront. Therefore I answered the woman who had complained, in a quiet but firm voice:

"Listen to me. I can't see where you are, I don't know whether you're old or young, but it's all the same. Could you tell me at what hour you asked the police to bring you to this hotel? I don't know why nor how you've come here. But I can tell you that I didn't come here. I was brought here, which is not the same thing. In any case, if the new guests bother you, I believe you can ask for a separate room; then you'll have no reason to complain."

There were some muffled whispers. Without knowing it, I had put one of the most feared women in the prison in her place. She was Manuela, a professional thief, capable of slashing you with a razor blade at the least provocation.

Nobody slept that night in the top deck—I, because the novelty of the situation would not let me close my eyes; my new cellmates, because they didn't want to miss the spectacle of the fight they expected between Manuela and me.

At six-thirty we were aroused by loud bells. The prisoners jumped off their beds and rushed to get dressed.

"Hey, you," said one of the women. "You're supposed to get up when the bells ring. The nun should be coming in soon."

"Let her come. I don't think she'll eat me."

They all came up to me except Manuela. They wanted to know who I was and why they had arrested me. The usual questions followed:

"Murder?"

"No!"

"Theft?"

"No!"

"Kidnapping?"

"Neither murder, nor theft, nor kidnapping."

"Then why are you here?"

"For being a Communist!"

They were all speechless. A Communist woman in that world, on the outside of society, was something nobody had ever heard of or seen.

"And what is that?" one of them asked.

"What do you think it is?" answered another, "that's politics."

"What do women have to do with politics?"

"C'mon, you mean you don't know? You're living in a cloud. Don't you know that the director of this prison—goddamn her! —is a woman."

"But, you're not one of them, are you?"

"No, I'm not. As you can see, the head of the Department of Prisons is a woman, and other women, like you and me are inside the prisons, for one reason or another."

"And, what do Communists want?"

"We'll talk about that later. Now let me get dressed."

I got dressed quickly and made my bed. Then I asked one of the women for a broom, so I could sweep the area around my bed.

"Not in a million years! You're not sweeping no prison floor! We'll take care of that." I told them I was used to working and that I wasn't going to have a heart attack if I did my part of the work. But they wouldn't let me.

After roll call, Manuela approached me, followed by the curious gazes of the other women.

"You'll forgive me for last night, won't you? One is always nervous in this dump and sometimes you speak before you think. I hope you won't have no hard feelings."

"Why should I have hard feelings? I understand how you feel. But you must also understand that none of us comes here voluntarily and that we are all disgusted at having to live inside these dirty walls. That is why we should avoid making it hard on each other."

"You're right, and let me tell you that in me you have a friend on whom you can depend."

"Thank you."

"Since they brought you later than usual you won't have a cup for your breakfast. Take mine. It's clean and I'm not sick."

"And how are you going to have breakfast?"

"Don't worry, I know the place and I know where to find what I need."

I took the cup. We lined up to go to the mess hall. When we finished I washed the cup and gave it back to her. We were friends.

That night, after the nuns made the last rounds and locked the door, the top deck became a lecture hall. I told them what communism was, what communism meant for women. I spoke to them about the Soviet Union, about women in the first Socialist country, comparing them to women in Spain and the causes that led to crime and prostitution.

One of them asked, "Can a woman like me become a respectable person?"

"Of course you can. And Communists will always try to help you."

"And how about a thief?"

"Yes, a thief too."

"And, won't anybody remind us of our past?"

"Nobody; and if anybody dares to insult you because of your past, they will be punished."

A few knocks on the window that connected our quarters with those of the nuns made it clear that our little talk had been overheard and that it was time to go to bed.

On the following day, after breakfast, the nun in charge of our section informed me, with the sweetest of smiles, that the Mother Superior had decided to transfer me to a small cell with a skylight where the kitchen help usually slept. In the Mother's opinion, the top deck was unhealthy, and she thought I would be more comfortable in the other cell.

I would have been more comfortable there but it was only too easy to see that they were trying to isolate me and put an end to my "lectures" on communism. I did not leave my cellmates. While waiting for the order that would transfer me to the Bilbao prison, I went to the shop where prisoners had to work from nine to one in the morning and from three to six in the afternoon.

The first day, intending to do some reading, I sat down on a bench next to a young girl who was straining her eyesight making a fine lace fan. She told me she would get 25 céntimos for a job that took her two days.

The director of the workshop, a Socialist professor, entered. She was substituting for the nun who usually was in charge of the shop; she sat down behind a table at the front of the room, as if it were a classroom. She noticed that I wasn't working. She rapped her knuckles on the table, demanded silence, and said:

"Hey, you, the new one, stand up."

I stood up. She looked at me from head to foot and asked me in an inquisitorial tone: "Why aren't you working?"

"I beg your pardon. When I went to school, my teacher called us by our last names. Aren't you ashamed to call us 'Hey, you'? I am not working because I am trying to learn a few things about prison life and because I will not allow you to exploit me as you exploit these women, forcing them to work for a few cents, ruining their eyes making embroidery and fans in this dim light. Do you now understand why I am not working? May I sit down?"

She did not answer and everybody in the shop was speechless. They went back to work and, after a while, the professor left the shop, on some pretext. She had obviously gone to get some information about me. When she came back, she looked pale. She was ashamed of her short temper and the rudeness she had shown toward the other prisoners in front of me, a Communist. One could not say that she or any of the other prison officials were inherently evil. But the job makes the man, and they were, first and foremost, prison officials.

When we were leaving for lunch, the professor took me aside. "I'm sorry. I didn't know you were a Communist. Since we often meet with resistance to the forced labor, I thought you were one of those rebellious women we often get here."

I smiled. "Well, you are not mistaken," I told her without resentment. "I did indeed rebel, like any other prisoner with a little self-respect, from working for such a miserable wage. Do you believe, as a Socialist, a woman and teacher, that such work should be so badly paid for? As a Socialist, because the labor made available by prisons, asylums and orphanages—which is bought for a few cents a day—devaluates the work done by workers outside. As a teacher, because you are well aware that authority, exercised with violence and, in this case, with spite, does not correct, but corrupts. And as a woman, because the spectacle of these women's wasted lives should give your work here a more human and maternal tone."

"It's just that we want to get them used to working."

"How do you expect them to get used to working, if after spending six hours in the shop to finish a pair of cuffs or collars, a bedsheet or a pillowcase, they then have to work in the courtyard and even in their own cells in order to get their 15 or 20 céntimos? I would even venture to say that there isn't a single woman here who will want to get a job when she gets out."

"It's true that we pay them very little. But without those céntimos, these women would not be able to buy stamps to send letters to their friends and relatives—those who have any; and those who haven't, wouldn't have enough to buy the few little things they need every day."

"That's not a very good reason. It's a justification for a disgusting exploitation. Tell me frankly, do the prison officials get any profit out of the work of the prisoners?"

"Yes! There's a commission, because the contract is made by the buyer with the prison officials."

"Now do you see what's behind this cheap charity? Why don't the prison officials, who always speak so enthusiastically of 'rehabilitation,' organize the work so that the prisoners themselves with your help could deal with the buyers and fix prices? This would be of real help to the prisoners. In the first place, because it would give them a human and social identity. And in the second place, because their wages would be several times higher than they are today."

"That's true. We inherited the present system from the nuns and the old administration and unfortunately we haven't replaced it."

"That's not the worst of it, Doña Carmen. The worst thing is that progressive women like you do not do anything to change the situation."

"What is your legal status?"

"I am waiting to be transferred to the Bilbao prison; the order could come tomorrow or a month from now. You never know. That's why I don't know how long I'll be here."

"Can I be of some help?"

"If you'd be so kind, I would like a book. In the prison library they only have 'morality novels.' "

"All right. I'll try to get you something."

During the time I spent in this prison waiting for my transfer to Bilbao, the atmosphere in the shop changed somewhat and a few prison officials began to take an interest in the prisoners' work, in spite of the opposition of the director, Don Luis Guzmán, a reactionary who ruled the prison like a feudal manor.

One day, while I was sitting in the shop, I received a note asking me to come to the visitors' room. I was taken by surprise, because I didn't know anybody in Madrid—I was arrested a few days after my arrival—and those who knew I was in Madrid were prudent enough not to risk coming to see me in jail. I asked the messenger if she was sure the note was for me.

"Yes! Yes! It's for you—a lady and a little girl, and they're very well dressed."

On my way to the visitors' room I was thinking that perhaps it was one of those society ladies who had come to lead me away from the path of evil I had chosen. I stopped at the door, trying to identify the face behind the double wire-mesh screens that separated the prisoners from the visitors.

A warm voice said, "Good morning, Dolores."

"Good morning. Whom do I have the honor of talking to?"

"A friend; my name is Estrella, and my little daughter's name is also Estrella. You don't know us. But we know you. I have two sons who begged me to come see you, and it's a pleasure to see you. While you are here, we will come every week to see you, if you don't mind."

I was surprised and moved, and I didn't know how to thank them.

"We brought you a few small things and we would like to know if you need anything, and if there are any other political prisoners we could help."

I thanked them. We talked briefly of life inside and outside the prison and I told her I was confident I would be free shortly. A prison official came to tell us that our time was over. I said good-bye, thanking her from the bottom of my heart for having come, and asking her to thank her two sons.

Who was this woman and where did she come from? They say that the mind's memory sometimes fails. But the heart's memory does not fail. And this unsung and heroic woman will live forever in my heart. The story of the Martinez family will carry me beyond the period I have just been describing.

On Fernando VI Street in Madrid there was a dental clinic directed by Don Daniel Martinez, one of the best and most renowned dentists in Madrid in 1930–31.

Daniel Martinez' family was composed of his wife—not Estrella, the name she had used in jail to conceal her identity, but Alicia López, two sons, Daniel and Wilfredo, and a daughter, Alicia. Daniel had a degree in dentistry and practiced in his father's clinic; Wilfredo was finishing his medical studies; and little Alicia, frail and sickly, lived surrounded by the love and attention of her family. It would be difficult to find a warmer and more united family.

The two sons joined the Communist Party on the eve of the establishment of the Republic. When the father found out, he raised some objections. He was dedicated to his profession and would have preferred that his sons should not meddle in politics. But the mother put an end to the argument.

"Let them go their own way. They feel that they have to be politicians as well as doctors and maybe they are right. We must help them and support them, without putting obstacles in their way."

Communist doctors would often meet in Daniel's or Wilfredo's rooms to discuss not only politics but medical questions as well. Those were difficult times indeed, when to be a Communist was to risk unemployment, jail and ostracism by one's colleagues. The Martinez family, since it was well-off financially, often helped Communist doctors who took care of the poor.

The old doctor remained true to his principle of non-intervention in his sons' political activities. He became used to it, and at times he even showed some interest. On the other hand, the mother—although she never joined the party—had a passionate interest in politics. She encouraged her sons to continue their professions, always trying to free them from daily chores and preoccupations so that they could have more time to devote to their political study and their work as Communists.

On July 15, 1936, the mother with her two sons, her daughter and a maid went to their summer house in the Sierra. The father, with a few of his clinic's technicians and one maid, stayed in Madrid, finishing some urgent dental work.

Daniel and Wilfredo did not manage to return to Madrid nor to send their mother and sister back there, for the fascists struck and the brothers joined the fight, together with a group of peasants whose only weapons were some old hunting rifles. Surrounded by rebels who were advancing toward Madrid, many of the peasants were killed in battle, and the rest—including Daniel and Wilfredo—were taken prisoner. They were tied to posts in a stable and beaten to death, after being brutally tortured and mutilated.

The mother was arrested and moved from jail to jail for more than 12 years. This tragic calvary took her from Segovia to Saturraran, then to Bilbao, and finally to the jail in Barcelona, where she met her daughter. She hadn't seen Alicia, who was also serving a ten-year sentence, since 1936.

When her mother had been arrested in the Sierra, Alicia remained in fascist territory, in the care of friends of the family. After the war Alicia Martinez went back to her father in Madrid. Don Daniel's heart was broken by the tragedy that had destroyed his family.

In those days "fascist death brigades" prowled Madrid like wolves, looking for Communists; someone informed the police that Communists were hiding in the Martinez home. So one night a group of Falangists came to their house and found Comrade Yagüe, of the Madrid Provincial Committee, and another comrade, who were hiding while they waited for an opportunity to leave Madrid. Don Daniel and his daughter were arrested and condemned to 20 and 10 years in prison, respectively, for hiding Communists in their house, while the two comrades were shot on the spot.

Don Daniel was taken to Burgos prison, where he died a few months later. While there, he did everything he could to cheer and give comfort to the other prisoners. More than a friend, he was an affectionate father to all his fellow-prisoners, who in turn tried to make the old man's last days less bitter and painful.

In 1948, when I was staying in Paris, I received a letter from Doña Alicia, who was in a Barcelona jail. Tears came to my eyes as I read the brief letter of a mother who—although everything that was dear to her had been destroyed by fascist brutality—still had the strength and spirit to express her faith in the ideals for which her sons had died.

This briefly, is the story of the heroic woman who, one day in October of 1931, came to visit me in the Women's Prison of Madrid, together with her little daughter, "so that she could learn to be strong in the fight for justice and liberty."

# 13

# Return to Madrid

At the end of November 1931, I was taken from Quiñones Prison in Madrid to Larrínaga Prison in Bilbao. And on December 8, as a protest against the government's refusal to free political prisoners after the Constitution was approved, a small group of Anarchists together with about 100 Communists started a hunger strike. It lasted four days, until the Vizcaya Provincial Committee of the party made us desist. In the first week of January 1932, Daniel Ibáñez, Ambrosio Arraras and I were brought to court. The case was dropped because of lack of proof, and all charges against me were also dropped.

After I left the prison I spent a week with my family, while I prepared my return to Madrid, where the party was preparing its Fourth Congress. In Madrid, Rubén and I stayed at the house of the managing editor of *Mundo Obrero*, who had agreed to put us up until we found a place of our own. But as it turned out I never had to bother to look for a house, because the police decided, as we shall soon see, to again provide me with free shelter, clothing and food at the "hotel" on Quiñones Street, whose ill repute was even sung about in Madrid music halls:

> Don't play the innocent
> or pretend to be decent,
> for you know quite well
> the walls of that Hotel.

At the beginning of March we went to Seville to lay the groundwork for the party's Fourth Congress, to be opened on March 17 in the Andalusian capital. The choice of Seville was not accidental. The Communist Party had won great influence there by its active participation in the fight against Primo Rivera's dictatorship. Among the comrades who had led this struggle were Antonio Mije, Manuel Delicado, Saturnino Barneto and José Díaz, who later was secretary general of the party for ten years.

In 1931 the Republican authorities had brutally tried to repress the Seville Communists, even going so far as bombing the *Casa Cornelio*, a restaurant frequented by many comrades, and invoking martial law in order to perpetrate the assassination of a group of young Communists in a public park.

The Fourth Congress was the first that could be held publicly and legally, with representatives of all the various local and regional organizations of the party. The situation had changed greatly since the time of the Third Congress, which had been held on the eve of the dictatorship's last crisis. Primo Rivera and his cabinet had fallen, dragging the monarchy down in their descent. The Republic had been established, but the new government was in no hurry to grant democratic rights to the people. As a result, the Spanish people began to show signs of disenchantment with the Republican-Socialist government, whose leniency toward reactionaries and harshness toward workers threatened to rob it of popular support. The government's attitude encouraged the reactionaries, who never forgave themselves for the moment of indecision and cowardice which had made the overthrow of the monarchy possible and who were determined to regain their lost ground.

The new conditions made it clear that the party had to change its strategy, putting an end to a sectarianism that was alienating the masses, and placing major emphasis on the struggle for the development of the bourgeois democratic revolution proclaimed by the Republic. The discussions and resolutions of the Fourth Congress dealt a sharp blow to the sectarian tendencies which had been cramping the development of the party and frustrating its attempts to consolidate the popular forces. But many unsolved problems that remained at the center of the party's latent crisis were still to be faced.

After the Congress of Seville, the day after I arrived in Madrid, I was arrested in Magdalena Plaza, on my way to *Mundo Obrero*. I complained loudly and resisted arrest. The cab drivers and workers who were in the Plaza knew from what I was saying that the police were not dealing with a common criminal, but with a Communist. Finally they seized me forcibly, threw me into a police car and took me to the General Bureau of Security.

When I had first been arrested, I had no "criminal" record. Therefore they simply held me at Security, until its chief got the bright idea of sending me to jail, after drawing up a file on me, with photographs and fingerprints. From then on I had a record.

This time, the day after I was arrested I was taken to the line-up room, where a group of rookie detectives made very thorough dossiers on me, each after his own fashion, in order to be sure not to overlook anything in their future persecutions. They obviously derived great pleasure from submitting me to such humiliation as having to stand there for half an hour under the inquisitive looks of the mangy rats who did the government's dirty work. Two more days in the detention cell, and then again to jail.

I knew what to expect. Since it had not been so long since my last stay there, I expected to meet some of the prisoners I had known before. I was not mistaken. Many of the old crowd were still there. There were some new inmates who stood out from the rest because of their fancy clothes. These were the "high class" thieves and criminals.

The prisoners knew me as "the Communist" and they all considered me a friend. And while they were happy to see me, they lamented the fact that I had been arrested again.

I went to the warden to demand that I be given the special privileges accorded to political prisoners.

"In the women's prison we treat you all the same."

"That is a very strange point of view. If there are women arrested for political reasons, why shouldn't they be given the same rights as male political prisoners?"

He got furious, and I told him a thing or two.

The following day was visiting day. The visitors' room was full of students and young Communists who had come to see me. They made a row about the fact that there were two iron grills between the prisoners and the visitors, making it almost impossible for people to see each other, and that the noise made by 25 prisoners all talking at once created an inpenetrable din.

My visitors left the room singing the International, and before they left the prison they made sure that the warden removed from the entrance the crucifix which was still hanging there in spite of the fact that the prison was a government building and that the Republic had proclaimed the separation of Church and State.

The following morning the warden came to the shop and very politely told me that, as a special favor, he would grant me special daily visiting privileges. I told him I did not want any favors. If he gave me my rights, I would accept them, but I wanted no favors from him. Without hiding his dislike of me but fearing that the episode with the young comrades would be repeated, he finally said between his teeth, "Take them any way you want."

The only change in the prison routine was that now I could communicate daily with the outside. This time I stayed with nine other prisoners in a cell with windows and not in the suffocating top deck.

But I had a new worry that tormented me. My son Rubén had been left practically to his own resources. To expect the family we were staying with to take care of him was like expecting a stone to have a human heart. My fears were confirmed. A few days after I had entered the prison, one of the guards told me that there was a child at the gate who said he was my son. I did not have to see him to know it was my son. He was lonely, living in an unfriendly house where nobody ever had a kind word for him. He came and stood under the shadow of the prison walls, trying somehow to see his mother.

I begged the guard to give him some fruit and pastries that the Martinez family had brought me, and a note telling him to go to the house of Navarro Ballestero's mother and stay there until I could find a way to send him back to Vizcaya. He followed my advice, and the mother of Comrade Navarro took good care of him until, a few weeks later, a truckdriver from our town took him to Somorrostro.

While he was in Madrid, Rubén came to the prison gates every single day, hoping that he would catch a glimpse of me or that I would see him. This grieved me enormously, because I felt impotent to protect my son and give him my love and attention. Again I saw how difficult it is for a mother to devote herself to a revolutionary struggle. My own life and liberty, were all very well but did I have a right to sacrifice my children, depriving them of a secure and warm home, of a mother's care and affection that they needed so much? In my life as a Communist, this has been one of the most painful aspects of the struggle, although I have seldom spoken of it, thinking that the best way to teach is by example, even if I had to shed tears of blood.

May was a month brimming with excitement in the women's prison. Days before its arrival, I began explaining the meaning of the First of May to my neighbors. I sang them some of the songs the workers sing on that day and even wrote down the words of the International, Red Banner and other songs, so we could all sing them in the yard on the international day of the working class.

There was a festive air in the prison on the morning of the first. Under tolerant eyes of the matrons, Socialist and Republican, the prisoners put on their best rags and went to the dining hall to have breakfast. The women had the day off, so the workshop was closed.

The evening before some of the old-timers, who had been in prison when it was run by nuns, sang a few religious hymns after dinner; some were very moving because of their sweet melodies, like the one that begins:

> Upon leaving Rome,
> They saw her fly
> Through the center of a beautiful cloud,
> Straight to Saragossa
> And down to the base of the cathedral of El Pilar . . .

All the prisoners assembled in the yard joined in, since everyone knew at least one or two stanzas of the songs. It never occurred to anyone to interrupt the singing.

This was not the case on the First of May. After breakfast, we formed a group in the yard with the women from my dormitory, who had memorized the International, and began to sing:

> Arise, ye prisoners of starvation,
> Arise, ye wretched of the earth . . .

We had not finished the first stanza when one of the office windows was thrust open and an employee angrily shouted:

"Quiet, please! By order of the director!"

Going to the front of the group, I answered: "Tell the director to come and give us the order himself."

We continued singing. The great Luis Guzmán, the director, was not long in appearing, as stiff as a board. Pale and nervous, he edged closer to the group.

"You wanted to see me?"

"Yes, we wanted to see you," I replied.

"All of you?" he asked menacingly, counting on the fear he had instilled in the common prisoners when he was lord and master of the place and could, with impunity, brutally punish a prisoner for the slightest show of resistance.

"I don't know about the others, but as for me, yes."

"And me," said Pura Cruz Salido, the sister of a Socialist leader, an important employee of the telephone company. Arrested with her husband, an Anarchist, as they were about to plant two bombs in the Congress of Deputies, she was waiting here to be transferred to the prison in Alcalá de Henares, where she would serve her sentence.

"And what would you like?"

"To know why the International can't be sung in the yard on the First of May."

"Because this is a government institution and the International is a revolutionary song."

"You must have two sets of regulations. Yesterday, you forgot that the prison was a government institution and let religious hymns be sung, in spite of the fact that under the Republic the Church is separated from the State."

"That's no business of yours. I make the rules here."

"Until you reach the end of your rope."

"Until whenever you like. But there is no singing in this prison today."

Pura Cruz Salido, a brave Andalusian, replied:

"Who's going to stop me from singing?"

Her fine, clear voice soared like the flight of a bird, to the applause of the prisoners, thus putting an end to the discussion.

> Twenty-five dungeons
> Has the jail in Utrera,
> I've been in twenty-four,
> The darkest still awaits me.

The director stalked off, furious, slamming the door so violently that it sounded like a clap of thunder. The First of May was still not over and Guzmán was a petty man, even in his vengeance. That evening he punished us with an inedible dinner. A loud outcry broke out in the dining hall when the food trays arrived, watery mashed potatoes drenched in paprika, with burnt codfish scrapings. Getting up, I said to the matron in charge of the hall: "We're not eating this garbage." All the women together pounded the table with the metal plates used in prisons, chanting: "Another dinner! Another dinner!"

We grabbed our plates and utensils and went into the yard, where the commotion continued.

I went up to the dormitory, positive that the matter wouldn't end there. Sure enough, in a little while I heard footsteps and voices on the stairs. The director appeared in the doorway with a prisoner and the nun who had wanted to undress me when I arrived in prison last time. The woman carried a plateful of the food we had all refused to eat. They came nearer to where I was sitting; behind them, I could see the women from my dormitory.

The director was visibly trying to control himself.

"Why haven't you eaten?"

"Because this food is repulsive."

His spectacles quivered on his nose.

"Look here, my patience has a limit, and I won't let this go on. Yesterday, it was the workshop; the day before yesterday, wages for the women and milk for breakfast. Today, it's singing and the food. Tomorrow, it'll be the man in the moon. But that's not the point. The point is that you have brought insubordination, disorder and subversion to the prison and I won't tolerate it any longer. Before you came the prison was calm; the women were meek and disciplined. Now, it's a hornet's nest of protest and rebellion."

"Before you reached all these conclusions, did you ever examine the actual conditions in this prison?" I replied. "It's perfectly possible that before I came the prisoners were treated humanely and correctly, that there was no speculation with milk, that prison funds were not used for business deals, that the sickroom was well attended, that work done in the shop was paid for according to standard wage rates, without rake-offs. But now that I'm here, living in the prison, I know that this was not so. And I protest because I think what you are doing is not only an injustice, it's robbery."

Making a tremendous effort to control his rage, the director answered: "I'm used to taming wilder horses than you, and it won't be hard to stop your activities by methods the law allows me."

"The law? You who break the law every day are now appealing to it? I'll demand that an investigating committee come here, and before that committee we'll all talk, you and the prisoners. Your threats don't bother me in the least. And as for your allusion to wild horses, I say that if horses are tamed with iron, brave bulls thrive on punishment. I have nothing more to say to you, Mr. Director."

"I warned you, and I intend to do what I say."

"Thank you, I'll keep it in mind."

He left in a fuming rage. The next morning when we went to the washroom, a prisoner furtively handed me a note. "If a quarrel breaks out among the prisoners in the yard, on the stairs or in the dormitory, don't interfere. The director has spoken to a group of old-timers and promised to help us in court if we give you a beating 'for meddling where it's none of your business.' "

I appreciated the warning and ignored the snide plans of the director, who had already shown his metal.

On the evening of the First of May, one of the sisters of Navarro Ballesteros arrived at the prison, along with two other comrades, Felisa Basterrechea and one of the Grado sisters. They were arrested for having protested police brutality against a group of workers after the May Day demonstration.

The Republic was revealing its true nature with each step it took. In the prison, the old dogs barked without daring to sink their fangs in. Outside in the streets they bit.

The comrades were released after two weeks. Once again I found myself alone in the midst of a sea of petty troubles and base passions, among women who were outcasts of society, defending at every moment what I thought to be right, protesting against injustice, discovering aspects of human degradation difficult to imagine in a society of normal human beings.

Under the Republic, nuns were removed from prison administration. Since this was done gradually, they were still around during the period of my first arrests. At that time, their duties were increasingly restricted and were being transferred to the matrons, the new corps of prison officials founded by the government.

The matrons deserve special mention. Most of them were from lower middle-class families, the widows or daughters of army men or civil service employees. The majority had worked before, so they were accustomed to earning their livings, and the job of a prison matron, with decent salaries and promotions on a seniority basis, was a desirable one.

The wide range of personalities, comportment and attitudes toward prison problems was only a reflection of the unstable outer world of the petty bourgeoisie, who behind a façade of spurious well-being, hide the futility of "keeping up with the Jones's"—their pathetic attempts to identify with the world of the big bourgeoisie.

They did not mistreat the prisoners, especially in the beginning, when they had to expedite the easing out of the nuns. The matrons hated one another, a fact which they were unable to hide from the prisoners, who were always on the alert to wrest advantages from any weak spot in the prison system.

A typical example of this intramural animosity was the case of the two head matrons, Miss Julia Trigo and Mrs. María Massó. Mrs. Massó was a cultured woman, a worker with a vocation and a family, a truly democratic person, who had come out ahead of Miss Trigo in the competition for the job of head matron. However, Miss Trigo was well connected with members of the court, and for this reason they were going to award her the appointment despite the obvious superiority of Mrs. Massó. The Trigo woman was much more "charming." Not one to be put upon, Mrs. Massó knew how to defend her rights and backed up by a solid case threatened to contest the appointment, thus forcing the judges to appoint them both.

Within the limits of her unpleasant assignment, Mrs. Massó carried out her duties as head matron in a humane manner. She was strict but not cruel, and knew how to listen when a prisoner came to her with a complaint.

Miss Trigo patrolled through the halls like a dethroned queen, looking at us from over her shoulder and speaking to the prisoners without the slightest expression on her heavily made-up face, lest it might ruin her careful handiwork. We hardly ever saw her. She used to arrive early in the morning, make her customary rounds to see that everything was all right, and spend the rest of the day in her office, sewing or chatting with the director.

And the prisoners? The only thing about the prisoners that interested her was some case of mental or physical deviation which would provide her with a lurid story that might be possible material for one of the novels written by her friends. She was really a stranger to the prisoners; nevertheless, they told stories about her which were no less obscene and repulsive than those she so avidly gleaned from the tormented lives of some of her charges.

# 14

## Political Prisoners

It was the middle of May, and there were rumors in the street that the monarchists were planning to overthrow the government on the 17th, the birthday of King Alphonso XIII. Instead, on May 17, the monarchists celebrated mass in one of the most elegant churches in Madrid; all the members of the aristocracy attended—the cream of Spanish gangsterism and prostitution.

Because of their ardent enthusiasm for Alphonso, the mistress of a duke and the lady director of a reactionary woman's newspaper were arrested. Shades of the Trojan War! How were they going to put these distinguished ladies with thieves, infanticides, pickpockets and charlatans, not to mention a Communist, the bane of the prison director's life.

They were taken to General Police Headquarters, naturally with all due respect because of their position, although it was claimed that the ladies were just ordinary prisoners, "like anyone else." Meanwhile, a strange and confusing event occurred in the prison. With the director's approval, the good sisters ordered some of the prisoners to mop, scour and scrub the room that I had once told the director to set aside for the use of political prisoners.

My roommates thought that because of the incident on the First of May, I would be put in that room to separate me from the rest of the women. But the director, in addition to having a lot of cards up his sleeve, was also a man of principle. Two beds with fine white sheets and wool mattresses together with cleaning utensils and all the comforts from the old convent were installed in the room: Basins, pails, pitchers, bowls, a dining room table, a small cupboard, a large rug, two armchairs and several other chairs. A de luxe hotel room!

No one knew what was going on until one morning the cards were laid on the table. There they were, snug in their warm nest, the aristocratic tramp, with her servant and sister in Christ—the commonplace director of *Nosotras,* a dull Catholic woman's weekly —more frightened than two lambs facing a ferocious wolf.

I didn't complain, because the prison finally had a section for political prisoners, even though the political opinions of the duke's girl friend were not exactly a product of her head, while those of the directress came along with her salary.

However, at breakfast, when all the prisoners were in line to enter the dining hall, I couldn't resist asking Mrs. Massó, the head matron, an innocent question.

"Are the two ladies who arrived last night sick?"

"No, they're quite well."

"Then why aren't they in line with the rest of us, even if they do have separate bedrooms?"

Pura Cruz Salido seconded my question, demanding that they should be treated the same as the other prisoners.

Of course, I wasn't right in this case. If the prison instituted a separate regimen for political prisoners, logically they would be exempt from all the obligations of common prisoners. But I was indignant that the director had discriminated against me, and I'm not one to turn the other cheek when I get hit. Neither was I going to sit by and watch the director, an open enemy of the Republic, brazenly protect the girl friends of his friends, whose moral fiber perfectly matched his own. They sold their bodies or their names. He was so abject that he served a regime he hated in order to reap the meager pickings that his position afforded him. Prostitution for the sake of prostitution. Whose was worse?

The head matron herself went to ask the ladies to join us. Joining the end of the line, they went down with the other prisoners but remained in the yard while we went to have the coffee and milk that was called breakfast.

The director was positive that I would start a violent protest, but he was wrong. In the afternoon, after we had washed our dinner plates and were in the yard waiting to be taken up to the halls, one of the employees came to tell me that the director wanted to speak with me in his office. "I haven't lost anything in the director's office," I answered. "If he wants to talk, we can talk in the yard in front of the prisoners, as we've always done before."

The director didn't come until the following day. Pretending he had casually ran into me in the yard, he said: "I heard that you've protested because I put the two ladies in the small hall."

"Well, you've heard wrong, Mr. Director. I haven't protested, because the separation of those ladies from the rest of the women is an implicit recognition of my own right to receive the treatment of a political prisoner. Only you choose to give special treatment to your friends. However small, it's still a start in the right direction. And since you're here, may I ask a question?"

"Go ahead."

"Are you a Catholic, a Christian?"

"Yes, I'm a Catholic."

"Then you know the works of mercy?"

"Of course."

"And how do you apply them?"

"According to my knowledge and understanding."

"And the theological virtues, especially the third, you know them too?"

"Is this an examination in Christian doctrine?"

"No, it's just a demonstration of your hypocrisy. And proof that Christ would have thrown you out of the temple just as he threw out the pharisees. Ever since the Republic was proclaimed and you knew the nuns would be leaving, you have been hiding everything of value, depriving the prisoners of many useful and necessary items. The arrival of two high-class ladies helped you to remember that you had tucked away certain things which were once used by the prisoners and haven't been seen for months now. Why didn't you put the wool mattresses in the sickroom? And what about the sheets and blankets?"

"Surely, you don't think that I would put all those things at the disposal of women like Millie the Cripple, for example?"

"And why not? Millie the Cripple is a sick woman, full of wounds, but a woman, a human being who has never enjoyed any comforts in her life and whom poverty has pushed on the road to delinquency. Whom should you show charity to, if not to the poor and the disgraced? On the other hand, all prison property is for the use of all prisoners, without exception. Why do you deprive those who need them of the few things that a jail can give, aside from confinement?"

The conversation ended with a promise that conditions in the sickroom would be improved. One thing was very clear. The director feared that news of his conduct with the lady monarchists would leak outside and create problems for his career. He organized a special program for them. Not only did they sleep and eat apart, but he also fixed up the kitchen yard for them to take sunbaths. However, an incident occurred that nearly cost the ladies the skin off their noses.

Smoking in prison was prohibited. Naturally, an exception was made in the case of the ladies who were tobacco addicts. The other prisoners were in despair, since they could smell a cigarette a mile away and had to content themselves with ones rolled from the straw mattress stuffing. Sometimes they hid in the washroom to steal a last puff on a butt they had found on the floor or to smoke a cigarette or two smuggled in among the clothing they received from the outside.

Next to the reception hall was a small room used to store the straw for the mattresses, which were always paper thin from constant use and the pilfering of their stuffing.

One afternoon, as our distinguished prisoners were on their way to the reception hall, one of them threw away a cigarette and in her hurry didn't bother to notice where it landed.

No one was inside the storage room; the door was open; the straw scattered over the floor; the cigarette landed in the most appropriate place and soon started its work. The ladies went up to their room and the prisoners to the halls. A few hours later we noticed a smell of something burning.

"It must be coming from the street," we commented.

In a little while we heard the siren of the fire engines and then the engines themselves pulling to a stop in front of the prison.

Thick curls of smoke were winding out of the window of the reception hall. In panic, the women started running down the stairs toward the yard. "We'll burn alive, the prison is on fire!"

A prisoner overheard one of the firemen saying that the fire had probably started from a cigarette carelessly thrown away in some corner. "No one smokes here except the monarchists," commented the prisoner, a woman who had always kept aloof from the rest of us.

This guileless remark traveled from prisoner to prisoner until it reached the women in the maternity hall, where it produced an outburst of hate and indignation. "They were the ones, it was their fault!"

The women charged up the stairs, heading for the room of the "political" prisoners. The women with babies were the most furious. "If this had happened at night, our children would have been burned to a crisp! Let's throw those strumpets out!" Followed by the prison guards, the director ran behind them to rescue his lady-friends. Using a bench as a battering ram, the women were already busy beating down the door of the prison "boudoir."

A few days later the ladies were released by special order; prison air had become too much for them. After a three weeks' stay in jail, where they were fed like pigs and had enjoyed all the comforts of home, with sunbathing and other special privileges, the commonplace directress of the commonplace Catholic weekly and her friend suddenly became martyrs. The directress published a horrid story in which one of the main characters was a terrible Communist who had made life unbearable for innocent victims of excess patriotic zeal confined in the inhospitable hotel on the Street of Quiñones.

On August 10, 1932, the monarchist uprising finally took place. The director, contrary to his custom, had been pacing around the yard since six that morning. The matrons made their rounds as usual. Those arriving on the morning shift brought the restless atmosphere of the street with them, but no one knew for sure what was going on.

As soon as the rumors began to get more concrete, the director ordered the prisoners shut up in the halls. We asked the matrons why, and they told us what they knew about the situation.

"I'm not going to be locked up in the hall," I said. "Why don't you take measures to prevent the prison from becoming a focus of rebellion instead of cooperating with the dishonest tricks of the director? Tell the prisoners what it's all about, tell them that the coup is an attempt to return to the old whiplash methods, to the dungeons with bread and water, to torture, and you'll see how long it'll take us to show him what side we're on."

Although the director had refused to permit it, Mrs. Massó ordered the flag of the Republic flown over the prison. Both the matrons and the prisoners were on the Republic's side. At noon the situation crystallized. The monarchist coup had failed, its leaders had been arrested. Later, the director went to the Ministry of Justice to make a public act of loyalty to the Republic.

Prison food had aggravated an old liver illness, and since I had to keep to a strict diet, I went on sick call in early autumn. Although this separated me from the rest of the women, I was still in touch with the prisoners and all the small daily events of prison life.

At that time, a new administrator arrived who promptly proceeded to trim down administrative costs. He reduced the number of bottles of bleach used in the laundry from four to two. Four bottles of bleach were considered a luxury, despite the necessity of disinfecting the clothing in a prison where 90 per cent of the prisoners had venereal diseases. The soap quota was also cut by half; the prisoners' money was collected and replaced by receipts issued by the administration. A blanket was taken off each bed, which left the women with only one, obviously insufficient to keep out the cold of a Madrid winter in that comfortless ramshackle building. This was the straw that broke the camel's back.

Why was a blanket taken off each bed? They told us that a recently opened prison in Jaén had no blankets, so it had been decided that the prisoners in Madrid would freeze in order that their poor sisters in Andalusia might be warm. This business of taking blankets from one prison to another was, of course, part of a crooked financial deal, since the government had allocated funds to cover these needs.

We decided to go on strike. All the prisoners, except those in the sick room, voluntarily assembled in the workshop, where they sat with their arms crossed. The kitchen and the laundry room were abandoned, the halls empty, the sewing machines idle. It was decided that I was to intervene only as a last resort, so that the prison officials could see that the women didn't need to depend on me.

The prison was quieter than a cemetery. The matrons were terribly nervous, waiting for the director to arrive. Very calmly, he went to the shop and asked why the prisoners weren't working.

One of the women told him why, and immediately broke into tears, overcome by her daring. The director began to speak to the women in a paternal tone trying to convince them of the abnormality of their behavior and assuring them that they could always count on his support and protection if they would only go back to being good girls.

The united front began to waver. One of the women stole out to tell me what was happening. I leaped up the stairs, quietly entered the room, sat down on a bench and listened. The director had his back to the door so he didn't see me. When he finished, I asked permission to speak, as if it were a union meeting. The director turned:

"What did you say?"

"I'd like permission to have the floor."

"What do you want to say?"

"I'd like to say that the prisoners are disgusted with the recent sanitary and economic measures you've taken, which are making life in this prison much harder and more unpleasant, not to mention creating an increased danger of contagion caused by insufficient materials to disinfect the prisoners' clothing. And to tell the truth, I don't think anyone here understands the affair of the blankets. Who do you think is going to believe your story that the government must rob Peter to pay Paul? All the prisoners say, and not without reason, that this is a cover-up for some dishonest deal and they're not going to put up with it. And they're absolutely right."

"But you're all wrong. The removal of the blankets is only temporary. As for the money, the soap, the bleach and the other things that have been changed, I'm sure the administrator will be happy to clarify the matter for you."

He walked out feeling very smug for having left the administrator holding the bag. The administrator ended the whole affair by promising to restore the soap and bleach quotas, to return the blankets before winter arrived, and to give money rather than receipts to those who wished it.

At the beginning of November, I was again taken to the prison in Bilbao, leaving Quiñones behind, with its prisoners and their chief caretaker, the hateful and hated Luis Guzmán.

The train ride to Bilbao was very unpleasant, but every bad thing has its good side. In this case it was that the other passengers treated us with kindness and respect, some because they hated the Civil Guard; others, out of sympathy for us prisoners.

At first everyone thought I was a common prisoner and, moved by pity, they threw copper or silver coins on my lap. Returning the money, I thanked them and explained that I was a Communist prisoner. Some women kissed me, their eyes full of tears, and cursed the government; the guards meanwhile were reading ABC, the monarchist newspaper, ignoring the people gathered around me. One of my guards, in a display of generosity, said that if he won the lottery he would buy me a trip to the Soviet Union so I could see for myself how "bad" communism was.

The guards, especially those who accompanied me from Miranda de Ebro to Bilbao in 1932, were not very happy about their job. From the North Station to the Larriñaga prison we had to walk a good distance through one of Bilbao's most populated sections, along the street of San Francisco, near the market of San Antón, where the women vendors are noted for their sharp tongues.

The guards feared that the sight of them would touch off a street fight. They had expected a pair of escorts to be waiting at the station to relieve them; instead, they found an orderly with the news that they had to conduct me to the prison.

They didn't bother to hide their fury. They begged me to walk ahead so as not to give the impression that they were escorting me. I refused, saying, "I haven't committed any crime, and if I'm escorted as if I were a criminal, let the others be ashamed."

"But you must understand our situation."

"I understand, but I'm still walking with you two."

After an uneventful journey, we arrived at Larriñaga, where I spent a little more than a month. I was released in January 1933, and once again returned to Madrid, this time with my two children, Rubén and Amaya, who, as usual, had had to suffer the consequences of their mother's Communist activities, and without whom I found it so hard to live.

It was not only worry about the children that had tormented me, nor the fact that I had spent months and months in prison, apparently abandoned by God and man. I never once received as much as a newspaper, because the party leaders, absorbed in the controversy that was to lead to their removal after the Congress of Seville, simply forgot I was in jail. At the same time, the committee formed to take care of Communist prisoners decided that it wasn't going to make the trip to the Street of Quiñones every day just for one prisoner.

Beyond these problems, I was deeply worried about the split within the party, since the majority of the members of the Central Committee was not in agreement with the tactics of the party leaders. Shortly before my transfer to Bilbao, a comrade from the new Politburo came to inform me of the outcome of the crisis, and to tell me of the attempts some lawyer friends had made to secure my release. He also wanted my opinion on the resolutions the party had adopted about the old group of leaders. I expressed satisfaction with the measures safeguarding the leadership and continuity of the party and correcting the narrow, sectarian policies which had converted it into a group of dedicated propagandists who admired the workers for their courage, but who somehow did not always identify with them.

The rapid increase in party membership and the movement's growing influence over the masses that took place after José Díaz became Secretary General of the party proved how just and necessary was the decision to remove from leadership those men who were incapable of ensuring the party's growth or of instituting policies based on the specific conditions in our country.

[15]

## Socialists at the Crossroads

The crisis that led to the Socialists' withdrawal from the government took place in October 1933. Rather than being an unexpected turn of events, this was the culmination of a process that had been publicly maturing for a long time.

The policies of the successive Republican-Socialist governments had been identical. Like Janus, they had two faces: A smiling one, which looked upon the old ruling castes with indulgence and weakness; and a brutal one which looked upon the workers and peasants with cruelty and stupidity. Because of their blandness toward the former, they lost the support of the forces on the Right; because of their severity toward the latter, they failed to gain the confidence of the people. The bloody repressions carried out in many Spanish cities and towns gave eloquent testimony to the "popular" policies of the Republican-Socialist governments.

At the end of 1932 and the beginning of 1933, the peasant movement of revolt against the large landowners demanded revolutionary agrarian reform, a program which the government was unable to carry out. As they had in the 19th century, Andalusia and Estremadura emerged as the centers of the agrarian reform movement, which sought to destroy the old semifeudal system of land tenure. From January to March of 1933 alone, there were 311 cases of peasants who had occupied the farms where they had been employed.

During this period, the Communist Party was doing an excellent job of propaganda in the rural regions. All the party leaders were going out to the various provinces. I went to Toledo, where we had a good Communist organization in the town of Don Fadrique. The mayor, Comrade Cicuéndez, exercised a well-earned influence not only over Don Fadrique itself but also over several other towns in Toledo. Later, I took part in propaganda work and in the organization of the party in the Andalusian cities of Cordoba and Jaen.

In reply to the working people's struggle for bread and land, the Republican-Socialist government had enacted the "Law of the Defense of the Republic," which was used by the Republic's most bitter enemies to crush the aspirations of the workers and peasants. In the partial municipal elections in April 1933, the Spanish Catholic Party (CEDA) managed to increase its hold in some provinces. This gave them an incentive to redouble their attacks on the government, whose ministers, caught up in the tide of events, showed determination only when it came to suppressing the fight for the workers' and peasants' rights.

After Hitler came to power in 1933, the danger of fascism in Spain became real and immediate. Fascist organizations began to operate openly, and as the Falange leader and son of the old dictator, José Antonio Primo de Rivera, declared, they "understood only the dialectics of the pistol." Soon the streets of Spain bore witness to fascist crimes that foreshadowed what was in store for the country.

To counteract the chauvinism and bravado of the fascist young people's organizations, the Communists called upon Spain's youth to form antifascist militia to defend democracy and the working masses. The party organized several antifascist demonstrations, which always ended in open rioting with the police.

During one of the demonstrations in 1933, as we were marching through the street of San Bernardo, near the university, a detachment of Assault Guards appeared and without any warning opened fire on us. Upon hearing the first shots, the people scattered in a panic. I hid in a doorway together with Comrade Guillén, a shoe worker from Madrid. A bullet hit him through the head. He fell slowly to the ground, without a sound, without a gesture.

At first, I didn't realize what had happened. But when I saw that he wasn't moving, I bent over him and saw a stream of blood flowing from his ear. I tried to lift him, and with my hands covered with blood, held him up and shouted for help, cursing his murderers. My cries brought other comrades who had taken refuge from the bullets; even some of the guards came running. They carried Guillén, to a car, but nothing could be done. He was dead.

Once I was arrested by the Civil Guards during an antifascist demonstration in Tetuán de las Victorias, but thanks to the protests of democratic organizations, I was later released.

While the Republican and Socialist leaders remained blind to the danger of fascism, the Communists created the Antifascist Front, a wide popular movement comprising all the sectors opposing the rising tide of fascism.

New elections held after the Socialists left the government brought the reactionary forces a great victory, giving them a majority of seats in parliament. The electoral law drawn up by the Socialists and Republicans was specifically directed against the Communists. Because of its provisions, in spite of the 400,000 votes we received, only one of our many candidates, Cayetano Bolívar Cortes, was elected deputy, on a coalition ticket by the workers of Malaga.

The Socialist workers were filled with consternation. They began to realize that the tactics of their own party were not leading to Socialism, as had been promised, but proved of help to reaction and fascism. The failure of Socialist collaboration in Republican governments, the increasing discontent of the people, the adoption of Communist positions by many Socialist workers, produced the serious and long-foreseen split within the Socialist Party. Three clearly defined groups emerged: Right, Center and Left.

The Left, headed by Largo Caballero, soon became the dominant group. Largo's attitude reflected the radicalization of the Socialist masses and their strong wish to reach an agreement with the Communists. Largo Caballero's leftist position, although not politically effective or correct, nevertheless represented a step forward in turning the Socialist Party toward again becoming a class-conscious workers' movement. It paved the way for an understanding between the two workers' parties, Communist and Socialist. This explains why the Communist Party, which had suffered so many blows at the hands of the Socialists, welcomed the change and worked to establish an alliance with the Socialists on the basis of the unity of the working class. Only unity would make it possible to offer serious resistance to the fascist threat, to ensure the safety of the Republic and of democracy.

On November 16, 1933, Alejandro Lerroux formed a coalition government backed by the Radicals and the CEDA, though the latter did not take active part in the administration itself. The period of reaction's overt aggression, known as "The Dark Biennial," now began. The financial and landowning oligarchies directed all their attention to the effort to superimpose a fascist regime on the institutions of the Republic and to destroy the victories won by the people in their long, hard battle.

After the November elections, the Socialist Party found itself in an extremely delicate situation. Following seven years of alliance with the military dictatorship of General Primo de Rivera, succeeded by three years of participation in Republican governments, where it had exercised a decisive influence, the Socialist Party could not easily make an abrupt transition from the ministers' bench to that of the opposition. Because of the special interests that had grown up while they were in power, the Socialists found it even more difficult to re-establish the party's class character, watered down during the years of collaboration with the dictatorship and petty-bourgeois parties.

Attracted by the participation of the Socialists in the government and by the anti-Marxist eclecticism prevailing in the party, its members included a great many petty-bourgeois intellectuals. While personally estimable, they contributed nothing positive to the party; on the contrary, they brought in opportunistic as well as liberal ideas, thus diluting the class character of the organization. The Socialist Party had no choice but to suffer the consequences of this influence. It was unable to counteract it or to rescue these intellectuals from their ideological weaknesses, because the party itself lacked a solid, revolutionary, Marxist theoretical base.

At the same time, Socialist leaders became aware of an alarmingly sharp decrease in party membership. In 1932, at the height of their collaboration with the government, the Socialists had numbered more than 80,000; at the beginning of 1934, this figure had dropped to less than 60,000. These significant losses produced serious divergences within the party. In January 1934, its Executive Committee, including Largo Caballero, Prieto, de los Ríos and others, openly broke with the Executive Committee of the General Workers' Union (UGT), which was under the leadership of Besteiro, Saborit and Trifón Gómez.

These divergences were of a well-defined political nature, touching upon both the tactics and strategy of party policies. The Socialist Party, headed by Largo, and supported by Indalecio Prieto, considered that a revolutionary movement directed by the party and the UGT, would enable the Socialists to seize power; while the directors of the UGT, under Besteiro, collaborated with fascist reactionaries to establish a political system based on state monopoly, as was being done in Italy.

In December 1933, at a meeting of the Socialist Executive Committee, Largo Caballero submitted for approval of the other members a plan for a revolutionary movement and a program to be carried out after the seizure of power by the Socialist Party. Both plan and program were dubious, because of their shortcomings from the standpoints of feasibility and content. Feasibility, because the Socialist leaders took into account only their own opinions and forces, ignoring those of Republicans, Communists and Anarchists who might or might not have supported their program; content, because the program was too limited. It ignored the existence of a national problem and the agrarian question. Without a solution of these problems, there could be no democratic revolution in Spain, much less a Socialist one. The truth is that the program was the wrong step in the right direction. At most, it represented an honest attempt to steer the Socialist ship on the proper course.

However, Largo Caballero, like Don Quixote, ran into some windmills, specifically three: Besteiro, Saborit and Trifón Gómez, who not only vetoed the plan, but also proposed a counterplan, a typically monopolistic and antidemocratic program drawn up by Besteiro. Under this program Spain's aristocracy and bourgeoisie would remain absolutely intact. It called for hydraulic works instead of agrarian reform, for the exclusion of the national problem, and respect for the established order, following the line of reasoning of Besteiro's favorite teacher, Hegel, who wrote "All that is real is rational." What was real in Spain at that moment was the ultrareaction. To prepare and carry out his plan, Besteiro proposed the creation of an assembly, on corporative lines, which, in his opinion, "should not have legislative powers, merely consultative ones . . . although, if deemed necessary, the powers of the assembly could be increased by legally instituting the appropriate constitutional reforms."

Such a man could not have acted otherwise. In answer to the proposal submitted by his friend Largo and all the other Socialist leaders who were determined to take a stand against fascism, Besteiro had said in December 1933: "Fascism is the sound of mice scurrying in an old house, frightening the weak and the cowardly. . . . There is no danger of fascism in Spain."

The Socialist leaders, especially Largo Caballero, began the long battle against the ultrareactionary positions of Besteiro, Saborit, Trifón and their followers. Eventually Largo, already president of the Socialist Party, became secretary of the General Workers' Union.

The united front antifascist policies proposed by the Communists were gaining ground among the masses. They attracted so many adherents from the ranks of the Socialists and the UGT that their leaders began to sit up and take notice of the Communist proposals. Largo, however, was not a man to change his opinions easily. Instead of objectively examining the proposals for a united front to organize the entire working class in the fight against fascism, Largo, without definitely rejecting an alliance with the Communists, as he had done in the past, accepted Trotskyite views and came up with a counterproposal calling for the creation of Workers' Alliances, in the hope that the Communist Party would refuse to participate in such a narrow, sectarian movement.

In this way, the Socialists, under Largo, hoped to attain several objectives: To counteract the growing popularity of the united-front proposals; to placate the Socialist workers who wanted to join forces with the Communists; and to throw on the Communists the responsibility for having rejected unity if they refused to participate.

Before the Communist Party could participate in such a plan, the Socialist leaders would have to change their ideas about the structure and purpose of the alliances. Membership in the alliances, as originally proposed, would have implied that the Communists had renounced an independent policy for an authentic united workers' movement.

Under the initiative of the Communist Party, a so-called truce was drawn up in July 1934, putting an end to public polemics between both parties. The official decision of the Communists to join the alliances was taken by the Central Committee in an assembly held in September 1934. The political situation in Spain had deteriorated considerably. It was dangerous to hold out any longer lest a reactionary coup take a divided working class by surprise.

When it joined the Workers' Alliances, the Communist Party declared that it had not renounced the fight to change the nature of the alliances, to convert them into Workers' and Peasants' Alliances, to unite the principal revolutionary forces of society, the proletariat and the peasants, in the battle for democracy.

After the elections in November 1933, I left for Moscow as a delegate of the Communist Party of Spain to the XIII Communist International Plenary Session.

Moscow was very different then from what it is now, but for one who viewed it with her heart, it was the most marvellous city in the world. Here, Socialism was being constructed; the earthly dreams of liberty fought for by generations of slaves, outcasts, serfs and workers, were becoming reality; the Soviet people were marching toward Communism.

I visited Leningrad, the cradle of the Revolution, and Smolny, where I could still feel the presence of Lenin who, in those memorable days that shook the world, had turned it into the nerve center of the Revolution. I heard Kirov speak at the party conference in Leningrad on the eve of the XVII Congress of the CPSU. I spoke with the workers of the Putilov factory, the old revolutionary workers' fortress, and with the workers of the Skorojod shoe factory. I attended the Party Congress, where I spoke in the name of the Communist Party of Spain.

With delegates from other countries, I visited a fishermen's co-operative in Rostov on the Don River, one of the first kolkhozes in the region. My impressions of the Soviet Union on my first visit have stayed with me through the years. As I compare the Soviet Union of today with what it was yesterday, my heart leaps with joy at the immensity of the changes wrought, at the incomparable greatness of its achievements.

# The Insurrection of 1934

The political situation was very serious when I returned to Spain in 1934. The danger of fascism, which the Communists had repeatedly warned against, was no longer a distant threat but an immediate one. The forces of the Right, decidedly fascistic in character, were gradually assuming control, utilizing Republican institutions and laws as a stepping stone to power.

According to Gil Robles, leader of the Right, the time would soon be ripe for action. "The positions we have adopted," he declared in Covadonga, "are the trenches from which we will assault and take public power."

After its electoral victory in November 1933, the tactics of the Right consisted of using the radicals as scouts to clear the way of obstacles. The Samper government was the first attempt at a governmental bridge to facilitate the seizure of power by the Right. When Robles realized that this policy was backfiring and could ruin his plans, he decided to take power openly. In a speech delivered on April 7, 1934, he said: "We are going to take power. With this government? With any government, no matter what it stands for, and by any method!"

This brief, concise threat constituted a program which precluded nothing, not even a civil war.

When the Cortes met on October 1, 1934, Gil Robles announced that the CEDA would no longer support the Samper government. The resulting situation was crucial. Fascism had the way clear, and it advanced on the back of the very laws of the Republic.

On October 4, a new government was formed under the demagogue Lerroux, a political adventurer whose shady police connections were public knowledge. The Spanish Catholic Party did not hesitate to collaborate closely with the anticlerical Lerroux, who had once called upon the "young barbarians" to tear the veils from the novices in the

convents and raise them to the category of "mothers." Were these
so-called Catholics interested in combating atheism? No! They were
interested in protecting the privileges of the big bourgeoisie and
the landowners by halting the advance of democracy in Spain.

Within the newly formed government, the CEDA controlled three
ministries: Justice, Agriculture and Labor. The Right began a new
stage in its ascent to power.

Meanwhile, Gil Robles kept to the sidelines, waiting for future
events. Thanks to the activities of the Communists and Socialists,
who had aroused its political vigilance, the working class was not
deceived by the smokescreen maneuvers of those who, under the
cover of Catholicism, wanted to establish fascism in Spain.

As we have seen, Largo Caballero, a man of great merit and unceasing activity in the workers' movement, was, nevertheless, a man
of fixed ideas, influenced by his own likes and dislikes. Neither political necessity nor obligation would make him change his ideas or his
obviously utopian plans, even when they were proved wrong in
practice.

The Communist leaders held Largo in esteem, despite his political defects and weaknesses. We wanted to join forces with him, to
help him for his own sake and for the sake of the workers he
represented. And we offered this help unconditionally, without any
ulterior motives. Unfortunately, he didn't see it that way; he considered every Communist proposal an invasion of his territory, an
infringement of his rights, or a maneuver to gain underhanded objectives.

Consequently, although the Communist Party was a member of
the alliances, Largo Caballero fled from discussions with the Communists on every conceivable occasion and insisted on following his
plan of December 1933 for a revolutionary movement directed by
the Socialist Party and the UGT. He tried to disown us and to
ignore the workers and democratic sectors in our ranks.

With the aims of his old program in mind, Largo gave the order
for a general strike when the Lerroux-CEDA government was formed
in the beginning of October.

The Anarchists' boycotted the October action, for which the
Communists criticized them. Objectively, the refusal of the Anarchists
to act helped the reactionaries and contributed to the failure of the
movement. But would the Anarchists have acted that way if they

had been consulted or included in the discussions prior to the insurrection? Instead, they were ignored, and it was taken for granted that they would march automatically behind the Socialist Party. After all, they did represent a numerous sector of the working class. This is a question that has remained unanswered, but the facts are plain to see.

It could be argued that the CNT (Anarcho-Syndicalist Trade Union) was not a member of the Alliances. On the other hand, the Communists were members. But what did the Socialists do after giving the order for a general revolutionary strike? They broke all relations with the Communist Party and hid from the police. While dodging police persecution was justified, the Socialist Party was certainly not justified nor correct nor revolutionary in failing to form a committee of alliance members to direct the insurrection and mobilize the masses. Instead, it let the battle run under its own steam, following Largo's theory that a revolution cannot be organized but that it spontaneously generates itself.

Meanwhile, although the Socialist leaders had not communicated their plans to us, the Communists plunged into the movement right from the start, fighting side by side with the Socialist workers. With the aid of the workers during the course of the battle, we transformed the Workers' Alliances into Workers' and Peasants' Alliances which, in some places like Asturias, where the Anarchists were alliance members, became true organs of power.

The insurrectionary movement of 1934 had an enormous educational value for the masses. The people were given the opportunity to see three different methods in action:

(1) The Socialist program, all-inclusive, professing to monopolize the leadership of an insufficiently prepared revolutionary movement and failing in the undertaking.

(2) That of the Anarchists who, because of their sectarianism, shied away from a battle which could have been decisive and thus played into the hands of the enemies of the working class.

(3) That of the Communists, who participated openly in the movement, leading it in some places, fighting for victory, and publicly assuming the responsibility for the insurrection.

Catalonia, under the leadership of President Companys, supported the insurrection and defended the interests and the democratic conquests of the Catalans, which the central government had begun to infringe upon.

The Communist Party of Catalonia took part in the fight and, although small in numbers, it was extremely active and combative. Among the most outstanding Catalan leaders were Comrades Sesé, del Barrio, Sastre, Montagut, and Lina Odena.

The strike was general in Madrid, Valencia, Seville, Salamanca, Córdoba, León y Palencia, Vizcaya and Guipúzcoa; important partial strikes took place in Murcia, Jaén, Segovia and Granada.

To suppress the insurrection, the Republican government sent General Franco, a monarchist who had distinguished himself in fighting against the people of Morocco in Africa. The most ferocious repressive corps in the country was unleashed against the workers of Asturias. The Foreign Legion, together with the Moorish *Regulares*, as well as regular troop detachments, were sent under the commands of Colonel Yagüe and General López Ochoa.

Seven columns marched against the insurrectionists, who were holding out in the mining zone. Troops were sent to "pacify" the Asturian towns of Oviedo, Pola de Siero, Grado, Sama de Langreo, Mieres and the valley of Narcea. The commanders who led the troops were Colonels Yagüe, Sáenz de Buruaga and Aranda, and Lieutenant Colonels Lafuente and Ceano. These names were to be heard again during the fascist military rebellion against the Republic. The most violent repression took place in Asturias, which was razed as if it were a rebellious Moroccan village. More than 4,000 people were killed during the insurrection and ensuing government repression in October 1934.

After October, the Socialist Party desisted from all public political activity in the hope that the storm would blow over. While its most important leaders were declaring that revolutionary struggles had now disappeared from Spain's social scene and denying responsibility for the revolt in Asturias, the Communist Party took full responsibility.

The antifascist forces dispersed by defeat began to reorganize feverishly and to resume the work of informing the people: *Red Banner*, the illegal organ of the Communist Party, was published; the organization in Madrid edited *The Soviet, Red Front* and *Red North*; Valencia put out *Combat*; Bilbao, *Red Banner*; Catalonia, *Red Catalonia*. The Communist youth organization, whose newspaper was called *Youth's Battle*, worked side by side with the party.

The first number of *Red Banner*, which appeared only a few days after the suppression of the October insurrection, carried an analysis of the defeat written by the Central Committee of the Communist Party. "The battle we have fought," declared the manifesto, "was not the decisive one. Let not the assassins of the working people crow victory. We have resumed our work with more confidence than ever in the triumph of the working class, ready to fight again when the time comes. We have gained experience from these events which will fortify us in the steady road to victory. . . . We call upon all workers to strengthen the ranks of the revolutionary movement and prepare to march toward new battles."

[17]

# Antifascist Women

In the middle of 1933, a delegate arrived from the World Committee of Women against War and Fascism, which had its headquarters in France, to visit the women's political groups in our country and study the possibility of creating a similar organization in Spain.

We talked with her and reached an understanding; the Communist women of Spain would be happy to help her. We began to work on the project immediately. Apart from myself, Irene Falcón, Encarnación Fuyola, Lucía Barón and other comrades whose names I don't recall participated in the meetings.

Since the World Committee delegate didn't have time to visit the Socialist women's groups before she left, which she had particularly wanted to do, she asked us to talk to them in her behalf. Complying with her request, we asked María Martinez Sierra, Socialist deputy and well-known writer, for an interview, to which she kindly agreed. When we arrived at the magnificent Martinez mansion, the doorman, casting a glance at our obviously unelegant attire, made us go around to the back door. Live and learn! Who says there are no classes?

Instead of María Martinez, we were met by María de la A, the widow of a former royal palace guard. In a slip of the tongue, I called her María de la O, the name of the protagonist of the latest song hit:

> María de la O,
> You're simply terrible,
> With so much of everything . . .

With the kind and sincere cooperation of Republican and some Socialist women, we organized the National Committee of Women against War and Fascism, with Catalina Salmerón as honorary president. Catalina was the daughter of an old Republican who had renounced the presidency of his country rather than sign a death sentence during the first Republic in 1873.

A group of intellectuals worked splendidly in organizing Women against War committees and in attracting important sectors of women from the middle class, who later played an important role in the organization.

We Communist women used to visit the Republican Party centers and hold pleasant conversations with the women members about the political situation and Republican government policies in general. Among the members of the Republican women's political organizations, in addition to Victoria Kent and Clara Campoamor, well known for their political activities, we found dozens of humble women who could have put some of their party leaders to shame with their excellent political capabilities, their understanding of Spain's vital problems and their determination to fight against fascism.

The sympathy that the Republican women showed with the political activities of their Communist sisters soon began to distress certain members of the Republican Union Party, who decided to put a damper on the cordial relations between their members and the Communists. They posted the police at the door to keep us out. But their plan backfired. The most politically active of their women members left the organization. Some joined the Communist Party; others became valiant workers in the Women against War. The first International Congress of the Women against War and Fascism was celebrated in Paris, in August 1934. I headed the Spanish delegation, which included Carmen Loyola, Encarnación Fuyola, Irene Falcón and Elisa Uriz.

On our return to Madrid, we received news that the government was planning to mobilize the reservists in connection with the war in Morocco. In a few hours, overcoming seemingly insurmountable obstacles with the help of Republican and Socialist women, who acted against the orders of their parties, a demonstration was organized protesting against the calling up of the reserve. Thousands of women participated, in particular the workers of the tobacco factory, who turned out *en masse*. Catalina Salmerón, as honorary president, and I, as acting president, presided over the meeting.

The mounted police tried to disperse the demonstration with their horses, but the women reformed their groups and continued marching through the streets of Madrid. Many were arrested and taken to General Police Headquarters, but were later released because of the protests lodged by several of the democratic organizations.

The Women against War Committee, operating in the principal cities and towns of Spain, passed its baptism of fire with honors during the repression of the insurrectionary movement in October 1934. Many women became outstanding political activists of the organization, among them, Emilia Elías, a professor in the Normal School of Madrid; Angeles Cruz de Mansilla, wife of a miner in the Basque Country, who later spent 18 years in prison under Franco; Juanita Corzo, laboratory assistant, who came from an Anarchist family, and hundreds of other women who helped defend the Republic against the military fascist aggression during the Civil War.

At the end of 1934, when the repression was erupting with bloody violence against the Asturian workers, I went to Asturias with two Republican women, Isabel de Albacete and Alicia García. The Republican Party could rightly be proud of these self-sacrificing workers who accompanied me in full knowledge of the risks involved.

We arrived in Asturias with a safe-conduct pass made out to the Committee to Aid Workers' Children, which was not yet known to the Asturian military authorities. A Republican woman had managed to send the pass to us from Asturias, where she was investigating how we could aid the families of the workers.

We arrived in Oviedo, and the Fierro family, restaurant owners, one of whom was a Communist and in prison, cautioned us against visiting the mining zone. Nevertheless, we went. We passed through several towns and visited many families who received us with open arms. The repression had not quelled the people's fighting spirit.

As we were returning to Oviedo, after having organized the departure of more than a hundred children, the authorities began to look for us. We were stopped at one of the mining towns, just before reaching Sama de Langreo, but when we showed our safe-conduct pass, signed by the military governor of Asturias, the guards let us go, thinking they had made a mistake.

There was another Civil Guard post at the entrance to Sama, but our miraculous pass didn't do us any good this time. They put us in a car that rode through the town at a snail's pace. We could see the terrified glances of the people along the way. We were taken to the Casa de Pueblo. It was now a prison where miners accused of participating in the insurrection were being tortured to death.

A lieutenant asked for our pass, and when he saw the official seal of his superior, he asked the guards indignantly: "Who was the idiot that arrested these ladies?"

The guards said they had acted under orders. The lieutenant telephoned to make sure, and when he received an affirmative reply, he turned to us and said: "Everybody loses their heads here. You're free. You may go on."

We weren't free for long. When we got to the next Civil Guard checkpoint in the middle of the road, our car was stopped and we were ordered inside the post. While we were waiting for the sergeant, a guard told us that they were looking for La Pasionaria, a dangerous Communist who was reportedly in the neighborhood.

My two friends went pale. Realizing that I couldn't keep up the pretense any longer, I asked:

"Who are you looking for?"

"La Pasionaria."

"That's me."

"What did you say?"

"That I'm La Pasionaria."

The guard almost had heart failure. "You're the one who was making propaganda for the Communists at election time last year?"

"That's me."

"You're the one who spoke on the radio from Russia?"

"That's me."

"Well, wait a minute."

He went to the other room and returned with two guards. "You're going to be taken to the prison in Oviedo," he told us.

"On what charges?" I demanded.

"We don't have to explain; they'll tell you there."

We protested, but it was no use. I told my friends not to worry, since I was the one they were after. We reached Oviedo at nine that evening. They took our documents and led us to the women's section, where we met some old acquaintances. There was no space to lie down. The other women made room for us in their bunks, and there we spent the night listening to them as they described the horrible details of the repression.

Shortly after being jailed, by a special method prisoners use to communicate with each other, we received affectionate greetings from the other prisoners and our spirits rose considerably.

The following day we were called to the office. A pair of Civil Guards handcuffed us as if we were dangerous criminals and took us to the General Staff quarters. We were received by a colonel who ordered the guards to take off our handcuffs. He asked about the purpose of our trip to Asturias. I answered: "There are thousands of families in the mining zone who don't have any means of sustenance. When you jail fathers and mothers, the children are the ones who suffer the most, the orphans you have deprived of the love and protection of their parents. Is it a crime to want to alleviate their situation?"

"No, it's not a crime. But by doing that you are contributing to the continuance of a state of rebellion. We want to pacify Asturias."

"Pacify Asturias? What do you mean by pacifying? Arresting and torturing to death men and women who have done nothing but defend their right to live as human beings?"

"The army doesn't do that. That's not our function."

"You know about it and tolerate it."

"It's out of our jurisdiction."

"But there's a state of war in Asturias, the army is in command here and the army, with its military tribunals, pronounces the death sentences!"

"Look, I've called you to inform you that you're free. You have 24 hours to leave Asturias."

"We'll go, but we're taking 150 children with us."

"Take them, but don't come back."

He returned our documents, and we left to pick up the children. They were placed in foster homes in Madrid with working- and middle-class families.

The Women against War held its first congress in Madrid in the summer of 1934. Delegates from all Spain attended; workers, peasants, employees, teachers, professors, journalists and artists. The congress gave testimony to the long road of achievements traveled in the brief but tempestuous period since 1933, when the first antifascist women's committee was founded.

(Later, during the Civil War, the Minister of Defense named a group of the organization's leaders to form the Women's Aid Committee, which played an important part in the conflict. In an impressive demonstration, it mobilized tens of thousands of women to demand that the government send those men who were in unessential jobs to the front. The women offered to take their places back home. In 1937, the Women against War held a national conference in Valencia with delegates from all Loyalist Spain—workers, peasants and intellectuals. Taking stock of the organization's activities during one year of war, the conference bore witness to the immense participation of women in the defense of the Republic.)

The Women against War became a great national organization of Spanish women, including many members who in times of peace had not only refused to join but had even fought the organization. The common struggle, although waged for different reasons, was the great melting pot of opinions. And we can say with all certainty that what was done yesterday in defense of the Republic and of democracy can also be done tomorrow in the reconstruction of a democratic and peaceful Spain.

[18]

## A Non-Tourist Trip

A movement of solidarity with the insurrectionists of Asturias spread throughout the world and was climaxed by the International Aid Conference held in Paris in the spring of 1935. Manuel Colinos and I attended as delegates from Spain. Since the Communist Party was then illegal, we had to leave Spain and return clandestinely.

The trip was difficult and risky. We had to cross the Pyrenees on foot, with a guide more adept at carrying contraband than escorting political delegates—not to speak of women. To avoid the guards at the border we had to take the practically impassable mountain paths which were not likely to be watched.

The itinerary was discussed at length before our departure. Some thought the way across the Basque-French border the safest, while others favored the route through Catalonia. I chose the latter, about which I hadn't the faintest notion. However, the Catalans we consulted assured us that the trip through that part of the Pyrenees was not very long and the guide was a good one.

Comrades Sesé and Arlandis, in charge of organizing the journey, met us in Barcelona, but neither knew anything about the route nor how long it would take to get to the other side. The guide had told them that the trip was more or less an easy one. However, as we found out later, our guide, while fearing encounters with the carabineros (customs guards), thought nothing of the craggy steep mountain paths used only by wild pigs, mountain goats and smugglers. He was an excellent person, who had saved dozens of Asturians from the repression by taking them out of Spain.

We left Barcelona in one of the trains going toward the border and arrived in Gerona. Comrade Arlandis had made us a map of the city showing where we were supposed to meet the guide, not an easy feat at night in an unknown city. After wandering through the city and walking around in circles several times, we finally arrived at the house indicated on the map. The party chief in Gerona opened the door and received us cordially. He would put us in contact with a driver and the guide.

After dinner with his family, we sat around waiting, since to avoid the risk of meeting anyone we couldn't begin our trip until the streets were deserted. The driver and the guide arrived later, and at ten o'clock sharp we were on the road going toward the mountains.

For an interminable half hour we drove over a road pitted with holes and ruts. The car jolted up and down mercilessly shaking its occupants, until we arrived at the place where we had to get out and start walking, skirting the sides of the Pyrenees.

It was a moonless night, cold and damp. The guide cautioned us: "Walk in silence, no conversation, no smoking. The night and the mountains have eyes. They can amplify and transmit echos in an astonishing way and the carabineros sleep with one ear cocked."

Useful advice, though difficult to follow. The prohibition on smoking didn't affect me. But when I began knocking my shins so hard against the rocks that I saw stars, or falling across a tree trunk and landing several feet away, or getting caught in brambles which tore my dress and scratched my body, silence was not easy.

We walked like blind men, guiding ourselves largely by sound and sometimes by touch, following the unfaltering steps of our guide, who never tripped. He knew the mountains as he did his own backyard and, like a cat, could see in the dark.

We walked for two long hours. Unable to bear the silence any longer, I asked the guide in a whisper:

"Do we have much farther to go?" He didn't answer.

"Far to go?" I insisted.

"The important thing is not the going, but the arrival," he replied, barely moving his lips.

The arrival, but where? How many more hours had we to walk, how many more hills to cross, valleys to pass, rivers to wade, before reaching the place where we could rest our tired feet?

No one had told us anything about the journey. The guide only made us walk and walk, at a trotting pace. But how could we walk fast if we couldn't see where to put our feet and might fall down a ravine, or if we had to stop and catch our breath, or tie our hemp sandals whose straps broke with every fall we took?

The sky began to lighten, and before us loomed the Pyrenees, like an inaccessible fortress. We walked and walked without stopping, mechanically. Even our thoughts were concentrated on walking.

Before dawn, the damp cold, the forced silence, which we dared not break with a word to lift our spirits, or an exclamation to release our pent-up emotions, or a complaint, was broken by something that meant failure, the possibility that we could not continue our trip. A howl? A roar? No, something worse. A bark!

A faraway bark, now clear, now indistinct. Bears, wolves, foxes, wild pigs, jackals, all the inhabitants of the mountains meant nothing to us. A bark at that hour and in that place meant not only a dog, it meant the carabineros, arrest, prison, missing the conference, not fulfilling our job.

We stopped. The guide listened with a hundred ears.

"What is it?" we asked, although we had no doubt what it was.

"Carabineros!" he said. "They're coming this way. We must head for the river. I wanted to avoid this, but we can't now. Let's go. The wind is in our favor, it's at their backs. But we have to run to get to the river and erase our scent before they get nearer."

Run? . . . We had to run and wade a river in the dark?

"And if we can't?" I thought out loud.

"We can," and the guide shot off ahead of us. We ran behind, praying not to lose sight of him. Leaving the path, we plunged through brambles, near the edge of gullies that we wouldn't have approached by day. Darkness prevented vertigo.

We stopped before a large ravine where the path ended and a steep incline opened up before us.

"Go down!" rapidly ordered our implacable escort.

His "it's not for women" had touched me. "Let's go," I said, getting up.

The guide gave me the small winebag hung around his neck. I drank a little and felt better.

"How are you?" I asked Colinos. He hadn't spoken a word during the entire trip.

"A little tired, but it doesn't matter. Now we have to cross the river. There's lots of water because of the thaw. But don't worry. I can swim and nothing will happen."

"Don't take your sandals off," said our guide, "the river bottom is stony and could hurt your feet. The waters are high, so be careful. Stay close to me. In the middle there are two big rocks set pretty wide apart. You'll have to jump over them. After that everything will go fine."

The guide went first, Colinos second and I went last.

"You have to jump over the rocks," I thought. If it had been by day I wouldn't have cared, because I'd know how far I had to jump. But now . . . if I don't jump far enough, I'll fall in the water where I'll surely drown. . . . And drowning would be a shame . . . especially drowning at night in a river in the Pyrenees . . . the height of absurdity.

The water got deeper and deeper as we went further out. The coldness made me catch my breath. I was extremely nervous. Wading rivers in the dark gives me gooseflesh. The water pressed against my legs, pushed me, dragged me. I took each step forward with difficulty, trying not to fall, straining against the force of the current pushing me.

I finally arrived at one of the famous rocks. Leaning on it, I rested a moment. From the top of the rock, Colinos wanted to help me up, but the matter wasn't that simple. I had one hand busy holding my skirt around my waist and I couldn't climb very well with only one hand.

Finally, I managed to get up. Now the jump over the twin rocks. I was paralyzed. The water breaking against the rocks made a furious whirlpool, producing a sound that froze my blood. I felt dizzy. I couldn't jump.

"Help!" I shouted nervously, forgetting about the dogs, the carabineros and all caution. Colinos waded back to the second rock and held out his hand. I could barely reach it. "Jump wide," he advised me. "I'll hold you if you slip."

I tensed my body and leaped. The hardest part was now over, and after wading some more we finally reached shore. I breathed easier. We renewed our march, which we found more strenuous after what we had just gone through.

Suddenly, someone fell into the river. I still don't know how it happened. Colinos had inadvertently strayed off the path and had fallen into the river. We gasped, stricken.

But when we arrived and, instead of shouts for help, we heard a volley of oaths and a mournful "Oh, my suit!" all my tension released itself in a nervous laughing fit. I roared with laughter. The more the guide told me to keep quiet, the more I laughed. I sat down and with my face on the ground laughed and laughed uncontrollably. I could have cried just as easily.

After the mad race, crossing the river, the carabineros, and the dogs, Colinos' unhappy wail broke the tension. The fact was that his suit wasn't paid for yet. When it was decided that Colinos would accompany me to the Paris conference, an urgent problem arose. He didn't have a decent suit. He had been out of work for a long time and his best suit, along with his other good clothing, had ended up in the pawn shop. One of our comrades had taken him to a tailor who made him a suit to pay for in installments.

Before we left Madrid, I had asked if he didn't have a pair of old trousers to put on for the rough trip to the border. "No," he answered, "I'll just have to be careful."

During the long trip from Madrid to Barcelona, his only worry was the suit—that it shouldn't wrinkle, that the crease in the pants shouldn't come out, and the like. When we began our trek through the mountains, he rolled up the trouser cuffs and fastened them with a rubber band so they wouldn't fray or get dirty.

He had crossed the river in his shorts. And in one second all his precautions had come to nothing. He came out with his trousers dripping; only the upper part of his jacket was relatively dry. I couldn't look at him, because, in spite of the pathetic situation, my urge to laugh was stronger than my will. I wanted to cheer him up, to say something nice, but I couldn't do it.

He wanted to take the trousers off, but our guide advised him not to. They would dry better and wrinkle less if he kept them on. After shaking out the jacket, he threw it over his shoulders and we started to walk again, this time with even less spirit than before.

Although I hadn't fallen into the river, I wasn't any drier than Colinos was. When I climbed onto the rock in the middle of the river, I had to let go of my skirt. Aside from the discomfort of walking with a cold, wet skirt swishing around my legs, I didn't particularly mind if my clothes were soggy. I had taken along a coat which was safely tucked away in the guide's satchel. The coat would hide my clothes. But Colinos? What would he look like when we got to the French border, not to speak of Paris?

The march was getting more difficult. We were tired and the path was getting steeper. From time to time I asked the same question, "Is it much farther?" only to receive the same answer, "No, not much."

We continued walking until we came to a huge hill. Our guide looked worried. He saw how tired we were, but the place was not safe enough to stop and rest.

"A last effort, comrades," he begged us. "We'll be there soon."

"We can't make it without resting for a minute," I answered.

Leaving the path, we sought shelter in the woods, where we couldn't be seen even if someone came up the path we had taken. I sat down, resting on a tree trunk. The guide gave us some bread and a little wine. Fatigue finally conquered my will and I promptly fell asleep. They let me rest for half an hour. And once again, onward and upward! From those heights at dawn, the Pyrenees were an unforgettable sight. But we weren't in the mood for landscapes.

In full daylight we arrived at the place where we were to stop. It was a cave dug out of the base of a huge rock by the rushing waters over the centuries. It was very small. We scarcely had room to sit down, and we couldn't stand because it was too low. Besides, it was located in the center of a slippery slope. There was a kind of wall made of earth and twigs built by the smugglers to prevent those who were forced to take refuge in the cave from falling down into the narrow valley extending across the foot of the slope.

The guide brought us an armful of dry ferns, which he had hidden in another spot, and we sat down. With the projecting rock above us, our feet reached the base of the wall. We didn't have anything to eat or drink; there was a far-off spring but it could be used only at night.

The guide suddenly announced that he was leaving. "I'm going to the cabin of some charcoal workers to bring something to eat. I'll return tonight. Don't even think of making a fire because the smoke can be seen from a distance and could bring the carabineros." We didn't know what to think or say.

"What'll we do if he doesn't come back?" I asked.

"What'll we do? Return the way we came," answered Colinos.

Not a very pleasant prospect, but we had no choice other than to wait and see. At nightfall we heard footsteps and sat up expecting to see our guide. We froze. The new arrival was a young man.

"Good evening," he said in a strong Catalan accent.

"Good evening," we answered.

"You're waiting?

"Yes, we're waiting."

Seeing our uneasiness, he introduced himself: "I'm the son of X (the name of our guide). My father will be here soon with provisions. But we won't make a fire until it gets darker." He told us that he had come from France the night before and he kept us entertained with some of the adventurous incidents of the smuggler's life, which he had lived since childhood as his father's helper.

When it was dark, our guide arrived with a chicken, which we plucked and roasted in the embers of our small fire. The chicken refused to get roasted. It was only singed on the coals and dirtied on the ashes, but after our close call at dawn and the daylong fast, the tough, saltless meat, burnt on the outside, raw on the inside, was an exquisite feast. Nothing tastes bad with a good appetite.

After we had eaten, they told us their plans. We would leave at three in the morning so as to arrive on the French side early. Our guide's son would take over. Once in France, the trip would be easier and less dangerous so far as vigilance was concerned. Father and son discussed the route to take, and the old man accepted the younger one's opinion. We would not take the path they usually used. The son had arrived via a new route which seemed safer although a bit longer. The advantage was that it could be used by day without risk of unexpected meetings.

We had no say in the matter and left it to their experience. What we wanted to do was arrive, even if it meant more walking.

The old guide said goodbye, wishing us a good trip. We put out the fire and settled back on the ferns. Worried about what the following day would bring, we couldn't sleep or even whisper, since it still wasn't safe. At three, the young guide rose and simply said, "Let's go."

Once again we began to climb up and down the mountains. The road was longer than we expected. Finally we reached French territory. We walked until noon, frequently wading through new rivers. It wasn't so hard now; at least we could see where we were going.

The route proposed by our young guide was blocked. The rain during the night had precipitated an avalanche. We had to choose between walking back to where we had come from, with the risk of having to spend another night in the mountains, or to climb over the rock slide through a fissure in the rocks some 50 feet above us, holding on to the roots of the shrubs that grew among the crags.

At first glance, it seemed impossible. It reminded me of the limestone quarries in Vizcaya, where the dynamiters, secured with a long rope, descended to the rocks below to bore holes for the sticks of dynamite. But we weren't dynamiters, and even if we had been, we didn't have rope and we had to climb up, not down.

What to do? If we turned back, we wouldn't arrive in time at the conference, which was to begin the next day. Climb? We ran the risk of breaking our necks, but there was no other way.

The guide climbed up first; I went behind him to see where he put his feet and Colinos went last to catch me if I slipped. When I finally put my hands on the top of the fissure, I suddenly sprouted wings. I felt so light. Fear is a heavy burden. Your legs become lead, your head turns to stone—sensations that I experienced several times during the trip through the Pyrenees.

Before entering civilized territory, we sat down by the edge of a stream to wash and tidy ourselves up a bit. At nightfall, we passed through the outskirts of a French village. Here we boarded the bus to Perpignan, where a French comrade was to give us our railroad tickets to the capital. We ate in his home, bade farewell to our guide and went to the station.

The next day we were in Paris. The first part of our trip was over. How would the second part, our return to Spain, be?

Before the conference, another French comrade, a doctor, attended to our cuts, scrapes and bruises. Everyone outdid himself in kindness. We were even promised help to return by a different route.

During the conference, we met Enrique Sánchez, the delegate from *Socorro Rojo* (Red Aid). He was a railroad worker, so he had left Spain without any difficulty, but he couldn't return the same way, so he decided to throw his luck in with ours.

The conference was a success, but—oh, human frailty!—when it ended, no one thought of the *malheureux* Spaniards who had walked across the Pyrenees to attend the meeting and who would have to return to their country in Joshua's chariot if no one took pity. No one did. We were told that it was extremely difficult to arrange for our return; there was nothing that could be done.

They gave us tickets to the south of France. From there we would have to fend for ourselves. We arrived in Perpignan and stayed at a friend's house. At dawn the following day, we began our trip to Spain by the same route, which was not any easier because of past experience, especially for our new companion Sanchez who was unaccustomed to the rigors of traversing mountains.

The VII Congress of the Comintern took place in Moscow three months later, in July 1935. This historic event had a decisive influence on the world Communist movement.

Dimitrov, Secretary General of the Comintern, known the world over for his noble, heroic stand against Hitlerism, struck out unequivocally against the old sectarian ills which were still plaguing the Communist movement, in spite of Lenin's devastating criticism of this weakness in *"Left-Wing" Communism, an Infantile Disorder.*

The congress brought about a basic change in the concepts, tactics and methods of all Communist parties, strengthening the international workers' movement and favoring the development of democratic forces in all countries of the world.

The United Front and Popular Front policies, as defined in the VII Congress and applied to the specific conditions of each country, taking into account national characteristics, still remain, in essence, a contemporary and efficient method in the fight for peace, disarmament, democracy and Socialism.

The People's Front policy was not concocted in a Moscow laboratory, as claimed by the priests of anticommunism. It was a logical step, arising from the need to counteract the danger facing the working masses; and it was also the crystallization of the political experience of various Communist parties—in particular the Spanish and the French which, by different routes, had arrived at the same conclusions.

While our French comrades in 1934 joined forces with the Socialist Party and other political groups to take specific actions against fascism, in Spain, for the first time in the history of the Communist movement, the Communists together with Socialists and Republicans elected a deputy to parliament in the 1933 elections in Malaga. Following the policy of unity, the Communists and Socialists entered an alliance for the common cause, an alliance which, despite its deficiencies, made it possible for the two parties to fight side by side during the insurrection of October 1934.

"We Communists," said Dimitrov in the closing speech of the VII Comintern Congress, "employ methods of struggle which differ from those of the other parties; but, while using our own methods in combating fascism, we Communists will also support the methods of struggle used by other parties, however inadequate they may seem, if these methods are really directed against fascism.

"We are ready to do all this because, in countries of bourgeois-democracy, we want to block the way of reaction and the offensive of capital and fascism, prevent the abolition of bourgeois-democratic liberties, forestall fascism's terrorist vengeance upon the proletariat and the revolutionary section of the peasantry and intellectuals, and save the young generation from physical and spiritual degeneracy."

Representing the Communist Party of Spain at the Congress were José Díaz and myself. The Communist Party of Catalonia sent Comrade Sesé, who was later murdered by the FAI (Anarchist Secret

Society) in the putsch of May 1937 in Catalonia; and Comrade Arlandis, killed in the bombing of Figueras in 1939.

Since the political situation of the Communist Party had not changed in the three months since my last adventure in the Pyrenees, we had to confront its lofty peaks, briers and precipices once more. I told party officials how difficult the journey was and even scolded our Catalan comrades for not having looked into the matter of a route more carefully. Teasing me, they said I was a disgrace to the Basques for scaring so easily. I laughed to myself, thinking of how *they* would have weathered the trip—one of them because of the extra pounds he carried around his middle, and the other because of a rather puny physique. And I even prepared a little joke for them.

I told our friends in Perpignan to give a bottle of quinine wine and a box of talcum powder to Sesé and Arlandis when they arrived, as a present from me—the quinine as a fortifying tonic, and the talcum to soothe the smarting of the cuts and scratches. I couldn't help laughing when I saw them in Moscow for, in spite of my gifts, they were in sorry shape.

This time I crossed the Pyrenees with José Díaz. The trek was easier since we could walk by day; and the fact that we were on our way to Moscow to attend the Comintern Congress made us forget all our complaints. We felt we could walk across the Himalayas if necessary.

We had the honor of being elected members of the Comintern's Executive Committee: José Díaz, our Secretary General, as acting member and I as alternate.

On our return trip we had to cross several borders, which frequently occasioned incidents, particularly in Austria, where we were held for several hours. We didn't have an Austrian visa and had to pay a heavy fine. This emptied our pockets of the little money we had and we arrived in Paris literally penniless.

We didn't get out of the train in Paris, but went directly south to a village near the Spanish border, where we waited for the arrival of a friend sent by Jesús Larrañaga, who was in charge of organizing our re-entry into Spain.

Larrañaga's plan was brilliant. We would go by boat from San Juan de Luz, the French port where we were staying, to San Sebastián in Guipúzcoa. We would use a yacht anchored in the Bay of San Sebastián whose owner was out of town. One of our comrades, a mechanic, knew the mechanic who took care of the yacht during the owner's absence. The mechanic in charge of the vessel was to be diverted by a gastronomic maneuver, a royal feast in a popular restaurant which a good Basque would never refuse, while his friend was to take the yacht out to pick us up.

We left the following day in a small boat captained by a sailor friend of Larrañaga's. However, the matter wasn't as simple as it had seemed to us on land. Huge waves began to rock the boat, lifting and dropping it as if it were a nutshell. During the moments of nausea and dizziness, soaring up and down with the waves through mountains of foam, I remembered the Pyrenees. At that moment they didn't seem so formidable.

Before sighting the yacht, we had a long, uncomfortable wait, while the turbulent waves threatened to capsize us at any moment. Boarding the yacht was no easy feat either, because of the high seas and our nonexistent nautical experience.

We finally sailed into San Sebastián safe and sound. The carabineros, thinking we were friends of the yacht's owner, let us pass without a problem.

The yacht belonged to Señor Luca de Tena, owner of the monarchist newspaper, *ABC*. And since we know how good and generous he is, I'm sure that he'll forgive us for having borrowed his yacht. It saved us, especially me, a weak woman, a long crossing of the Pyrenees.

[19]

# Generous Aid

As I recall those hazardous days, I would like especially to express my gratitude to the sincere and decent people who helped us, who offered us their homes and their solidarity in the face of government persecution.

The sympathy that men and women from all walks of life showed toward the Communist Party, harassed and hunted, was all the more important and appreciated since, contrary to bourgeois political practices, no one expected anything in return for his aid. The Communists lacked political influence and did not have government jobs or favors to hand out.

In one of the streets going from Rosales to the Glorieta de Quevedo, there was a stationery and tobacco shop where I used to buy my writing supplies. During the time that I frequented the shop I had never spoken to the owner more than was strictly necessary for my purchases.

One day, at the beginning of 1935, as I was buying some notebooks, the shopkeeper asked me amiably: "How are things going?"

Surprised, I looked at him and said, "I don't understand your question."

"Pardon me, but I know who you are. I would like to express my sympathy for the cause of the Communist Party and also my indignation for the conduct of the other parties. I'm an old Republican and I'm ashamed and outraged at the situation that our governments have put the Republic in. You can count on me for anything. Both my shop and my house, where I live with my sister, are at your disposal if you need a place to work in, or for your meetings."

I thanked him, but we had no need to take him up on his kind offer. As Communist policies were being more and more accepted by the masses, we had many, previously nonexistent facilities for our meetings—workers' homes, and even houses whose appearance allayed all political suspicion.

There was a Republican-Radical-Socialist circle in the street of San Bernardo whose president was a small industrialist, a sincere Republican and democrat. When the persecution was at its height and all the party meeting halls had been closed down by the police, some of our members accepted the assistance offered by Republican friends in this circle and went to the street of San Bernardo at night to meet with other comrades who lived far from the center of town.

This alarmed the president of the circle—not because he feared for himself, but because of his Republican moral scruples. He thought it would be shameful for them as revolutionary democrats, if the Communists whom they admired and respected were arrested by the police in the clubhouse.

One evening I went there in the hope of meeting a comrade whom I urgently needed to see. The president of the circle called me into his office.

"Look here, Pasionaria. I know that your friends come here for a reason. However, the police also come here, and I'm afraid that one of these days we'll have a problem. I sincerely want to help you. I know that you have no place to meet, so let me offer you my home. You can meet there, no one will bother you. The apartment is at your disposal all day long. I'll tell the concierge to give you a key and you can go there freely at any time, beginning tomorrow."

I thanked him for his generous offer and told the comrades about it. The next day I went to the address he had given me and without even asking my name the concierge gave me the key. The apartment was perfect for the meetings of the Politburo. We met there several times, until the political situation finally improved.

At the end of October 1934, the police began looking for me in the district where I lived. I had to move out of my house quickly and take an apartment in the street of Blasco de Garay, which seemed relatively safe.

However, my situation was becoming increasingly difficult, especially in regard to my children. They were frequently neglected while I was active in clandestine party work.

When I returned from the prison in Bilbao and met again with the leaders of the party, I told them I wanted to return to the Basque Country. There, I could work for the party and still be with my children, which I could not do in Madrid. But the party thought it important that I remain in Madrid to work among the women, an activity which up till then had been neglected. In any case, my work in that field was temporarily suspended by a new arrest in March 1932. I was released in January 1933.

My two country-raised children were used to the fresh air, the sea and the mountains of the Basque country. I couldn't bear to see them cooped up in a stuffy, dark Madrid house, or lost in the crowded city selling *Mundo Obrero*, without knowing anyone but a small group of Pioneers, without being able to attend school, and constantly worrying about their mother. The party leaders thought the matter over and proposed to send my children to the Soviet Union, where they could lead a normal life together with the children of Soviet workers, even though they would not have the presence and comfort of their mother.

It was another sacrifice I had to make. I accepted it with the confidence that the pain of separation would be mitigated on both sides; they would enjoy a child's normal life, and I would be at peace knowing they were well cared for.

In the spring of 1935, Rubén and Amaya left for the Soviet Union. After a brief stay in the Pioneer Camp in Artek in the Crimea, Amaya entered the international children's home in Ivanovo, and Rubén became an apprentice lathe worker in the Stalin Automobile Works in Moscow. A few months later, he was enrolled in an aviation school.

A few weeks after the children had gone, the concierge knocked at my door. I received her warily. I had signed the lease in the name of my husband, a "sailor" who was always away at sea; my name didn't appear on the lease. The visit of the concierge, with whom I never had any dealings, was highly suspicious.

She had scarcely crossed the threshold when without preamble she blurted: "Are you La Pasionaria?"

Since denying it would have been idiotic, I answered: "Yes, madam, I'm La Pasionaria. I hope you'll understand why I don't carry my name on a label pinned to my coat. Why do you want to know? Do you have any complaints? Don't I pay my rent on time?"

"Forgive me for the intrusion. But it's not that at all. The police were here asking for you. I told them you didn't live here because I really didn't know. And if I knew, I wouldn't have told them anyway. They gave me your description and I've come to warn you to be careful. My family isn't Communist but we admire those who defend the workers. We'd like to help you."

She warned me to be cautious with some of my neighbors and told me that there were some apartments on my floor where I could hide in case of trouble. In one of them lived an employee, an excellent person, not affiliated with any party. A Socialist embroiderer lived in the other. She had already spoken to them and they were willing to cooperate.

With all the natural ingenuity and lively intelligence of the saintly and self-abnegating women of Spain, the concierge traced out a defensive plan to foil the police. A kind of anti-police cordon was formed around me, extending from the concierge's family and my sympathetic neighbors to the owners of a café in the street. When someone suspicious entered, they hung in their window a previously agreed upon signal which meant, "Attention! Pirates in sight!"

Every morning when I left, the concierge's aged father, a former peasant from Valladolid, who stood guard at the door, would say: "Just a minute, my child, let me see if it's raining." He would go out to the middle of the street, look at the sky, spit, and return rapidly: "Go quickly, nobody's in sight."

The solidarity of these people warmed my heart. Because I was a Communist persecuted by the police, they looked upon me as one of their own, someone they had to protect and take care of.

I used to tell the porters when I would be coming home late, and they would stand guard with the door open, until I returned so I wouldn't have to wait or call. Weeks went by like this and the police were stumped. I would really have been safer somewhere else, but my moving out would have offended them. Besides, where else would I find such generous and unselfish people?

I decided to stay in spite of the risks. The police arrived one evening, wanting either to search all the apartments in the building or to have the porters name all suspicious tenants. The porters declined the first proposal, claiming it was illegal and, as for the second, they showed the police an apartment whose occupants were very well known to everyone in the building.

Thinking that they had discovered the person they were looking for, the police entered the apartment. They came down snorting with anger. The porters were waiting for them with serious expressions on their faces.

"Did you find her?" they asked full of interest.

"No," answered the chief curtly. "We're looking for a woman, and we found a pair of queers."

"Are you sure you haven't seen La Pasionaria?" insisted the police chief.

"Look," answered the concierge, "she *could* have come here. You know that Escanilla, the Communist you arrested, used to live on the sixth floor. She could have visited him once or twice. But we can assure you that she doesn't live here."

After checking the names of all the tenants, the police left. Unconvinced, they returned the next day and put guards on the stairway, hoping to catch me as I entered or left the building.

Under pretext of cleaning my room, the concierge came to see me.

"Don't go out," she said. "They've left a guard downstairs. If you need anything, my daughter will bring it. She'll use a special knock. Don't open the door for anyone. I'll tell your friends. I'll go to

*Mundo Obrero* (which was nearby) and tell them of your situation so that no one will come to visit you. Don't worry, we'll get you out of the mousetrap."

A week passed by. The guards changed shifts, but La Pasionaria didn't appear. Finally the concierge and I decided to "cross the Rubicon." The police were looking for a woman dressed in black, and they paid more attention to those who entered the building than to those who left.

I told Hermenegilda, the concierge, to buy me a few yards of white material for a dress. She made the dress and gave me a wide-brimmed hat, long earrings, sunglasses and lipstick. We had a taxi waiting downstairs. Leaving the police calmly seated on the stairway, a more-or-less elegant lady dressed in white left the building to spend a few weeks up north. There I was, masqueraded, in a taxi, driving around Madrid, a little undecided as to where I should go.

Under no circumstances could I go to my friends' homes lest the police were following me. I decided to go to Alcalá Street, to the office of the lawyers who were defending the Asturian workers. A comrade found me a safe lodging, far from my old neighborhood. There I lived and worked, always running the risk of being arrested, until my departure for the VII Comintern Congress.

[20]

## Victory for the Popular Front

> Who are you that, sweetly singing the
> praises of a cruel ruler, hope to imprison
> the golden wings of a free spirit?
> —Curros Enríquez

Although the insurrection of 1934 had failed, Spain continued in a state of revolutionary turmoil. The economic crisis was worse; unemployment in industry and agriculture was soaring. Poverty was more intense and widespread. There were reasons for the country's never-ending ordeal: 30,000 families had no breadwinner. Spain had

30,000 political prisoners! The fever of rebellion was spreading through Catalonia, now deprived of its autonomous rights. The winners of the last elections were less united, less stable than before their victory. But the spirit of the working class was unbroken. The mere rumor of a strike or a protest demonstration was enough to send the government into a panic.

Despite the evidently superior political potential of the forces on the Left, there was one fatal flaw—lack of unity. Opposing the forces on the Right were several Republican parties, allied for a common purpose with many well-known leaders and considerable influence over the country but without large, effective organizations.

The Socialist Party included in its ranks workers with a long fighting tradition. Its leadership was varied and reform-minded, but it lacked the cohesive power of a revolutionary theory. Spain's two rival labor unions, based on different principles, followed different methods of battle. Outside of the trade unions there was an amorphous mass of millions of unorganized workers, especially in the rural areas. The Communist Party's influence was growing, but it was still too small to play a decisive role. These were the forces aligned on the side of democracy, with which Spain had to build the dam to hold back the fascist tide.

The Communist Party of Spain undertook the construction of this historic dam with its Popular Front policy. It was no easy task to overcome the multitude of obstacles that emerged to block the way. Special interests, ambitions, rivalries, incomprehension, personal feuds, all these problems came to the surface in the ranks of the Republican, Anarchist and Socialist parties to prevent the unification of popular forces.

The fight for an alliance of left-wing groups, for the creation of a joint democratic front against the fascist danger, had been tenaciously carried on for some time by the Communist Party, in spite of the reserve with which this policy had been viewed by some of the old-time Comintern leaders before Dimitrov became secretary of the international Communist movement.

In a meeting of the party's Central Committee in Madrid, in April 1933, the party's new political orientation was clearly defined: Unity with all the working-class and democratic forces, thus breaking with previous limited and schematic formulas. Chavaroche, one of the Comintern leaders, came out against this position in a series of articles, only to admit later that we had been right. Since we knew the situation in Spain better than Chavaroche did, we continued to fight for an alliance of the workers' and other democratic forces.

In the VII Comintern Congress, our policy of unity was fully approved, along with the Popular Front policy of the French Communist Party, whose activities were considered a model for all Communist parties.

In a meeting held in Madrid on June 2, 1935, prior to the VII Comintern Congress, José Díaz, in the name of the Spanish Communist Party, exhorted all the antifascist forces to unite, and proposed specific activities. The Communists were not renouncing any of their aims. On the contrary, the party was showing its revolutionary nature by adapting its tactics to the actual political situation in Spain.

"In these moments of danger, with fascism controlling key government positions," José Díaz said, "we declare our determination to fight together with all antifascist forces, united on the basis of a minimum program which all members of the Popular Front will be obliged to carry out. . . . We propose the formation of a provisional revolutionary government that will satisfy the demands of all the workers, the popular masses and antifascists, and pledge itself before the people to fulfill the program approved by the Popular Antifascist Alliance."

When Dimitrov, at the VII Congress, launched the new international Communist policy, and our tactics were approved, we were immensely happy.

At this point, it would be impossible not to mention an Argentine comrade, Victorio Codovilla, who helped us enormously both then and later to overcome our political weaknesses, to eliminate sectarian methods of work and to organize our party. The name of Codovilla is inextricably linked with the difficult moments of Spain's Communist Party and its evolution.

From the congress, we returned to Spain full of enthusiasm, determined to move heaven and earth to reach an agreement with the various working-class and democratic organizations in our country. The Communist Party became the new revolutionary force, capable of successfully joining all the forces on the Left, since it was not branded with failure in the eyes of the people, as were the political groups responsible for the revolutionary sterility of the second Republic.

In a meeting held in the Pardiñas Coliseum on November 3, 1935, José Díaz once again called upon left-wing forces to put aside their differences and to unite on one basic point, the defense of the Republic and of democracy, and to constitute an antifascist Popular Front to do battle with the most ferocious enemy of liberty, fascism.

Denouncing the reactionary governments, their antidemocratic and antipopular laws, their corruption, exemplified in the *straperlo* (the financial scandal involving public men), Díaz welcomed the renewed activities of the Left, a recent speech by Azaña and the policy changes adopted by the Socialist Party in favor of unity. He called enthusiastically for the alliance of all antifascist forces.

Speaking directly to the Socialists, Díaz publicly exhorted them to unite with all democratic forces, to work for political and organic unity with the Communist Party and to halt the growing schism in the workers' movement. "We want to march side by side with you in the coming battle," said José Díaz to the Socialists. "We want to march side by side with you until we merge into one single party."

The Communist Party carried this urgent call for unity to all the cities and villages of Spain. It called upon all Spain's workers, intellectuals and democrats to renounce their hostilities and misgivings in favor of unity and confidence in the victory of workers and democrats over the forces of reaction.

At the end of 1935, the party sent me to Galicia to take part in some propaganda meetings organized by the Provincial Committee of Coruña.

Before I left, José Díaz briefed me on the characteristics and chief trends of the workers' movement there. His advice was of immense value, even though this wasn't my first trip to Galicia—the cities of Pontevedra and Vigo were already old friends of mine. The revolutionary firmness of Galicia's workers, peasants and fishermen, and especially of the self-sacrificing women who worked in the fish canneries, had made an indelible impression on me.

Galicia is one of the most attractive regions in Spain. The beauty of its rivers and banks, the perpetual verdure of its mountains, the mild climate and the hospitality of its people take hold of a visitor to such a degree that when he has departed he feels a deep nostalgia and a profound desire to return. Only after seeing Galicia, after meeting the people, seeing the landscapes and the sea, can one understand the melancholy of Galicians who have been separated from the land where they were born.

So I returned to Galicia with joy. But I had to work, and to work hard, to overcome incredible resistance.

Coruña's Communist Party held its first propaganda meeting in the theater named after Rosalia de Castro, the famous singer who sang so wonderfully of Galicia's beauty.

The meeting took place on January 1, 1936. The people of Coruña knew that the Communist Party was the standardbearer in the fight for a joint people's front, and they came to the theater with the hope of hearing new arguments in favor of the unity which they themselves also thought indispensable.

This was the first Communist meeting in Galicia since the October insurrection and it gave the people an opportunity to express their bitterness at the repression. "UHP!" (Union of Working-Class Brothers!), the rallying battlecry of the Asturian combatants, was heard everywhere. Thousands of men and women acclaimed the Communist Party. Workers arrived at the theater in huge groups, singing the International and The Young Guard.

The meeting's success, to say the least, irked the reactionaries and their favorite allies, the Anarchist small-town politicians. In the name of "liberty" they plotted to disrupt the meeting. Friends told us of the underhanded plans being hatched by these groups, who saw their old feudal political powers in jeopardy. We proceeded calmly, thinking their bark would be worse than their bite. But those who had warned us were right. The provocation was carefully prepared. As the first speaker was about to begin, he was rudely interrupted.

"We want nothing to do with politicians!" shouted a provocateur from the balcony. And the 20 or 30 men in his claque repeated in a chorus, "Nothing!" over and over.

The audience was indignant. A dockworker stood up and shouted: "Sons of bitches! How much did they pay you to yell?"

Repeatedly interrupted by the commotion, the first speaker managed to end his speech. The same thing happened with the second speaker. But the crowd wouldn't take any more. A group of comrades began to throw the troublemakers out. "Cowards! Firebrands!" shouted the women angrily.

After a time the shouts quieted down, and it was my turn to speak. I intended to ignore the interruptions. I spoke from my heart to the men and women present, the peasants, fishermen, cigarette workers, the simple, brave and heroic housewives, to all the people of Coruña, rebels and revolutionaries.

I reminded them of the thousands of prisoners in the jails of Spain waiting for their freedom, freedom which could only be obtained by the united action of all progressive forces. I reminded them of the martyrdom of the heroic workers of Asturias, the firmness and unselfishness of its men and women and, finally, I spoke about the necessity for unity against the dangers of reaction.

Before I could go on to denounce the maneuvers of the reactionary forces, the provocateurs tried to start another riot. I went on energetically, telling the audience that the instigators were the tools of those who opposed unity. The claque fell into a moody silence.

And then something happened which clearly showed the collusion between the provocateurs and the police. What the provocateurs had not succeeded in doing by disruption, the Assault Guards were to do by violence. They broke into the theater and, before the audience realized what was going on, began to strike out savagely left and right, regardless of whether they were hitting men, women or children.

The riot was undescribable. People wrenched their seats from the ground and began beating off the guards. "Criminals! Cowards! Murderers!" screamed thousands of voices. The people in the balconies threw down everything they could find on the guards below.

The theater was quickly emptied. An officer accompanied by some guards tried to get up on the stage from which we were shouting at them, but we managed to push them down the stairs. The fighting continued in the street. The guards fired their rifles, and the workers replied with a volley of stones. I was arrested as I left the theater. "She's the one who threw the officer down the stairs," raged the guards.

Suddenly I saw a guard beating one of our comrades. Pushing aside my guards, I jumped on top of the other man in an effort to stop him. Workers came to my aid. When they found out I was being arrested, hundreds of them formed behind us on the road to the police station.

The news of the disrupted meeting spread like wildfire through the city. Everyone was out on the street, protesting against the instigators, the instruments of reaction. Fishermen, workers and sailors of the CNT told our comrades of their disgust and indignation at what had happened. The workers' political organizations formed special committees to visit the governor to demand the liberty of those who had been arrested and to protest against police interference.

We were released later in the afternoon. As we passed through the streets of Coruña, workers came up to us promising solidarity and inviting us to visit a score of other towns in the province. The cause of unity in Galicia had won a battle.

When I returned to Madrid, I found the party working fervidly on the creation of the Popular Front.

Some Republican leaders were still holding on to their senseless positions and resisted any idea of an alliance among democratic forces. The unfruitful discussions continued. Everyone thought he was right, and blamed everyone else for all the ills of the Republic. No one bothered to examine his own errors. No one raised the question of restoring the power of the Republic by fighting against the forces in power. The Socialists blamed the Republicans for not having supported the October insurrection. The Republicans blamed the Socialists for wanting to monopolize the leadership. Everyone was so busy attacking everyone else that they forgot about the crumbling Republic.

The political oracles prophesied the fall of reaction without anyone having to move a finger. It would happen as naturally as a rotten apple falling off a tree. Republicans and Socialists expected political panaceas to appear by chance, from the spontaneous "natural" activities of the masses. They expected a repetition of April 14, 1931.

Up to 1936, political alliances between the working class and the bourgeoisie of Spain had been like putting the lion to bed with the lamb. Or, to use another metaphor, the bourgeoisie got the chicken and the workers ended up with the bones.

The Popular Front policy represented something very different. The working class had acquired considerable experience since 1931. Asturias had demonstrated that unity was the decisive weapon in the workers' struggle against reaction. In October 1935, with the government crisis at its zenith, the Communist Party, in a letter to the newspaper *Claridad*, made the following proposals to the left-wing Socialists:

*At a mass meeting in Oviedo, 1936,*
*Dolores Ibarruri warns the Asturians*
*of a possible fascist rising.*

*Main street in Gallarta,
the mining town where
La Pasionaria was born.*

*Bilbao, Basque capital and center of strikes and political strife.*

Crowd gathers in the Puerta del Sol, the historic Madrid plaza, to hear news of the birth of the Republic, 1931.

*Asturian women shovelling coal.*

*"Land for those who work it!"*

*With Pandit Jawaharlal Nehru, Barcelona, 1938.*

*A demonstration celebrating amnesty for prisoners who took part in 1934 insurrection. Plaza de Toros, Madrid, 1936.*

*1936: "Madrid will be the tomb of fascism!"*

*Posters in Barcelona appeal to women to respond to the call to arms.*

*José Diáz,*
*Secretary-General*
*of the Communist*
*Party of Spain.*

*With*
*Indalecio Prieto.*

*Largo Caballero, Socialist leader.*

*Manuel Azaña, President of Spain*

*Buenaventura Durruti,*
*Anarchist leader.*

*General Emil Kléber,*
*International Brigade commander*

*With General Walter
at the Guadarrama front.*

*(Below) On Madrid front
with Antonio Mije, Pedro
Checa (left of La Pasionaria),
and José Diáz.*

*Comforting a soldier who had just lost his brother.*

*With soldiers at the front.*

*The poet Miguel Hernández speaks to militiamen.*

*Women of Madrid demand the defense of the capital.*

¡TODO EL RAMO DE LA CONSTRUCCION a fortificar MADRID!

*"Without culture and discipline, a powerful army isn't possible."*

*With Juan Modesto, Enrique Lister and Luis Delage.*

*Lincoln Brigade heroes Dave Doran and Robert Merriman, killed in Spain, flank Professor J. B. S. Haldane of Great Britain.*

*James Lardner of the Lincoln Brigade, killed in the battle of the Ebro.*

*Thousands cheer Soviet ship arriving with food donated by Russian workers, Barcelona, 1936.*

*Barcelona after German and Italian air attack.*

*University City, a major front in defense of Madrid.*

*Desolation.*

*Flight from horror.*

*La Pasionaria with her granddaughter, Dolores.*

*With Elizabeth Gurley Flynn in Moscow, 1960.*

(1) To unite the labor unions by merger of the Communist-influenced General Confederation of United Workers (CGTU) with the Socialist-led UGT; (2) to promote a policy of alliances; (3) to create a Popular Antifascist Front which would be directed by the working class; (4) to strive for the organic unity of the Communist and Socialist parties, taking as point of departure the resolutions of the VII Comintern Congress. These proposals were received favorably by many Socialist sectors.

At the end of the year, the government and parliament were completely shorn of their prestige. The President of the Republic, pressured by public opinion and the workers' movement, dissolved parliament and called for new elections in February 1936.

The Spanish Communists' theory had been confirmed. The people by their actions and their unity had destroyed the plans of the reactionaries to seize power. They had forced the holding of new elections. There existed the possibility of restoring a democratic situation by pacific, electoral means. There was a possibility of creating a solid block of workers and democrats. Republicans, Socialists and Communists directed all their activities to these ends.

The forthcoming election was to be a political catalyst. The electoral law itself favored the coalition tickets. Leaders of the Republican parties began to renew their old pacts with the Socialist Party. The Communist Party could no longer be ignored, since in 1936 it represented a political force of first rank that would have to be reckoned with.

After lengthy negotiations, stalled by the conservatism of some Republican leaders, a pact of unity was signed in January 1936 by the petty-bourgeois Republican parties, the Socialist and Communist parties. The Popular Front was born. Millions of men and women came over to the democratic camp. Spain was on its way to rebirth.

The Popular Front program was not exactly what the Communists would have wished. It had serious weak spots and deficiencies, in particular its ambiguous stand on the agrarian reform question. But in spite of its shortcomings and the ulterior motives of a few political shysters, the Popular Front represented something more than a mere election-ticket coalition. It was a weapon of unity wielded by the workers and the democratic forces in the electoral and postelectoral fight to restore and consolidate democracy in Spain.

When the Communist Party accepted a limited and unsatisfactory program, it did so in full awareness of its responsibilities. The party believed that while a more acceptable program would have been a good thing, this common democratic front on a national scale was an even better thing. This would clear the way for the united action of the masses in the forthcoming crucial elections and for later political struggles. The elections of February 1936 were a great political battle. Reaction and democracy would fight it out to see which would rule over the nation.

The people won their victory. The Popular Front elected to parliament a majority of left-wing deputies: 158 Republicans, 88 Socialists, 17 Communists and some other deputies from small parties, as opposed to the 205 delegates elected by the Right.

The triumph of the Popular Front in Spain had a tremendous impact all over the world, and confirmed a phenomenon which had become especially evident after the Asturian revolt of October 1934— that the chief forces of resistance against fascism in the capitalist countries of Europe were concentrating in Spain.

[21]

## I Become a Deputy

I returned to Asturias in January 1936, after my visit to Galicia. With me went Juanita Corzo, the 20-year-old daughter of a Madrid family of Anarchists. She was a member of the Women against War, an admirable person in modesty, energy and intelligence and in her determination to learn and to fight. Juanita did not join the Communist Party until later. She was arrested in 1939 and sentenced to death for the crime of having worked with me. The sentence was commuted to 30 years, of which she served 19 in the prisons of Malaga and Alcala. She was released in 1958, a white-haired lady, physically destroyed but morally unbroken.

Together we took about 200 children to Madrid. The political climate in the capital was red hot, and thousands of persons met us at the North Station to welcome the children of the Asturian miners.

Everyone wanted to show his respect and admiration for the children's parents, the combatants of 1934. We took them to the Tobacco Workers' Federation, where they were given to their new families.

I was then arrested by the police, who had been waiting for me at the door, and taken to General Police Headquarters. After being subjected to a few hours of police vulgarity, I was transferred to the Women's Prison on the street of Las Ventas.

My short stay in prison, from January to February 1936, was not like my other arrests. The prison director was the poet Manuel Machado. And while his beautiful romantic poetry did not bend prison bars, life in prison was at least more humane.

After my release on February 6, I went to Asturias to campaign for the Popular Front ticket, including my candidacy for deputy. Ten days of campaigning, with several speaking engagements each day, together with Socialists and Republicans, throughout Asturia's mining zone taught me many things.

During the first meetings held by the antifascist coalition, I noticed that the Communists always spoke first, as if they were the least important. Republicans spoke second, and the Socialists always wound up the meetings with the key speeches. However, what usually happened was that since the Republicans and Socialists always spoke of legal, constitutional and other irrelevant issues, of which everyone was sick and tired, many people would leave as soon as the Communists had finished speaking.

Tactics were then changed and the Communists spoke last. It took a lot of patience to listen to the interminable discourses of the jurists and propagandists to whom popular issues were less important than their own fame as orators, especially in Asturias, which is noted for its great speakers and high cultural standards. The Socialists, more used to dealing with the people, knew how to play on their sensibilities, even though they repeated certain themes so often that they lost all emotional appeal.

However, I envied their eloquence and tried to imitate them. And one day I outdid them, not with a set speech, but with a factual description. One of our meetings was held in a movie house in Candás, a town with a population half-peasants, half-fishermen. All the town was there. Six or seven orators had already spoken. Since I was the last, it was almost midnight when my turn came. As I walked to the stage, the chairman of the meeting whispered: "Be brief. It's very late."

In a few words, I described the party's position on Spain's political situation and the importance of the Popular Front, not only in the elections, but also to carry out a democratic program afterwards. Then, mindful of the nature of my audience, I said: "Since I know you'll be interested, I want to tell you about my visit last year to a fishing cooperative in Rostov, on the River Don in the Soviet Union."

Exclamations and applause broke out through the audience, showing the interest that the people had in hearing a first-hand account of a fisherman's life in a Socialist country. I told them what I had seen of the peaceful lives and secure future of Soviet fishermen. Everyone asked questions and wanted to hear more. What kind of boats did they use, what kind of nets and bait, did they fish at night, did they use dynamite, how did the fishermen live, how was the fish distributed?

I tried to answer all questions, and when I reminded them of the late hour, they shouted: "Never mind! We'll stay here till morning."

The chairman was beside himself. Ringing the bell, he called for silence and told the audience that the speakers were tired and would have to continue the campaign early in the morning. The meeting was adjourned. As we were leaving, a group of workers, waiting for me at the door, thanked me for what I had told them. They asked me to return after the elections and tell them more about the Soviet Union and the mutual problems and interests of the workers in both countries.

Election day finally arrived, and the Asturians inflicted a roaring defeat on the reactionary forces, the instigators of the repression of 1934. All the Popular Front candidates in Asturias won, including the two Communists on the ticket, Juan José Manso, who had been sentenced to 30 years in prison for his participation in the insurrection, and myself.

The day after the elections in Asturias, the prisoners in Gijón rebelled, demanding their freedom. I went to the prison with a group of comrades from Oviedo. We found it completely surrounded by the Civil Guards.

The prison director authorized us to visit the Communist prisoners, whom we had advised against the revolt, since it could be used as an excuse for repressive action. We promised to do everything possible to obtain their liberty before parliament convened.

Meanwhile the prisoners in Oviedo had also rebelled, but the authorities managed to keep the news quiet for several days, until they could no longer deny the facts. Groups of workers and relatives of the prisoners were arriving in Oviedo from the mining zone in response to a rumor that the prisoners would be freed.

We decided to visit Oviedo also. There was a huge crowd of people in front of the jail waiting for the release of their relatives, friends or comrades. Armed with rifles, the Assault Guards stood at every door.

The Mayor of Oviedo, pale and nervous, suddenly appeared at the main entrance of the prison. When he saw me, he came over, shaking his head with his hands, lamenting: "It's terrible! The prisoners have rebelled. They want their release. I don't know how we can solve this problem without bloodshed."

"I know how," I said, "it's very simple. Release all the prisoners."

"What?"

"It's the only logical thing. Open the doors of the prison."

"Come with me. Let's talk with the other deputies and officials and see how we can straighten out this mess."

The first deputy we found was Moreno Mateo, a Socialist, who agreed with me that the only correct and just solution would be to free the prisoners. Together we went to the home of the Republican deputy, Dr. Luis Laredo, an honest, highly respected democrat. He wasn't home, but we found another Republican deputy there, Mr. Albornoz, an ex-minister, celebrating the recent electoral victory with Laredo's family.

After learning about the prison revolt, Albornoz said indignantly: "It's intolerable! Here we've only just defeated the Right, and the law is being broken again, the same thing that led to the defeat of 1933. Let them be patient and wait a while until parliament declares an amnesty."

I objected: "They won't wait and neither should we wait. The people of Asturias voted for us on the platform of liberty for the prisoners. We have the obligation, regardless of what the law says, to free the prisoners. They were the ones who by their resistance and martyrdom made it possible for the Republic to triumph."

"I can't do anything that's against my conscience or my position as an upholder of the law."

"Well then, we'll do it. We may not know anything about the due process of law, but we do know what the people want, what Asturias wants."

Laredo's wife came with us to the door. She was upset by the incident and said: "Go to the Deputy House. Go on, Dolores, my husband is there. He'll go with you and do everything possible to release the prisoners."

We went to the Deputy House, but Laredo wasn't there. Meanwhile the mayor located the deputy Maldonado who agreed to join us in our attempt to free the hundreds of workers clamoring for their liberty. We went to see the military governor, Caballero, a notorious fascist, leader of the repression, a rabid declared enemy of the Republic. He told us that he had received orders to release only 60 men. And that even if the earth opened up to swallow him, he wouldn't free one prisoner more.

His menacing tone convinced us that he would use all his power to maintain law and order. Actually, he had virtually no real power because of the results of the election, but officially he was still governor.

When we returned to the prison we found that he had re-enforced the guards and ordered the people waiting for the prisoners to move out of the proximity of the building. We asked the administrator (the director had fled after the elections) to let us speak with the prisoners. He opened the huge iron doors, behind which was a vestibule leading to the galleries. All the prisoners were assembled in the vestibule. Howls of derision greeted us.

"Are you bringing our liberty?" they asked.

"No. That's what we want to talk to you about."

"Let's hear it."

Maldonado spoke first. He told them about our visit to the governor and the 60 releases.

"We don't want just some of us freed. It's everyone or no one!"

Moreno Mateo spoke next and agreed with the prisoners, but explained that the order would have to come from Madrid, since the new government was still in the process of being formed.

"And what does Pasionaria have to say?" asked the prisoners.

"Pasionaria says you're right. We promised you your liberty come

what may, law or no law. Your families are outside waiting for you
and I think we can set you free."

"Can you? Hurry up! We're tired of cells and bad food."

When we left the prison we learned that some encounters had
taken place between the crowds and the guards. The people kept
moving closer to the prison, threatening to enter by force. The
administrator came out to calm the crowd's growing excitement.
"The deputies are speaking with the prisoners. Wait a while."

"We want La Pasionaria! She'll tell us what's going on inside."

Terrified, the administrator asked me to pacify the crowds.

"Pacify the crowds! Release the prisoners and they'll be pacified."

"I can't do it. They'll shoot me."

"If you don't do it, they'll come after you."

I spoke with the people on the street. I told them of the prisoners'
revolt and the attempts we had made to obtain their release. I
promised to set them free, I asked the people to wait and to move
back from the prison to guard against any incidents. "We have faith
in you, Pasionaria. Let them return our sons and husbands," shouted
the women.

When I entered the prison again I was met by an unwelcome
surprise. In front of the main entrance were two soldiers with
machine guns. The prisoners were forcing the locks on the massive
iron doors. I jumped over the machine-gun nests and reached the
gates of the door. "Comrades," I screamed. "They're going to shoot
you! They have machine guns pointing at the door."

Without realizing it, I had climbed up on the gate and the
prisoners were pulling at my feet trying to make me come down.

"Go away, we're going to open the doors."

"I won't go away, I'm staying with you."

The bolts gave way and the doors were flung open by the thrust of
these men who had been so unmercifully tortured and beaten. The
administrator quickly let down the outer gates. I was locked inside
with the prisoners.

"Now for sure I'll stay here until everybody gets out," I said.

"We're happy to have you. Did they give you a scare?"

"I'll say they did. I thought those savages would shoot you."

The other two deputies were in the director's office, along with the
mayor and the administrator. They didn't know what to do. They
had spoken to Madrid, but the central government couldn't help

them. Its members were either no longer ministers or not yet invested in office.

In short, justice was tied hand and foot waiting for someone to unbind it. They decided to consult with me again. The administrator came to the gates. "Friends," he said. "We're going to make a decision and we have to talk to La Pasionaria." Suspecting a trick to make me come out, I refused to go. "She'll leave when we do," said the prisoners.

"I swear that we're going to make a decision and that she'll return."

"Can we believe you?"

"I give you my word of honor that she'll return."

I went to the director's office, where they told me about their calls to Madrid. "Gentlemen," I said, "one thing is clear. The only way to settle this problem is to release the prisoners."

The administrator asked: "Who will assume the responsibility for the order?"

"I will, as deputy for Asturias."

"But there are common prisoners among the others. What will we do with them?"

"Release them too. You could have made a distinction before, but you can't now."

"Here, take them and open the doors," said the administrator, handing me all the keys. I grabbed them and ran through the halls of the prison, shaking the keys above my head and shouting, "Comrades! Everybody out! Everybody out!"

The moment was undescribable. I was so excited that I couldn't open the lock. The prisoners had to do it themselves.

They rushed into the street. Everyone wanted to hug me at the same time. Pandemonium broke loose when the prisoners appeared. Mothers, wives, friends, comrades ran to meet the men who had fought so firmly to prevent Spain from becoming one huge fascist jail. For the first time in the history of the Oviedo prison, the officials, wardens and guards had absolutely nothing to do.

# The Communists in Parliament

With the victory of the Popular Front and the creation of a Communist minority in parliament, the party now had new prospects and new opportunities to carry out its political activities.

The forces on the Right did not accept defeat easily. As soon as the election results were known, they began plotting against the Republic. Their maneuvers were repeatedly denounced by the Communist deputies, who toured Spain from north to south, alerting the people against reaction and urging them to redouble their support of the Popular Front and the government.

José Díaz and I went to Asturias in May. In a huge meeting in Oviedo we called upon all Asturian workers to be ready to defend the Republic at any moment. "Keep your powder dry and sleep with one eye open. The enemy lurks everywhere and we must be prepared," I told them.

When Parliament convened in April, the Communist deputies met with José Díaz in one of the chambers to discuss the organization and distribution of work among the party's deputies in the various committees. Unlike the Socialist minority in parliament, the Communist group was not independent of its party. The Communist deputies were under the control and leadership of the Politburo and subject to strict party discipline. Their job was to defend in parliament the interests of the workers, peasants and the working class in general, and to turn the parliamentary tribunal into a forum for the defense of democracy.

During the meeting a telegram arrived from our comrades in Asturias informing us about the situation of the workers in the "Cadavio" mine in Sama de Langreo. The miners had gone on strike several days earlier because of the company's refusal to meet their demands. When they went out on strike, the miners decided to stay down in the mines. This had happened a few days ago, and it was apparent that the miners' health was being endangered. Some of them had already been taken to the hospital gravely ill.

The party decided to bring the matter up in parliament and also to send me to Asturias to get a first-hand look at the situation and, with our Asturian comrades, to do whatever was necessary to aid the strikers.

The news of my arrival spread quickly through Sama. The families of the strikers came to see me, asking help. I went to the mine with a group of women. It was cordoned off by the strikers. At the entrance, two workers came out and asked me what I wanted. I told them who I was and why I was there. They told me to wait a moment, one of them went inside and returned with a horsedrawn wagon. "There's a lot of mud down here. The miners sent you the wagon so you won't get dirty."

I climbed on and rode in darkness until we came to a group of miners in a small clearing lighted by lamps hung from the shorings. They were extremely pleased to see me. They explained their position, and I told them briefly of the general political situation. I told them I would remain in the mine with them until the strike was settled.

The news that a Communist deputy was in the bottom of the mine with the strikers spread like wildfire through the mining region and reached the ears of the governor of Asturias. He communicated the fact to the government, which received the news with some indignation.

The strike leaders, Anarchists from the *Sindicato Unico*, called for a general strike in the mining zone in solidarity with the strikers in Sama. But the sectarianism of some of the Anarchist workers inside the mine upset their leaders' plans.

At first, the opinion was unanimous: "Sure, let Pasionaria stay. That'll help us end the strike quickly and successfully." But after a while they began to complain that since I was a Communist, my participation would give a political overtone to the strike, and if the strike were won the credit would go to the Communists.

Our Communist comrades told me of what was going on and asked me to leave, to avoid giving anyone any reason for saying that the party was exploiting the situation. I didn't agree but, on the other hand, I didn't want to start a conflict among the miners who had already spent days inside the mine.

"Listen, comrades," I told them after I had learned about the

Anarchists' feelings. "I've come here to help you win the strike regardless of the fact that most of you are Anarchists. You're workers, and for me and for the Communist Party that's the important thing. If my presence here displeases you and leads to friction between you and the Communists, I'll leave. Stay united down here and I'll help you win the strike on the outside."

When I returned to Sama, the Anarchist leaders didn't understand why I had left the mine when they had already prepared everything for the general strike. "I've left the mine to prevent division among the strikers. If you want, I'll go back, but one of you will have to come with me to convince your friends that they're wrong."

They didn't think returning would be a good idea and asked me what I was going to do. "Right now, I'm going to the governor to explain the situation to him and ask him to persuade the mine owners to cede to the strikers' demands."

I went to Oviedo and spoke with the governor, Señor Bosque, an old-guard Republican, who was later shot by the fascists in the Civil War. He promised he would do everything he could to help the strikers. "Go to Madrid," he said, "and put pressure on the government there not to contradict my orders here. I promise you to settle the matter in 24 hours."

He lent me his car and I left rapidly for Madrid. I told our party leaders of the situation in Asturias. We brought the matter up before the government, and that same day the strike was settled in favor of the miners.

Brief indeed was the relatively tranquil period in which the parliament, constituted after the elections of 1936, was able to function. Nevertheless, it was long enough to instruct those who like ourselves were novices in parliamentary debate in the many avenues of action open to deputies of workers' parties. That is, if they don't forget they are the representatives of the people and don't get inflated egos that lead them to put themselves and their position above that of the workers or to look down upon those whose votes carried them to the tribunal.

When parliament opened its doors, great numbers of delegations from towns and villages, especially from the provinces, arrived daily to petition their deputies for aid. But, to the discredit of some deputies, the people were not always received by the men for whom they had voted.

Consequently, an interesting phenomenon began to take place.

When a delegation arrived from the provinces and was not received by its own deputies, who would plead urgent work, a meeting, or heavy duties, the people would be so disappointed and disheartened that the parliamentary ushers began to advise them to talk to the Communist deputies.

At first the visitors were uncomfortable and wouldn't venture to do this, since they hadn't voted for the Communists; they belonged to another party. In a short while, however, asking to speak to a Communist deputy in the waiting room became routine procedure.

One afternoon, an usher told me that someone wanted to speak to me over the phone. I left the hall and discovered that the call was from a group of tenants in a tenement neighborhood. With anguish they asked me to come to see them. Most of them were being evicted for nonpayment of rent. They told me of pitiful cases of sick people and children left in the street, surrounded by all their belongings.

"We've called our deputies," they told me, "but they won't come. They say if we didn't pay our rent, what do we expect them to do?"

"Hold on! Don't let them throw anyone out. We'll be right over."

I returned to the session hall and told our comrades of the situation. Another Communist deputy went with me to the scene of eviction. We arrived by taxi in a matter of minutes. The street entrances were guarded by mounted police. The evicted tenants were picking up their humble belongings, which had been scattered all over the street by the evictors.

When we arrived, they were carrying a sick man in an old broken-down chair out of a house. "What are you doing?" I asked the men who were casually going about the business of rendering one of their fellow men homeless.

"Following orders," they replied, shrugging their shoulders.

"Who gave you these orders?"

"Who do you think? The company and the court."

"Well, neither the company nor the court can do anything, if the people refuse to let themselves be trampled on. You put that man back in his house this minute!"

The determination in our voices made the men hesitate. They were simple employees who would be fired if they didn't carry out their orders.

"Who are you?" they asked us.

"We're Communist deputies."

They didn't know what to do, and we understood their position. "Go home," we told them, "we'll take him back." I grabbed the chair and called two evicted neighbors standing nearby to help me.

The sick man was crying silently, the tears rolling down his emaciated, sallow face. We brought him back to his room, fixed his bed and put him in it.

I went out to the front of the house. "Friends," I said, "put all the furniture back in the house. Nothing, no one, on the streets!"

"They've taken the keys," said the eviction victims.

"Break the locks!"

They wouldn't do it.

"Let me have a hammer." I broke the first lock and after that everyone began smashing the others. Within a few minutes every tenant was back in his apartment.

The court employees were frozen with terror. Finally, recovering their voices, they said: "We'll have to make a report on this."

"Make all the reports you want and tell the gentlemen from the company that next time they had better come down themselves to throw people out on the street. But tell them to let us know beforehand, so we can come down too."

The guards at the street entrances had come nearer to the scene. We could see that they were on our side. All the tenants from that street and from many others came to greet us and thank us.

"Form tenant committees to defend your rights! Unite in the fight against the bloodsucking companies. Don't forget that your strength lies in union!" we told them, and left. The guards also left as soon as we had gone.

Prior to the Franco uprising, I lived in Madrid in the home of a non-Communist railroad worker. He ran a modest boarding house and restaurant in front of the *Mundo Obrero* editorial offices on Galileo Street.

I was the only boarder. The household treated me warmly as one of the family and did everything to make my stay pleasant. Their regular customers, too, always had a smile and a kind word for me.

Little by little my room was turning into a branch of the post office because of the large amounts of mail I received, usually from people asking help, although there were many letters of a different sort. I could have easily compiled an anthology of obscenity and threats from the letters sent to me by so-called respectable people.

I had spent the First of May in Asturias. When I returned to Madrid I found a man waiting for me at the door of the restaurant. He was a worker, but dressed so poorly (even poverty has degrees, a truth I learned from my own experience) that I immediately knew misfortune had singled him out for special attention.

He said: "I'm a hod-carrier, but I've been out of work for several months. Look!" And he took a stack of pawnshop tickets out of his pocket. Everything he had owned, from his mattress to his shoes, had been pawned. "But this isn't the worst. Right now I have a problem, but I don't know what to do. I'm so desperate that I'll try anything. My wife was in the maternity home and they've thrown her and another woman out. She's due to have the baby any time now. We don't even have a bed; the baby will have to be born on the floor."

"Why were they thrown out?"

"For refusing to pray."

"Where are they now?"

"Sitting on a bench in the park."

"Come in and wait a minute. I'm going to wash up and comb my hair." I told the owners to serve him some breakfast, and I fixed myself up quickly. I called a taxi and we went to pick up the women. We then headed for the maternity home. I left the women in the car and went to speak to the director.

A nun received me. I asked for the director.

"What do you want?" she asked.

"I told you I wanted to speak to the director."

From the tone of my voice, she knew she wouldn't get anywhere with me. The nun left and returned shortly with a man as big as an ox, dressed in a white gown. His manner wasn't at all friendly.

"You wanted to speak with me?"

"Yes, if you're the director of the home."

"I am."

"Can you tell me why two women who are about to give birth were thrown out of the maternity home?"

"And who are you to be asking?"

"Dolores Ibarruri, Communist deputy."

"I'm the director here and I do what I think right."

"And you think it's right to throw two women practically in childbirth out on the street? Doesn't your conscience bother you? Two women abandoned to their fate without a roof or a penny to their names? Mr. Director, I ask you to admit them again."

"I don't want to admit them."

I turned to the nun: "Can't you do anything so that these poor women will have a bed and a meal and can bring their children into this world decently?"

"The director is the one who decides," she answered, lowering her eyes.

I couldn't control myself any longer. "You're despicable!," I shouted, "Where's your charity, your love of your neighbor? This home is supported by the people precisely for women like these and not for you who live at its expense. We'll see if you can or can't admit them." I left, slamming the door behind me.

I went to the taxi and told the women to wait in the home's reception room. "Stay here with them. I'll be back soon," I told the husband. I headed for a nearby Socialist club.

The porter told me that the district chief had gone to lunch but that I could reach him by phone. I called him, and he replied that he would be there in an hour. An hour was too long to wait. I went to a group of young people in the club, told them what was happening and asked them to come with me. Without hesitating they all came. When we arrived at the maternity home, the hod-carrier's wife was already in labor.

Opening the first door I found, I started shouting for a doctor. The director ran out.

"Look at that woman," I said, "she's in labor!"

He denied this obvious fact and refused to have her on the premises. Ignoring his diagnosis, I told the husband and the young Socialists: "Help me. We'll take her in and find a bed." Making a seat out of our hands we carried her into the halls.

A nurse who had witnessed the disgraceful scene came to our aid. She told us she belonged to the UGT and instructed us to put the woman in the delivery room. Our diagnosis was confirmed, the woman would give birth very shortly.

"You're responsible for this woman," I told the nurse. "If anything happens to her or the child, the maternity home won't hear the last of it."

"Don't worry, Pasionaria, I'll take care of both women."

"Now we have to carry in the other one."

This was easier to do. The incident with the director had spread through the neighborhood. There was a large crowd of people in front of the home ready to drag him through the streets because of his heartlessness.

Meanwhile, at my request, one of the young Socialists had called Comrade Recatero, a young, well-known Madrid doctor. His father, also a doctor, who came in his place, apparently knew the director of the home. I wasn't there when Dr. Recatero arrived. The director immediately told him his version of the incidents. "You can't imagine the scandal that Pasionaria made, she acted more like a cook than a deputy."

I laughed when Recatero's son told me what the director had said to his father. Inadvertently, the director had hit the nail on the head. I not only had once worked as a cook and knew how to make a codfish dish good enough to make you lick your fingers, but I also knew how to put the kitchen in order and even clean the soot from the director's chimney, which undoubtedly was extremely dirty. And not to lose one's character or personality even when one is a deputy is a fortunate thing—something that doesn't happen to everyone.

An hour after I returned home, the nurse at the home called and told me that the woman had given birth to a girl. The father, a member of the CNT, had named the baby Dolores after me. Both mother and daughter were doing fine.

[23]

## Sowing the Tempest

Parliamentary life in Spain did not last long after the electoral victory of February 16, 1936.

The defeated forces became more aggressive as the left wing consolidated its unity and seriously undertook the task of a democratic revolution, which the reactionaries had succeeded in stifling during the Dark Biennial.

The threatening political atmosphere was felt throughout the country. The bloody incidents at Yeste, where 16 peasants were killed by Civil Guards in the service of the landowners, had shaken all Spain. One question was perpetually on our minds. What were the reactionaries up to?

In the middle of June, CEDA announced that it would demand an official explanation from the government about the state of public order in Spain. The effrontery of these reactionaries knew no bounds. It was perfectly intolerable that those who lowered workers' wages in industry and agriculture, who set the Civil Guards on starving peasants, who told them they preferred losing a harvest to paying the wages fixed by the workers' organizations, who armed mercenaries to assassinate men of democratic principles—that the elements themselves responsible for disorder would dare ask the government to explain the disorder.

Such insolence could be understood only if one examined the political position of the Popular Front parties. The Front's weakness was the enemy's strength. It was no secret that certain Republican leaders and even some Socialists were averse to the idea of restoring workers' rights. Statements like those of Albornoz in Asturias about the excessive impatience of the prisoners could be heard only too frequently in conversation and in the debating chambers of parliament when wage increases and improvements in the living standards were discussed.

The CEDA deputies were the third ear of the landowners and the capitalists. They heard the slightest sighs of the Republican Mary Magdalenes, whom they were using in an attempt to open a breach in the left-wing block.

The announcement of CEDA's motion on public order was like a slap in the face for the government and the Popular Front. The Right insisted it would go all out when it presented this motion to parliament. The forces of the Left grouped themselves around the government for the coming battle.

The atmosphere in the Spanish parliament was one of all-out war that afternoon of June 16, exactly one month before the military uprising. The reporters took notes, and the photographers took pictures. Everyone had the impression that this session would be historic. Either the government would be defeated, meaning the failure of the Popular Front, or the Right would be repulsed in their open attack on the government.

Each side prepared its weapons. The Communists met at noon and outlined the main points of my speech, since I would take part in the debate in the name of the Communist Party. Enrique de Francisco would speak for the Socialists and Marcelino Domingo for the Republicans.

Before the session began, the halls and corridors of parliament were a beehive of activity. People coming and going, comments, predictions, discussions, looks charged with hate, ironic smiles, wrinkled brows, unrest, deputies preparing to defend, deputies preparing to attack.

The Communists' chief worry was that instead of the government's taking the initiative against the Republic's enemies, the latter would exploit the Republic's tolerance and launch the attack themselves. Up until then it was the Communist minority whose firmness had given a new tone to parliament. That afternoon our weapons would be measured against those of our most vicious enemies.

I was very nervous. I knew that the session would be a crucial one for the Republic, and that the Communists would have to be the shock troops in the fight against CEDA and all Spanish reaction, represented by Gil Robles and Calvo Sotelo, who had engineered the showdown.

The session began. Some routine measures and the first article of a bill modifying the old Public Order Law were passed. The President then announced the reading of CEDA's motion asking the government to explain "the subversive state in which Spain lives."

Gil Robles defended the motion. After an enumeration of events attributed to the Popular Front parties, he ended by saying that he didn't want to break up the Popular Front. What he wanted was to destroy all the parties composing the Popular Front, affirming that "we are present at the funeral of democracy."

Enrique de Francisco spoke next, in the name of the Socialist minority. Politely he excused himself because he, so unimportant a delegate, was obliged by a painful duty "to debate with a man so outstanding as Señor Gil Robles." His speech left the chamber cold and outraged many Socialist deputies, who expected a stronger and more politically minded speech from their representative.

The Right grew bolder as they observed the changing mood of the chamber. When the former minister of the Primo de Rivera dictatorship, Calvo Sotelo, delivered his speech, bristling with threats and challenges, everyone thought the government was on its deathbed. In a clever and demagogic discourse, the right-wing leader warmly praised the CNT, whose leaders had unmistakably been playing along with the Right since February 16.

Casares Quiroga, prime minister of the Republic, ably answered Calvo. Referring to the threats made by the ex-minister, Casares held Calvo Sotelo responsible for the activities of the Right against the Republic and against the people.

I spoke next, exposing the maneuver of the Rightists who were pretending that they were the victims while they were really the authors of the events they were denouncing. I exposed their plots against the Republic, and the shipments of contraband arms that were being smuggled across the border in Navarre, arms which were destined for a coup. I analyzed the events prior to October 1934 and defended the memory of those assassinated in the repression, denouncing the Jesuitism and hypocrisy of the forces on the Right, which did not hesitate to spread the most vicious lies, in order to produce in the masses a feeling of revulsion toward the glorious insurrection of October.

I then examined the causes behind the strikes and the state of unrest in Spain, and ended my speech by saying:

"Neither the attacks of the reactionaries nor the thinly disguised maneuvers of the enemies of democracy will destroy or weaken the faith of the workers in the Popular Front and the government it represents.

"But the government must take heed and make the full force of the law felt for those who refuse to live within the law—in this case certainly not the workers or peasants.

"If there exist reactionary generals who, at an opportune moment, encouraged by elements like Calvo Sotelo, may rise against the government, there are also heroic soldiers who can keep them in line.

"When the government begins to carry out, more rapidly than it has done up to now, the program of the Popular Front and initiates the Republic's offensive, all Spain's workers will be on its side, determined, as they were on February 16, to crush the forces of reaction and once again carry the People's Front to victory."

Speaking directly to the Prime Minister I said: "Señor Casares, in order to avoid the 'perturbations of the peace' that cause such distress to Señores Gil Robles and Calvo Sotelo, in order to end the state of unrest which exists in Spain it is not enough to lay the blame for what may happen solely on Calvo Sotelo or his associates. The government must begin by jailing those who refuse to abide by its laws.

"The government should jail the landowners who keep the peasants in poverty and starvation, as well as those who, with unheard-of cynicism, come here, still bloodstained from the October repression, to demand condemnation for deeds which have not been committed.

"And when this work of justice is carried out, Señor Casares and Honorable Ministers, there won't be a government more popular or stronger than yours, because the people of Spain will rise to fight against all those forces that in all conscience should not be seated here today.*

Events followed one after another rapidly. The Right was in a hurry to get into action. The earth was moving under their feet, and they wanted to stage their charade once and for all. The tactic they used was one of attack, in line with the old Spanish proverb: He who strikes first, strikes twice.

Jesús Monzón of Navarre arrived in Madrid to inform the party of the political situation in his region and to denounce before parliament the activities of the Navarrese reactionaries, who were openly preparing for war.

The political history of Navarre has always been different from that of other provinces in Spain. Navarre was a fortress of reaction where neither the restoration of the Republic nor the progress of Spain counted a farthing. It had been traditionally resistant to democratic forms of government, a resistance which the successive Republic-Socialist governments fostered. Fearful of a confrontation with long-entrenched reaction, they abandoned the Navarrese workers and peasants to the hands of their enemies.

Navarre had hardly changed from what it had been in 1876. The

---

* I want to emphasize this part of my speech and rub it into the noses of the Franquist writers who for 24 years have been spreading the infamous lie that I instigated in parliament the assassination of Calvo Sotelo.

only difference was that in 1936 it was armed, not with the old muskets and pistols buried at the end of the Carlist Wars, but with modern Mausers and machine guns.

In Navarre there lived the descendants of the old Carlists, organized in armed bands called Requetés, characterized by iron discipline, religious fanaticism and untouchable hierarchies. A combination military, Carlist and fascist organization, the Requetés, held constant drills, target practice, military parades and maneuvers, to which the authorities shut their eyes.

The elections in Navarre were held under the pressure of these elements. In spite of the Popular Front and the tireless efforts of the Socialists and Communists in Pamplona to change the picture, the Carlists continued to rule over the region. When the military fascist uprising against the democratic elements in Navarre began, the criminal assault of the Requetés and fascists was launched with a savage violence that left in its wake hundreds of mourning families.

Comrade Monzón, representing the Popular Front of Navarre, arrived in Madrid to denounce the arms shipments constantly arriving in Spain through Vera del Bidasoa and other points along the Navarrese Pyrenees. Monzón planned to ask the government to take measures to stop the activities of the reactionary organizations and to disarm them. I went with him to see Casares Quiroga. Although the prime minister promised to do something about it, he acted as if the fascist danger were a big joke, since he thought that Communists always imagined fascists lurking behind every bush. In the face of such irresponsible attitudes, fascist activities in Navarre remained uncurbed. When the military fascist uprising took place several thousands of Navarrese Requetés became the shock troops of the Franco army, especially in the North.

Since the government was constantly in hot water as a result of the economic and political sabotage committed by capitalists, the high financiers and landowners, voices prophesying doom began to be heard within the ranks of the Popular Front. This lowered morale, paralyzed the people's revolutionary impulse, stifled the initiative of the government and created a political climate favorable for concession to the Right. The Communist Party attacked the spirit of pessimism, and urged greater unity around the Popular Front to fight reaction. Mundo Obrero wrote:

"The Popular Front should aid and encourage the government,

both in and outside of parliament, to carry out an economic and social program which will satisfy the just demands of the workers and
peasant masses and crush the sinister plans of the reactionaries. If
this is done, we are certain that the prophets of doom will have less
and less evidence upon which to base their predictions."

Each day brought new unrest. The flight of capital was undermining the country's economy. Special undercover agencies were organized for the express purpose of sending money abroad. Hundreds
of millions of pesetas were being deposited in French, English or
Swiss banks. The value of the peseta was falling; import prices were
soaring, along with the cost of living. The poorer sectors of the population, especially the working class, were suffering an increasing deterioration in their living conditions.

The government attempted to intervene and to confront the mer-
chants of hunger and money speculators. It ordered the arrest of some
20 persons involved in black-market operations. Some measures were
passed to prevent the flight of capital, which was destroying the
state's economy and impoverishing the people.

Every Spaniard who formed part of the Popular Front or sympathized with its policies went to bed wondering what the next day
would bring. The storm weather stirred up by the Right created
such a feeling of uncertainty and danger that everyone wanted to
tear the curtain aside to see what it was they had to contend with.
The idea of resistance and defense in the face of a possible reactionary coup was taking hold among the people.

*Politica*, the organ of the left-wing Republican parties, wrote on
June 28: "He who wants to seize power and wield it against the people must fight it out in the street with the legitimate government.
And in the street he'll find the people. All the people, because the
army, deep inside, is also people."

On July 11, in Valencia, a group of Falangists seized the Union
Radio station. After having cut the telephone wires to prevent interference, they broadcast the following message:

"Union Radio, Valencia. At this moment the military forces of
the Falange are occupying Union Radio station. Take heart! The
Syndicalist Revolution will break out in a few days. We take this
opportunity to greet all Spaniards, especially our followers."

What did the authorities do in the face of this warning, this alarming demonstration of the fascists' insolent statement of intention?

They simply played the Riego hymn several times on the air, along with a speech made by the governor of Valencia.

But what the authorities failed to do was at least in part done for them by the people in their own fashion. Valencia's Central Right-Wing Casino was assaulted and set on fire. The people even stopped the firemen from putting out the blaze. An enormous crowd marched to the editorial offices of the monarchist newspaper, *La Voz Valenciana*, where they were prevented by the police from doing the same thing. Later, the restaurant "Vodka," the meeting place of the Falangists, was completely destroyed by the workers.

The police arrested some of the Falangists who were suspected of attacking the radio station. Rightist clubs and casinos were burned, and some persons were wounded on the outskirts of Valencia's capital. The people's reply to the provocations of the Falangists was just a sample of what would occur several days later in answer to the lawless military rising.

Madrid was in the grip of strikes. Maintenance men, elevator operators and construction workers had walked out two months earlier. The most important strike was that of the construction workers comprising more than 80,000 workers. The strikes were being prolonged because management wanted to maintain the state of unrest in the country in order to discredit the Popular Front and push the workers to the end of their economic rope.

The plan of the Right was taking shape. Our comrades in the post office intercepted letters from the provinces addressed to right-wingers in Madrid, disclosing things like this: "As you know I have a Smith revolver, but I want to exchange it for a better weapon. As *the time is drawing near*, all right-wing men and women must be ready with their arms, as they are in their hearts." Deposits of arms and Civil Guard uniforms were found in some Falangist and Spanish Renovation clubs in Madrid.

Lieutenant Castillo, a young officer of the Assault Guards, known for his democratic and antifascist ideas, was assassinated by Falangist gunmen on July 12.

With the Right becoming more belligerent, the Communist Politburo met to examine the situation and take urgent measures. It published a note protesting fascist provocations, calling upon the government to take a more energetic stand against the enemies of the Republic and to intensify its fight.

"Reactionary and fascist elements are speeding up their preparations to destroy popular liberties," said the note. The assassination of Lieutenant Castillo and many provocations, it continued, "are part of a foul plan to breed unrest in the country and create an atmosphere in which a reactionary coup can be perpetrated."

A meeting requested by us was attended by José Díaz and Vicente Uribe, representing the Communist Party; Manuel Lois, from the UGT; Edmundo Domínguez, from the Casa del Pueblo of Madrid; José Cazorla and Santiago Carrillo, from the Federation of Socialist Youth; Lamoneda, Jiménez de Asúa, Cruz Salido, Vidarte, Prieto and others, from the Socialist Party. All agreed that the political situation was grave and that joint action would be necessary to meet any eventuality. Representatives of all the organizations formed a committee to visit the President and offer aid in the defense of the government against a subversive attempt to overthrow it.

At the same time, the workers' organizations of the Popular Front published a declaration:

"The intentions of the reactionary enemies of the Republic and the working class having been made known, the political and labor organizations represented by the undersigned have met and unanimously agreed to offer the government the support and aid of the masses herein represented, in whatever capacity, for the purpose of defending the government and repelling all attempts against the regime.

"This unanimity is not merely provisional; we have every intention of making it permanent, insofar as conditions make it advisable, in order to strengthen the Popular Front and satisfy the aspirations of the working class, now in danger from its enemies and the enemies of the Republic."

The declaration was signed by Manuel Lois, UGT; Santiago Carrillo, Socialist Youth Federation; José Díaz, Communist Party; Edmundo Domínguez, Casa del Pueblo; Jiménez de Asúa, Socialist Party.

The government suspended some reactionary newspapers and arrested several groups of right-wingers. But at this stage this was not sufficient.

On July 13, rumors that Calvo Sotelo, the right wing's most important leader, had been killed were circulating in Madrid. Who put the weapon in the hands of his assassin? One might quote the poet who, upon the death of the Count of Villamediana, said: "the killer was Bellido and the sovereign impulse."

The direct responsibility for the death of Calvo Sotelo belonged to those who fanned the flames of hate and civil war in Spain. The Communist Party was not to blame, as the Franquists viciously asserted; it was rather those who armed the assassins of Lieutenant Castillo, Captain Faraudo and Señor Pedregal; it was those who had attempted to murder Jiménez de Asúa and Largo Caballero.

It was evident to the Communists that the death of Calvo Sotelo did no service to the cause of the Republic; on the contrary, it produced new antidemocratic arguments for the counterrevolutionaries. The right-wing forces made a martyr of him and used his death as a rallying cry against the Republic. The government met these maneuvers by suspending the sessions of parliament for one week—a step violently opposed by the Right.

In the meeting of the Permanent Committee of the Cortes called by the President of the Chamber to declare a "State of Alarm" for all Spain, incendiary speeches virtually amounting to a declaration of war were made by representatives of the Right, particularly by Count Vallellano and Gil Robles.

The document read by Count Vallellano, in the name of the conservative and the Spanish Renovation minorities composing the so-called National Front, contained such grave allegations that the President of the Permanent Committee warned that it could only inflame passions and that therefore it would not be published.

In that historic session, the representatives of the Left tried to demonstrate the responsibility of the Right for the unrest in the country, calling upon the National Front to reconsider its actions, while the latter announced its intention of withdrawing from the parliamentary government. In an apocalyptic oration, the Right broadcast the imminent advent of a plot they had been preparing since their defeat in the February elections.

José Díaz answered the cynical and insolent statements of the reactionary delegates, as did the Socialist and Republican representatives before him:

"You cannot deny," said Díaz, "that you are plotting, that you are preparing a coup. But be careful! We are all watching to prevent you from putting Spain on the road to repression, hunger and shame.

We shall do all that is necessary to safeguard the Republic in Spain
We will never consent to the destruction of gains won by so much
bloodshed and so much effort."

That same day the Politburo published another note, directing al
its organizations to contact the regional, district and local bodie
of the Popular Front and to be prepared for any future event
Far from disregarding the threats of the Right, the party strength
ened its ranks, allied itself with other forces, started conversation
with loyal military men and fortified the workers' and peasants
militias. "The events of the past days have shown," declared the note
"the scope of fascism's bloody plans, which our party has long been
denouncing, and the Right's intention to impose by force a savage
criminal dictatorship."

On July 16, the maintenance men and elevator operators success
fully ended their 72-day strike in Madrid. The wood-industry worker
also returned to work after having won a victory the same day.

But the counterrevolutionary fuse was lit. It was only a matter of
hours before the great explosion.

As a political lesson for the future, which demonstrates the neces
sity for deeper analysis and earlier recognition of changes developing
in the relation of forces in the enemy camp, and adapting policies
accordingly, I want to briefly mention the role which, somewhat
rigidly and subjectively, we continued to attribute to Gil Robles as
the head of the anti-Republican conspiracy at a time when, important
though he was, he was no longer a decisive figure.

Since the Right's failure in the February elections, the political
importance of Gil Robles had declined considerably, although this
was not publicly admitted by the interested parties. He could indeed
make great pompous speeches; he was a man of reaction, represent
ing government repression, a combination Thiers and Galliffet.* But
he was neither the figurehead nor the leader that the extreme re
action needed.

And this was all the more true when the political battle was trans
ferred to the arena of open violence against the Republic and to
civil war. Gil Robles was not the most appropriate person to direct

* Adolphe Thiers (1797–1877) and Gaston Gallifet (1830–1909), President and General of France, respectively; responsible for the crushing of the
Paris Commune in 1871 and the massacre of the Communards.

this new battle. The Right had not forgiven Robles for having left the Ministry of War nor for the electoral defeat of February.

It was to the military that the Right turned. And it is no co-incidence that practically all the threads of the conspiracy were in the hands of the military, although Franco was not yet in the picture. He was biding his time, and when the moment arrived he pushed aside, with the help of Hitler, all the Right political forces that had backed the rising.

Although the Communist Party was the first to denounce the criminal plans of Franco and his crew and the clear danger to the Republic, perhaps it did not realize the full, tragic extent of that danger.

# PART THREE

# he Uprising

> *Before we become slaves, the rivers will*
> *flow with enough noble blood to redden*
> *the sea.*
>
> —Basque song

The optimism of many Republican and Socialist leaders was ab-
urd. Stubbornly closing their eyes to the danger, they called the
Communists alarmists because we insisted on taking precautions
gainst a possible coup.

The Socialist leaders had called for a meeting of the UGT Execu-
ive Committee, headed by Largo Caballero, to discuss confidential
eports concerning the conspiracy. The call for the meeting, sug-
ested by Indalecio Prieto, was received with disdain by Largo
Caballero, who did not believe in the possibility of a reactionary
prising. "There are no conspirators in Spain!" he said. "If the re-
ctionaries want to launch a coup, let them do it if they dare! We'll
ee what will happen."

For days the Communist Party had been keeping a permanent
guard in its meeting halls and offices throughout the capital. As part
f our vigilance, we also kept watch over the Right centers and
nilitary posts, as well as the homes of the most important Right
eaders and those known for their reactionary ideas. Men and
vomen from the antifascist militias were on a 24-hour vigil.

Every bit of information, every rumor, every suspicious troop
novement and all out-of-the-ordinary comings and goings of visitors
o reactionary homes were duly reported.

We spent many nights without sleep, in a state of extreme fatigue.
When a comrade was ordered to rest, he would firmly refuse. There
vas no way of convincing any of our comrades to go home. Their
ale faces, burning eyes and furrowed brows, reflected the uneasiness
ll of us felt.

The storm, which had been threatening for so long, finally broke;

Spain woke up with a shock on the morning of July 18, 1936. The first shots were fired in Morocco. They were soon heard throughout Spain. From mouth to mouth, house to house, street to street, the alarm was raised: "The army in Morocco has rebelled against the Republic!"

The fragmentary information, which was being spread by every possible means, brought tens of thousands of people into the street all over Spain in an attempt to learn the truth and to show their patriotic support of the government and the Republic. The leaders of the political and workers' organizations, both those within the Popular Front and those who were not members, swiftly met and agreed to take appropriate measures to meet the extremely grave situation created by the military rebellion, the import of which escaped no one.

Only Casares Quiroga, prime minister of the Republic, a Galician lawyer and member of the left-wing Republican Party, to which President Azaña also belonged, tried to belittle the uprising. He considered it just one more of the many military revolts which had plagued Spain during the 19th century. For this reason, Casares thought the revolt would be easy to quell.

But what had happened in Morocco when the Foreign Legion and the Moroccan Army launched the Civil War was not just an ordinary military revolt.

The so-called army revolts or revolutionary movements of the 19th century, such as those of Lacy, Porlier, Torrijos, Riego, and the revolution of September 1868, which dethroned Queen Isabella II, sprang from patriotism and the desire to bring liberty and progress to Spain.

After the restoration of the monarchy in 1875, the army began to lose its popular and progressive character and became a praetorian guard, a palace army at the service of the monarchy and the ruling class. This was all the more serious since Spain's army was excessively large. The War of Independence (against France, 1808–14) and the successive civil wars had attracted to the army a considerable part of the intellectual and petty-bourgeois youth. When peace was established, they preferred to stay in the army and enjoy a secure though mediocre future rather than return to the economic uncertainty of civilian life.

The overgrown army, a great strain on the national budget, became a permanent obstacle to the exercise of civil power. Always ready to use force, the army rejected the slightest restriction of its salaries and privileges.

When Spain still had Cuba, Puerto Rico and the Philippines as a source of wealth, these colonies, especially Cuba, were a paradise for ambitious military men dreaming of careers. A "mission" or an appointment as military proconsul in a colony was payment for court services and palace flattery, and kept the number of aspirants to government posts in the metropolis fairly low, while it crowded the already impoverished colonies with thousands of officials and military men. These, like plagues of locusts, devoured the colonies' sugar cane, coffee and tobacco, and pauperized the native population while filling their own pockets.

The return of the colonial armies to Spain after their defeat in the Spanish-American War created a serious problem that could be solved only by reducing the armed forces and thereby lancing the military abscess which was infecting all Spain. But who would bell the cat? The King himself, when he assumed the throne in May 1902, based his power on the army, putting it before all the social forces forming the foundations of Spanish society. This policy was reinforced by the Law of Jurisdictions, which made it a crime to criticize the army and removed so-called crimes against the country and the army from the civil to the military courts. What government leader would risk his political career and even his physical safety by proposing that the army's dead or useless branches be cut away and that it be transformed into an efficient corps at the exclusive service of national defense? As Fernández Almagro wrote in his *History of the Reign of Alfonso XIII:* "The King and the army rule national life. Relatively new social forces, plutocracies, officials, the press, serve one and imitate the other, submit to or exploit both."

All the governments under the monarchy inherited the oversized army. To avoid problems, they all let the snowball roll on and grow larger. Since they confined themselves to treating the military abscess with hot packs rather than with a scalpel, the abscess continued to fester.

So far as Morocco was concerned, the great powers ceded to Spain territory in the north of Africa which was not theirs to give. To protect the theft of a foreign territory from the Moroccan people, Spain needed an army to stand guard over the so-called protectorate.

This army was quartered by force in the north of Morocco against the wish of the Spanish people, who more than once had rebelled against this military adventure.

Thousands of soldiers were sent to Morocco to establish a military protectorate. Consequently, any pacific or political solution of the Moroccan question was impossible because the King and the army with their imperialist ambitions, which Franco was to adopt, were opposed to it. G. Maura y Gamazo wrote in his *Brief Historic Sketch of the Dictatorship:* "The Spanish protectorate, as established in international treaties, was perhaps an impossible concept to begin with. But the use of bayonets essentially adulterated it, transforming it into a military conquest."

The Moroccan situation, which constituted a permanent drain of men and money, dominated the national scene, strengthening the praetorian character of the army. This was especially true in the case of the Moroccan army, whose generals were highly esteemed by Alfonso XIII. He showered them with promotions and favors which only caused discontent and protest in other sectors of the army and ended in wholesale demoralization.

Such is the background of the "African" generals who played such a notorious role in the history of Spain throughout the 20th century. They had to their discredit the terrible disasters of Melilla, Barranco del Lobo, Monte Arruit and Annual in the Moroccan wars which cost Spain the lives of tens of thousands of soldiers, recruited to fight for a cause repugnant to the whole country but satisfying to the sick colonialist vanity of "Alfonso the African" and his palace generals, among them General Franco.

These African generals, who had brought neither glory nor benefit to Spain, headed and organized the armed rebellion against the Republic. They were backed by the castes which up to 1931 had been in power and by Mussolini's Italy and Hitler's Germany, without whose intervention the revolt would have been rapidly crushed.

No steps were taken to abort the uprising. On the contrary, in a delirium of irresponsibility, the government named General Mola commander of the armed forces in Pamplona, thus paving the way for a coup in Navarre. This gave the rebellion the combat strength of the *Requetés*, without which it would have been very difficult for Franco to keep the battle going.

During the hours following the revolt, the government still believed it could control events, and, to the exasperation of everyone, issued official communiqués on the situation which certainly were not based on the facts.

The leaders of all parties were alert, each in his home, listening to the news and waiting to act. The people were preparing for the fight. Workers wanting instructions and demanding arms crowded the meeting halls of all the organizations.

Representatives of the Popular Front asked the government to arm the workers' militias. Casares stated that he didn't think this was necessary, since the government was sufficiently strong to control the situation.

As the hours passed, the news became more alarming. Reports were coming in that all Spanish possessions in Africa were in the hands of the rebels, that Valladolid and Palencia had joined the revolt, that Burgos, Avila and Galicia were occupied by the rebels, that something unusual was happening in the military posts in Madrid and Barcelona.

The government finally had to admit it could no longer handle the situation. The clamor of the people for arms and the pressure of the Popular Front organizations forced it to arm the workers. Casares Quiroga sent his resignation to the President of the Republic.

While the political crisis was being resolved, the workers' militias and the Assault Guards who had remained loyal to the Republic occupied all the strategic places in the city. Madrid, and indeed all of Loyalist Spain, resounded with a single clamor: "Arms! Arms!"

Trucks, buses, taxis and cars went through the city at breakneck speed, carrying arms to the workers who were leaving their jobs to take up rifles.

The news being broadcast by the government announced that the revolt had been crushed in several places. The people were jubilant.

On the evening of July 18, I spoke on the air for the Communist Party from the Ministry of the Interior radio station: "It is better to die on your feet than to live on your knees! *No pasarán!*" From that moment, "They shall not pass!" became the battle cry of the resistance movement.

Everyone was tense and nervous. The streets of Madrid and of all the important cities and towns in Spain became military camps. To take leave of a street meant to abandon it to the enemy, who lurked everywhere. The sight of armed women won the applause and admiration of everyone.

# 25

# The Soldiers

In the early morning hours of July 19, after the resignation of Casares Quiroga, Spain learned that a new, distinctly right-wing government had been formed, headed by Martinez Barrio. One of the members of the cabinet was Sánchez Román, who had once refused to join the Popular Front.

A wave of indignation swept over the masses. Cries of "Treason!" began to be heard from those willing to fight and die for the Republic.

Were the arms to drop from the people's hands? A government of capitulation? No! A thousand times no! Protests rose like a tidal wave even up to the President of the Republic. Azaña was frightened. The government which had just been born was already dead, thanks to the instinctive wisdom of the people, who sensed that the Martinez government was not one that would lead the battle for the Republic. The workers were not willing to capitulate.

Within 24 hours, the people of Spain looked into their hearts and found themselves. The new government was now out, ousted by the people who had the right to be heard.

A few hours after the flash-in-the-pan Martinez government resigned, another was formed, similar to the Casares Quiroga cabinet, with left-wing Republican Giral as president, General Castelló as minister of war, and General Pozas, former head of the Civil Guard, as minister of the interior.

For the moment, the Giral government had the confidence of the people, and its first communiqués brought renewed determination to those who were ready to make any sacrifice to prevent the triumph of reaction.

Tension reached its height in the capital when, in the early evening of July 19, news came that the military posts in the suburbs of

Madrid—Carabanchel, Leganés, Getafe, etc.—had rebelled and were preparing to fight it out in the street.

Soldiers and Falangists inside the Montaña Barracks in the heart of Madrid were already firing on groups of workers in adjacent streets.

As the danger of a rebel take-over increased, so did the determination to fight. On July 20, Madrid woke up to the sound of intense gunfire. The militia and loyalist forces were battling it out with the rebels in the Montaña Barracks. One of the bravest fighters was the militiaman Bárzana, a young Asturian schoolteacher, who in 1934 had taken active part in the October insurrection.

Two old cannons were dragged out and placed near the Plaza de España, but their projectiles bounced off the walls of the fortress without doing any damage.

White flags appeared in the windows of the rebel fortress several times. When the Republican militiamen came out and advanced to accept the apparent surrender, they were greeted by machine-gun fire. With expert aim, a Republican airplane dropped several bombs on the fortress. This was a daring act and caused a wild panic among the rebels. They raised the white flag again, this time not as a dirty trick, but in earnest. In a dramatic scene the militiamen dashed through the half-open doors of the structure that had come so close to turning into a bastion of reaction.

General Fanjul, disguised in the uniform of a common soldier, tried to escape through the window, but was arrested along with dozens of other officers and Falangist civilians who had slipped into the fortress hours before the revolt to help the rebels. Several hundred militiamen were armed with the weapons taken from the barracks.

The rebels in Montaña were not the only ones to be defeated that day. The rebel garrisons in Carabanchel and other fortresses were also subdued.

Madrid was Republican! Madrid was the capital of the Republic and the heart of Republican resistance!

And it was not only in Madrid but elsewhere that fighting was going on. Barcelona, San Sebastián, Gijón, Oviedo, Málaga and Córdoba were also in the line of battle.

Queipo de Llano took over Seville by trickery, in spite of the efforts of the Communists to organize the resistance, which had held out in Triana for days, halting the advance of the rebels to Huelva.

The popular resistance in Galicia, headed by the workers and democrats of Vigo, lasted several days. Socialists and Communists fought together under the leadership of Vigo's mayor, Botana, an old-time Socialist, and Eustasio Garrote, an old Galician Communist. The military superiority of the rebels broke the popular resistance, and its heroic leaders were killed by the insurgents. Botana was shot. Garrote was so badly mutilated that it was impossible to recognize his body.

Virtually all northern Spain was Republican, including the coal mines of Asturias, the iron-ore mines of Vizcaya, and Spain's powerful steel industry, as well as a large part of Castile's wheat zone, Levante, parts of Aragón, Estremadura, Andalusia and all of Catalonia.

The rebellion of the fleet was rapidly crushed by the sailors. On July 21, the newspapers carried the following headline: "The crew of *Jaime I* overpowers the rebel commanders and seizes the battleship." This was followed by two laconic telegrams, one from the crew to the Admiralty:

"We have had serious resistance from the commanders and officers on board, and have subdued them by force. Killed in the fight were one captain and one lieutenant; gravely wounded were eight corporals, one lieutenant, one ensign, one artillery corporal and two sailors. Urgently ask instructions about bodies."

The Admiralty's reply was even more concise: "Admiralty to crew *Jaime I*: Lower bodies overboard with respectful solemnity. What is your position?"

There is no doubt that the lack of decision on the part of the officers of Montaña Barracks, who preferred to fight from strongly fortified positions inside the fortress rather than out on the street against the people, led to their isolation and defeat and strengthened the resistance in the capital. But Madrid had other fortresses whose commanders were involved in the uprising and who were waiting for the order to strike against the Republic.

I returned on the afternoon of July 20 from the Guadarrama mountains to report to the party on the unstable situation of the Popular Front in that region. It was composed of badly armed workers, without organization or discipline; on the other hand, the enemy was perfectly armed and trained to march on Madrid. We began a discussion as to what course should be pursued in those critical hours.

The government no longer had an army. To which side would the military units still confined inside the fortresses go? If the situation was to be saved, this question had to be answered within a matter of hours.

The Communists took charge of the districts with fortresses and immediately began to contact the soldiers to seek a reply to this question which meant life or death to the Republic. The No. 6 Infantry Regiment and the Battle Vehicles of the Pacific Regiment were swiftly enlisted on the side of the Republic.

With Comrade Lister, I went to the No. 1 Infantry Garrison, the former Wad Ras, where, in addition to the soldiers, a large number of Civil Guards were quartered.

We thought that we wouldn't leave the place alive when we entered the barracks and saw the looks of hate on the faces of the Civil Guards—or were they looks of despair and frustration?

We asked some guards: "Where are the soldiers?"

"In the barracks," was the reply.

We went to the first barrack. The door was open. We were greeted with curiosity. Lister spoke with a rebel corporal who wanted to know who we were.

We told him our names and political affiliation and of our wish to speak with all the soldiers in the fortress. To our surprise, he made no objection and sent some men to tell the others to come.

When most of the soldiers were assembled, the corporal called for silence and told the men: "Two delegates from the Communist Party, La Pasionaria and Enrique Lister, have come to have a word with you."

"Let them speak!" cried the soldiers, some curious and others indifferent.

The soldiers came nearer to where I was standing in the center of the room. One of them brought me a bench which I used as a makeshift platform so I could be seen and heard better.

I told them who we were and what we wanted from them, who the rebels were and what were their objectives. Ninety-five per cent of the soldiers were peasants. One of them asked: "Comrade Pasionaria, if the Republic wins, what will it do with the land?"

That simple peasant wearing the uniform of the Republic had every right to ask this question, for it epitomized all the deceptions and hardships that the peasants had suffered since the Republic was declared. The government had promised them much but delivered little.

"The land? The land will go to those who work it. Absentee ownership will be eliminated, so will the latifundium. A broad agrarian reform will give the peasant the land he has dreamed of owning for so long."

"And who guarantees this?"

"You do!"

"We do?"

"Yes, you. The reactionaries have brought us into a war; they have rebelled against the Republic, despite the fact that the Republic never touched any of their basic privileges. With the defeat of the reactionaries, you will not only have the right to your claims on the land, but also the arms to defend your right and to impose it. The workers will be on your side, backing you up, the most progressive men in Spain, the Communist Party. But you must never forget that you yourselves are in the driver's seat now. You with your fighting, with your determination, will be the ones to decide the future of the land and with it the future of Spain."

There was a moment of suspense. The soldiers had to make a decision and they decided. The corporal called the standard-bearer and gave him an order. A strident call for formation filled the barracks, extended into the yard and out into the street. The soldiers of the Wad Ras regiment would fight for the Republic!

They dressed rapidly and formed their ranks in the yard. The corporal told them: "We're going to the front to defend the Republic against its enemies, our enemies. Don't let the Republic down! Long live the Republic!" The soldiers answered with enthusiasm. They automatically looked upon the corporal as their chief. Lister informed the party of the event and organized the transportation of the soldiers to the front. We took the trucks and buses which for "safety's sake" had been hidden in a huge garage by their owner, an enemy of the Republic.

A captain from the antifascist Military Union took charge of the convoy, along with the corporal, now promoted to lieutenant by unanimous decision of the soldiers. Lister and I went with them.

We arrived in Guadarrama late at night, and while the soldiers were organizing themselves in the plaza in front of the town hall, we went to the General Staff Headquarters, which was under the command of the notorious Colonel Cabrera, who was later to "shorten" the front of Málaga and deliver the city to the fascists.

We found the "loyal" military chiefs in a small room lit by a lamp, bent over a military map, "studying" enemy positions which were no more than two steps away from them, virtually within arm's reach.

We told them that we had brought an infantry regiment to put at their disposal. They answered indifferently: "Let them spend the night in the plaza. We'll see about them tomorrow."

I couldn't believe my ears. Respectfully, and with the greatest control, I said: "I don't know anything about the science of war, but I have a very strong impression that if we leave those men there, the fascist planes won't leave one soldier alive to wake up tomorrow. Don't you think it would be better to take them to the front tonight so that if the enemy decides to attack tomorrow, he'll find a surprise —a trained and organized military regiment?"

"We're not familiar with the road to the mountains and don't have any guides."

The Mayor of Guadarrama offered his services: "I can show you the way to go without being seen by the enemy."

"Then discuss it with the chief of the regiment," answered Cabrera.

Lister and I exchanged quizzical looks. Were these the "loyal" commanders who were going to defend the Republic? Or were they preparing its collapse so that they might be rewarded for their treason?

## [26]

## Nonintervention

The widespread popular resistance movement obliged the government to supply material and technical means for the Republic to defend itself. The government, therefore, requested the aid of friendly nations with whom it had treaties.

In 1935, the Spanish government had signed a trade agreement with France. One of the clauses stipulated that in case of need the Spanish Government could not purchase arms from any country other than France. With this agreement in its hand, the Republican government appealed to the French for the arms and equipment needed to protect the nation from aggression. The French government flatly refused to sell (not to give, loan or aid, but to sell!) to the Republican government the arms it so desperately lacked. The Republican government never asked France for assistance or active aid, but simply to sell it the arms it needed.

Both France and Britain closed their eyes to Spain's wounds, to the heroism and sacrifices of its people. And let it stand on the record that Spain did not complain. The facts speak for themselves.

The French bourgeoisie and the British capitalists did not want the Republic to triumph, for various reasons, among them the fact that they needed Spain as a poor, backward neighbor on whom they could impose onerous and extortionist treaties. They saw Franco as a defender of Spain's aristocratic and reactionary caste privileges. They aided the reaction, easing its way, and tied the hands of the Loyalists, denying that they even had the right to fight.

Very revealing is the fact that the nonintervention policy emerged at a time when Germany and Italy began to aid the rebels openly. Both these policies came into being when Franco's forces were being routed by the popular resistance during the first weeks of the war.

While the legitimate government was being denied the right to purchase any type of arms, the insurgents were receiving all they needed from Germany and Italy. The so-called democracies did nothing to stop it!

The British government attached more weight to the words of Count Grandi in the nonintervention committee who insisted that the report of Italian participation in the war was a lie than to the irrefutable facts provided by the Spanish government.

The British government's disregard of the Spanish people, a stand encouraged by Britain's Labor leaders, sank to the low level of sending committees to Spain to investigate the nationality of the bombs being dropped on Spain's people and cities. It was not too long after the crushing of Spain's resistance that the people of England learned the hard way who had been manufacturing the bombs that the Junkers had hurled on the battlefields and on the defenseless civilian population of Spain.

Completely disregarding the facts, and exaggerating the kind of incidents of violence which had always characterized Spain's social struggles—so much more numerous and violent under the monarchy than under the Republic—the rebels and their foreign allies justified the revolt which was bleeding Spain as a national necessity to fight the danger of an imminent Communist take-over.

The truth was that on the national scene, the chief reason for the Civil War lay in class hatred on the part of the landed aristocracy and the plutocratic oligarchy. These economically linked castes refused to accept democracy in Spain or, for that matter, the most minute encroachments on their class privileges.

On the international scene, the uprising was encouraged and supported by Italy and Germany, where the promoters of the revolt had put the finishing touches on their conspiracy and obtained generous but far from disinterested help. The strategic position of the Iberian Peninsula, as a bridge between Europe and Africa, its mineral wealth, its proximity to the American continent, and its influence on Latin American countries amply warranted the aid given to the Spanish reactionaries and the sending of hundreds of airplanes and tanks, thousands of machine guns, technicians and soldiers.

After the first victories of the popular forces in Spain's principal cities and industrial centers, the war of positions began. For the Republican forces, resistance meant gaining time to organize, to create an army, to speed the wheels of war industries and to mobilize the country's resources to meet the demands of the conflict.

For the rebels, the Republican resistance would have meant defeat, if they had had to count on their own resources. The zone controlled by the rebels could not provide the necessary materials since there were no important mines or steelworks in any of the rebel zones.

When the powers behind the scenes of the counterrevolutionary movement realized that a rapid victory for the rebels was impossible in the face of the popular resistance, they openly and brazenly began to take over direction of the war.

German and Italian units, chosen from among fascist youth groups, were sent to Spain. With them they brought the most modern war equipment—fighter planes, bombers, heavy and light tanks, artillery, machine guns, rifles, ammunition, hand grenades. German and Italian battleships were sent to the rebels. United States petroleum companies supplied Franco with all the petroleum needed to carry on the war. Hitler's generals openly participated in

Franco's General Staff meetings. The military technicians were either German or Italian.

According to official Italian data, some 150,000 of Mussolini's soldiers fought in Spain. Although the Germans never published the number of soldiers they sent to Spain, we can get a good idea of Germany's participation in the war from the fact that 25,000 nazi commanders, soldiers and officers of all branches of the armed forces, received special gold, silver or bronze medals for bravery and zeal in the fight against the Spanish people.

Italian and German airplanes destroyed Guernica and Nules. German cannons shook the Republican fortifications at Sierra Pandola and bombarded Madrid from the Cerro de los Angeles. Italian troops marched on Málaga; German warships showered Almeria with cannon shells; German airplanes bombarded Barcelona and Madrid dozens of times; Italian troops entered Spain in the north and marched to Santander; Italian military units were defeated in Guadalajara; Italian Blackshirts surrounded the last remnants of the Popular Army holding out in the port of Alicante. These were the forces of so-called Nationalist Spain—not to mention the Moors, the Portuguese and the human dregs recruited in the sewers of other gilt-edged societies—against whom the people of Spain fought in their heroic resistance from July 1936 to March 1939.

The aid of the fascist powers gave a special character to the war begun in 1936. It overflowed the boundaries of a civil war to turn into a national revolutionary war against domestic and foreign fascism. Herein lay the international importance of Spain's resistance against fascist aggression. Hitler was using Spain as a training ground for his aviation and soldiers in preparation for an attack against Europe and the world.

It was the people of Spain, morally sustained by the sympathy and solidarity of the working class and democratic forces of the entire world, who had the difficult task of fighting and containing the forces of aggression and war in Europe, and of demonstrating that the advance of fascism in the world could be checked and liquidated.

Confronted with the plain, outrageous facts of the intervention of fascist powers, Spain's government and people made urgent calls for solidarity to the democracies. They were voices crying in the desert.

The international forces of reaction openly built a wall around Republican Spain. The press, the radio, all the immense network of propaganda of the reactionary forces in all the countries of the world thundered against Spain's epic struggle. With the most bare-faced lies they tried to cover and justify the military rising and foreign intervention.

To expose the infamy of the vested interests, the distortion of the facts, I spoke on the official radio station on July 29, in the name of the party's Central Committee. I appealed to all the democracies, telling them the truth about Spain and the danger which the defeat of the Spanish people would mean for them.

I explained the country's situation and called on the people of America and the workers of Europe to come to the aid of the Republic and its people:

"The battle of the Spanish people is the battle of a people that has risen against the criminal aggressions of the reactionary military castes.

"It is a battle for peace; it is a battle against the instigators of war.

"Help us prevent the disappearance of democracy in Spain. For if this should happen, it would inevitably mean the beginning of a world war which we all want to avert.

"Stop the hand of the interventionists! The government of Spain is a legal government deriving its powers from the elections of February 16. We, the Communists, support and defend this government, because it is the legitimate representative of the people who fight for democracy and liberty."

Unfortunately, the defeat of the Spanish Republic did mean the beginning of the war, as the Communist Party had foretold. Five months after the Spanish resistance was crushed, World War II broke out in all its tragic fury.

# 27

# In the Crucible

From the outset of the rebellion the Communist Party had had to change its activities completely. Every Communist had only one concern: To defend the Republic and prevent a fascist victory.

When fascist columns from the north were marching on Madrid from several directions, the antifascist militia, led by Líster, Modesto, Juanito, Peña, Captain Benito, Abad, Andrés Martín, Bárzana, Heredia, Evaristo Gil, Barral, Sender, Ariza and others, sped to the Guadarrama Mountains to cut off the enemy's advance.

The organizing ability of Pedro Checa, the political intelligence of José Díaz, the propagandistic ability of Antonio Mije, the political maturity of Vicente Uribe, the fighting spirit of the United Socialist Youth under the leadership of Santiago Carrillo and Trifón Medrano, all came to the fore during those critical days.

The resistance became a proving ground for all political forces, and the revolutionary quality of the Communist Party emerged fully. It didn't take long for the masses to realize that if it hadn't been for the party the forces of reaction would have gained their objectives without meeting the slightest resistance.

After Hitler rose to power in 1933 and the danger of a fascist coup became a real threat in Spain, the Communist Party had proposed the creation of antifascist militia as armed units to defend workers' organizations, democracy and the Republic.

Many men in the Republican camp failed to understand the need for the militia. Communist proposals were considered alarmist and were interpreted captiously and erroneously. The party was thought to have ulterior motives.

A good part of the youth, however, did not share the opinions of the old Republican leaders, nor those of the bureaucrats, who were stultified by dogmatic legalism and incapable of understanding the changes operating in the world and the new forces lining up on both the national and international scene. The leaders of the United Socialist Youth, headed by Santiago Carrillo, who proved to be a true revolutionary leader, broke the bureaucratic ties that had confined the organization. Both young and old Socialists joined the fight together with the Communists. They were a tremendously important factor in maintaining popular unity and resistance.

With its own forces and the aid of some military chiefs, the Communist Party formed the Antifascist Workers' and Peasants' Militia (MAOC) in 1933 in nearly every province of Spain. Militia chiefs in Madrid were Líster, Modesto, Captain Benito and others. Their immediate superior was Pedro Checa, the party's secretary of organization.

After the Communist Party had formed its antifascist militia, the Socialist Youth followed suit. The militia had its baptism of fire in the Asturias insurrection of 1934. Under the battlecry of UHP! (Union of Working-Class Brothers!), they were the shock troops against reaction and fascism in Spain.

It was these militiamen, sharply opposed at first by the Republican government, who stopped the insurgent army in its advance toward Madrid, giving it battle in Somosierra, Navacerrada and Alto del León. They were the cornerstone of the Popular Army.

During the first weeks of the war, our main concern was defending the roads to Madrid, blocking all enemy attempts to reach the capital. As long as Madrid was in the hands of the Republican government, victory was assured. Every party, every organization, including those which in 1933 had tenaciously fought against the creation of the militia, now formed its own militia units at full speed.

From the start it was evident that the militia, organized on a volunteer basis and given the most elementary military training, was not able in spite of its heroism to sustain a drawn-out battle. The militia could not cope with the disciplined, well-equipped army that was besieging the Republic.

The Anarchists of Levante organized the "Rose Bush" and "Iron" Columns. Together with honest Anarchist workers, common prisoners released by the Anarchists from the San Miguel de los Reyes prison also became militiamen, as well as some fascist elements who revealed their true colors when they assaulted the Communist Party offices in Valencia. They received such a sound thrashing that they never had the strength for a repeat performance.

In an attempt to create the indispensable army of its own that the Republic should have had, the Communist Party began to merge its militia. The party's activity made up for the government's lack of initiative, aiding it to overcome many difficulties. The Giral government, which history and the people will remember as one of noteworthy merit, decreed the militarization of the militia. Although this in itself was not enough, it was a step toward the organization of a Republican army.

Martinez Barrio, whom the Communists never hesitated to criticize when they thought his policies were damaging to the people's interests, accepted the presidency of the Supply and Recruiting Committee of the Militia. Knowing its usefulness to the Republic, he accepted this not very glamorous post with a modesty that honored him. Martinez set an example for many "peacock" politicians to whom politics only meant an opportunity to display their feathers and bask in the limelight of the nation or in diplomatic missions abroad.

One day in August 1936, José Díaz and I went to the Chief-of-Staff headquarters of Colonel Asensio in Guadarrama. There we found Casares Quiroga, the former prime minister of the Republic, with a rifle slung over his shoulder.

A few weeks before the revolt we had visited him to denounce the situation in Navarre, where the Requetés were openly preparing for a coup. With typical Galician slyness, he had answered us: "You Communists are terrible! Imagining fascists and conspirators everywhere!"

I reminded him of his political dodging during that conversation and his mockery afterwards when, in the corridors of Congress, he had once teased me saying: "You scare me!" Now I asked him:

"Were there fascists or weren't there, Señor Casares? Did the Communists invent them? Or were you politicians deliberately playing the ostrich? Whom are you scared of now? Them or me?"

He tried to justify himself, mentioning superiors who had influenced his actions and policies at the time.

"To whom are you referring? To Azaña?"

"That I can't say, but the responsibility was not mine alone."

We spoke with Colonel Asensio about the situation on the front, which was in the process of stabilizing itself. "By the way," he said, "do you want to see the Fontan barricade? It's just one large depression in the ground because of the constant enemy fire on that spot."

(Asensio neglected to tell us what he, who was responsible for the Guadarrama front, was doing to stop the enemy now fighting desperately night and day to control that key position protecting the road to Madrid. Apparently it was a military secret, one that covered many sins.)

"Fine," said Díaz, "but how do we get there?"

"In an armored car."

The armored car we rode in was one of the many being built by the Loyalists. It provided about as much protection from bullets as a sheet of paper. As we were advancing on the road toward the barricade, enemy batteries spotted us and let loose some volleys. Had they reached our famous armored car, they would have riddled us like Swiss cheese.

At a corner of the road blocked off by barbed-wire fences, Asensio told us to get out. The enemy was still firing. The car drove back to Guadarrama, while we ran toward the barricade through the barbed wire. Many times it tore into my skirt as if it wanted to hold me there as a witness to the stoicism of a handful of men who preferred to die rather than cede one inch of ground to the enemy. I thought of the criminal indifference of Asensio's General Staff who, with a "what-do-we-care" attitude, let the town bleed to death because the militiamen were not the regular disciplined troops they were used to commanding.

We arrived at the barricade where under the burning sun a small group of grimy soldiers, with feverish eyes, swollen lips and dry throats, many of them wounded, were fighting against the enemy, conscious of the importance of their sacrifice.

They were all happy to see us. Crawling behind the parapet of sandbags protecting them from the enemy, they came to shake our hands and greet us. Captain Fontán told us of his admiration for these heroes. "With these men, we can conquer a world. They don't know military regulations, but as for combativeness and resistance, they're unbeatable." The soldiers felt the same affection for Fontán, their commander, a professional soldier well known for his Republican sentiments.

We spoke with all of them, informing them of the situation, expressing our confidence in victory, cheering them up. They took out their identification cards, personal documents, photographs of their mothers and sweethearts so we could sign them and write a kind word, an expression of affection and hope.

We spent a long time with them under constant enemy fire, which was never answered because the barricade didn't have a cannon.

It was growing darker, the shooting had calmed down a little and Fontán advised us to leave since there was always the possibility of a nocturnal attack. We bade farewell to those heroes. We parted with handshakes, hugs, letters to be mailed and family messages.

"Go quickly! before they begin again."

We left rapidly, but the enemy artillery was even more rapid. We ran an unbelievable obstacle race until we finally reached territory which was out of their firing range. Avoiding the road, we walked back to Guadarrama and then returned to Madrid.

We never saw Captain Fontán again. The day after our visit, an enemy bullet deprived the Republic and the people of Spain of one of their most faithful soldiers, one of their most honest and best men. Fontán's barricade had been defended with his life and to the end of the war his kind of heroism was characteristic of the men of the Popular Army which bore his name.

Also unforgettable were the days of the battle of Somosierra in Guadarrama, a terrible battle fought between badly armed men and a well-organized and directed Army.

Alto de León! Silent witness of the heroism and sacrifices of its militiamen.

As I have said, the war completely changed the nature of the party's work. After July 18, the party put all its efforts into organizing and maintaining popular resistance on both the battle- and home-fronts.

Comrades vied with one another in sacrifice and effort. From our gravely ill Secretary General, José Díaz, down to the humblest member in a faraway province, we were all obsessed with the war, with doing more each day to assure the victory of the Republic.

The Communist deputies took part in this unselfish labor with the greatest zeal.

Some of them came to Madrid only for the sessions of parliament, so the revolt took them by surprise in their own constituencies. Comrades Eduardo Suárez Morales, deputy for Canarias, and

Bautista Garcés, deputy for Córdoba, were arrested and killed in their home districts by the Falangists. Comrades Suárez Cabrales and José Ochoa Alcázar, who were in Canarias organizing a party conference, were savagely tortured; then, still alive, they were put in sacks and thrown into the sea.

Comrade Leandro Carro, who had gone to Galicia two days before the revolt to attend a regional meeting, took part in the fight, together with Benigno Alvarez, the party chief in Orense. After heroic resistance, they managed to escape with a group of guerrillas into the mountains, where Alvarez later died. Carro spent more than two years with the guerrillas. At the end of the war he escaped to Portugal and later went to Mexico.

Juan José Manso, deputy for Asturias, Comrade Angelín and the Roza brothers participated in the fight in Asturias, organizing the resistance and working on the home front. Party chiefs killed in the war were Horacio Argüelles of Asturias, Carlos Vega of Gijón and Herminio Argüelles of Oviedo.

Several of our deputies became militiamen, among them Antonio Pretel of Granada who, with Lina Odena, fought on that front.

Daniel Ortega, deputy for the province of Cádiz, was one of the organizers of the Fifth Regiment. He was very active in Madrid throughout the war. The Falangists shot him after the capitulation of Casado.

Cayetano Bolívar, the party's first deputy in 1933, was commissar of the militia in Málaga. At the end of the war he was shot by the Falangists.

The deputies Adriano Romero and Pedro Martinez Cartón joined the militia and later the army. Romero was the Quartermaster General in Andalusia, and Martinez directed a military unit in Estremadura, his constituency.

Most of the members of the Politburo were deputies: Antonio Mije who worked in the War Commissary; Vicente Uribe and Jesús Hernández, who were ministers with Largo Caballero and Negrin; and finally myself.

As with all the comrades, my main concern was the battlefront, but neither could the work on the home front be neglected. Our wartime tasks were many: helping the people who had been evacuated from the rebel occupied zones; organizing nurseries and children's food centers; aiding nursing mothers; creating sewing centers to supply the army with uniforms; setting up special organizations to help the soldiers at the front and in the hospitals; supplying food to workers in war industries; and participating in the Women's Aid Committee, which cooperated with the Ministry of Defense in solving the multiple problems arising from the war.

In addition, the party carried on intense propaganda work in the battlefields and at home. We had to attend numerous meetings, conferences and demonstrations, as well as sessions of parliament, where I was now vice-president.

The party sent me and other comrades to the fronts of Guadarrama, Somosierra, Ciudad Universitaria, Aragón, Catalonia and Estremadura, into the very line of fire, wherever the party's voice and help was needed. I must confess that I felt more at home among the soldiers than with the civilians.

For whatever was accomplished by us the credit belongs entirely to the party, whose strength was behind each one of us and whose political activities inspired and helped us overcome our own shortcomings and weaknesses.

The Communist Party produced an endless stream of combatants. Who were Líster and Modesto? Who were Cordón, Márquez, Prados, Hidalgo de Cisneros, Recalde, Cristóbal, Marquina, Ciutat, Marin and the many other soldiers and militiamen who fought so bravely?

Who were the heroic commissars Diéguez, Del Campo, Fusimaña, Bahamonde, Delage? Who were "the first to advance and the last to retreat?" Who was Celestino García, the simple peasant of Morata del Tajuña, who destroyed four Italian tanks and took their drivers prisoners? Who were the antitank fighters, Coll, Cornejo and Grau, the embodiments of determination and courage?

Workers, peasants, students, soldiers, sailors—all of them were men of the Communist Party. Deputies, members of provincial and local committees, of the Politburo and Central Committee. The entire Communist Party with a single purpose fought the war and defended the liberty and independence of Spain, the Republic and democracy.

# 28

# The Fifth Regiment

The first militia recruiting center was organized in the Salesian Convent in Madrid. Here the Fifth Regiment of the militia was born, comprising the following battalions and columns: Local Militia, the Workers' and Peasants' Youth, October, Thaelmann,* Iron, Red Lions, Red Bullets, White Arts, The Pen, FUE (*Federacíon Universitaria Española*, the Spanish student union), Asturias, Condés,† Captain Benito, Leningrad, Paris Commune,‡ Madrid Commune, Victory, Sailors of Kronstadt,** Jaén (a province in Andalusia), Líster, PUA, José Díaz and the Steel Battalion.

Recruiting went so well that new additions were made to the Fifth Regiment: United Socialist Youth battalion, named La Pasionaria, and the Mangada and Galán Columns. In Catalonia, the United Socialist Party (PSUC)†† organized the Karl Marx Column and later the 27th Division.

* Ernst Thaelmann (1886–1944), German Communist leader, was imprisoned by the Nazis as soon as they came to power; he was executed in Buchenwald after several years in the concentration camp.—Ed.
† Named for Captain Fernando Condés of the Civil Guard, accused of assassinating Calvo Sotelo, the Monarchist leader.—Ed.
‡ On January 8, 1871, with the city beleaguered by the German army, the Parisian proletariat proclaimed the Commune when the central French government in Versailles attempted to disarm the National Guard. Marx and Engels, and Lenin after them, considered the Paris Commune the first worker's government. After two months, the Versailles troops took back control of the city, executing 17,000 men, women and children.—Ed.
** Kronstadt, a small island base near Leningrad, was the scene of naval mutinies which played key parts in the Russian revolutions of 1905 and 1917.—Ed.
†† On July 23, 1936, the Catalan Communist Party, the Catalan Workers' Party, the Catalan Federation of the Spanish Socialist Workers' Party and the Socialist Union of Catalonia united to form the United

The militarization of the militia, the government's first step in organizing its forces, permitted the miltia to train under experienced commanders and military technicians such as Arellano, Marquez, Gallo, José Galán, Barceló, Bueno and others, who won the respect and admiration of the militiamen under them.

The Fifth Regiment, which was emerging as the most solid and serious military organization of the Republic, included all those who sincerely desired a victory for the Republic. Civilians and soldiers of many different political shades belonged to the Fifth Regiment, thanks to the order and discipline established by the Communist Party among the combatants.

When they organized the Fifth Regiment, the Communists did not organize the men in units concerned with military matters alone. It also carried on intense political education, publishing newspapers, some of which, like *Popular Militia*, achieved a circulation as high as 75,000 copies daily.

Bulletin boards graphically depicting current events were posted in the forts and trenches.

The Fifth Regiment created a military sanitation unit and a quartermaster's office which later served as models for the army.

An incipient war industry was begun which supplied the militia with hand grenades and armored cars. Shops were set up to repair weapons. Model hospitals were organized, along with rest homes, sanatoriums, homes for the orphans of militiamen and sewing shops where hundreds of women worked.

The Fifth Regiment created military training schools for artillery and infantry men. The first tank drivers and aviators of the war came from the ranks of the Fifth Regiment. The Fifth Regiment thus organized on a small scale what the government should have done on a nationwide basis many months earlier.

It was an honor to belong to the Fifth Regiment, a feeling captured by the poet Rafael Alberti in his short poem, "I'm From the Fifth Regiment."

> Tomorrow I will leave my house,
> I will leave my oxen and my people behind.
> Good luck to you! Where are you going, tell me where?

---

Socialist Party of Catalonia (PSUC), which was to contribute greatly to organizing resistance and counteracting Anarchist tendencies within the Catalan workers' movement.

I'm going to the Fifth Regiment.
To march without water
Up hills and over fields,
Singing songs of glory and triumph,
    For I belong to the Fifth Regiment!

Among its achievements were the Steel Battalions. The Steel
Battalions were composed of unselfish, brave men and women, determined at the cost of their lives to win victory for the popular cause.
The poet Luis de Tapia wrote this poem about these legendary
batallions:

The Steel Battalions
Go to their death singing!
They're hard and fierce,
With the air of warriors
And the ways of heroes.
The Steel Battalions
Are made of steel
And will triumph!

In the crucible of war where the steel is forged,
They unite with one purpose:
The worker, the peasant,
The rude guerrilla
The invincible captain!
The Steel Battalions
Are made of steel
And will triumph!

The Steel Battalions
Go into battle singing!
In their soldiers' song
They sing to their captain: If I die,
It will be so that
My children will be spared!
The Steel Battalions
Are made of steel
And will triumph!
Warn the men of the past, they shall not pass!

The propaganda work carried on by all the Popular Front organizations, especially by the Communist Party and the Fifth Regiment, played a most important role in stimulating the resistance movement. Newspapers, posters, pamphlets and broadsides describing Republican conquests and our people's fighting spirit were to be found everywhere on the battlefields and at home.

*Mundo Obrero* and *Frente Rojo*, both party publications, were excellent examples of wartime revolutionary workers' newspapers. They were messengers of hope and faith, the meeting place of antifascist opinions, and a source of direction for all Communists, reflecting the Communist policy of unity.

Many soldier journalists worked on *Mundo Obrero* and *Frente Rojo*. Among the most outstanding were Manuel Navarro Ballesteros, Eusebio Cimorra, Rejano and Izcaray. Ballesteros was shot by the insurgents. His journalistic work was a genuine and passionate expression of his vocation. He worked tirelessly and was always willing to undertake any task, despite his responsibilities as director because, above all else, he was a Communist. Eusebio Cimorra's activities included such political commentaries and war chronicles as his remarkable description of the assault on the Montaña Barracks. Comrade Rejano worked with *Frente Rojo*. He was a man of broad culture, sincere modesty and diverse talents. Comrade Izcaray, who also worked for *Frente Rojo*, wrote vivid articles which were read and discussed everywhere. The editors of both these newspapers, with their intensity and their tireless work—not always exempt from error because of their great zeal—made up for the lack of more seasoned journalists still in the process of formation in our camp.

The United Socialist Youth, under the intelligent leadership of Comrades Fernando Claudín and Víctor Velasco, published the dailies *La Hora* in Valencia and *Ahora* in Madrid. These were the young patriotic voices of Spain, guiding and educating the youth. Manuel Azcárate also actively participated in these projects.

Writers, poets, artists, painters, sculptors, offered their talents and work to the Fifth Regiment, which, in turn, provided them with an inexhaustible source of inspiration for their work. Many of them wielded the pen and the sword alternately.

The democratic journalist, Antonio Zozoya, well known in Republican literary and press circles, impressed by the heroism of the militiamen, described his decision to fight in their ranks in these expressive lines:

> Militia! Shining name
> Which does honor to our country,
> And deserves all honor.
> A soldier is always a hero
> When he does his duty bravely.
> A hireling can be enslaved,
> Used against the people who are his kin,
> But never a militiaman, no!
> And when war is declared
> Against an enemy's onslaught
> He doesn't ever cry, in fear,
> "Mother, they are making me go,"
> Instead he says, "I go
> To answer my people's call!
> I go joyfully to fight
> Against treason and tyranny
> To protect what is dearest to my heart:
> Your hair turning gray
> The memory of my father.
> To help free my long-oppressed people
> To decorate with laurel wreaths
> The fields where I was born
> And the beams of my house.
> And so, unafraid and joyful,
> United with my brothers,
> I go to triumph.
> And if I should die,
> I will die like a militiaman!"

Antonio Machado wrote the following in honor of the popular hero, Líster, whose bravery was legendary in all Spain:

> *To Líster, Chief of the Embro Army*
> Your letter—oh, noble heart who keeps the vigil,
> Unconquerable Spaniard, strong fighting arm,
> Your letter, gallant Líster, lightens
> The burden of death that weighs on me.

Your letter brought me the sounds of
The sacred battle on the Iberian fields;
My heart, too, woke up
To odors of gunpowder and rosemary.
Where the marine seashell announces
The presence of the Ebro, and on the
Cold rock from which this Spanish cry bursts forth,
From hill and sea, these are my words:
"Were my pen worthy of your valiant sword,
I would die content."

When the enemy-surrounded capital was tense with horror, fighting to keep from its soil the beast who discharged his fury in
monstrous bombing raids, the voice of Herrera Petere, the soldier
poet of the Fifth Regiment, was heard calling the people of Madrid
to prepare for its heroic last stand:

### Alarm

Madrid, Madrid, at your very doors,
Before your very eyes, at your very houses,
The black snout comes closer and closer
The black beast comes straight at you.
To arms, people of Madrid!
The times are far from calm!
The air smells of iron,
Bullets streak across the blue sky,
Cannons shake the city
And the earth rises
In deadly spurts
Of black, metallic dust.
Planes unleashed by the fascists,
Are borne in on the winds.
Men, women, young, old,
Are struck down by their bombs.
Madrid, Madrid, at your very doors,
The black beast comes right at you.
There still is time, Madrileños.
Quickly, very quickly, to arms!
The assault has been made ready
By traitorous mercenaries

> In the service of the nazis.
> To arms, people of Madrid!
> At your throat the claw of
> The great fascist beast
> Prepares to close.
> Men who aspire to life,
> Liberty and hope,
> Bread for your children
> And a peaceful tomorrow;
> Men of heroic Madrid
> Look out the window!
> The times are far from calm.
> Now, tonight or later,
> In the cold dawn,
> The fascist army
> Prepares to seize
> In one swift, murderous blow
> Spain's great capital, Madrid.
> I warn you, people of Madrid.
> I warn you, comrades,
> The Fifth Regiment
> Has sent me to warn you.
> These are the moments of decision,
> For the fate of our country.
> Quickly, very quickly, not a moment's delay!
> The rifles are waiting.
> To arms! To arms!

Singing the praise of Comrade Modesto, the Popular Army's first general, forged in the Fifth Regiment, first as commander of the Steel Battalions and later as commander of the Thaelmann Battalion, the poet Emilio Prados wrote:

> *To the Comrades of the Thaelmann Battalion*
>  *and to Modesto Guilloto, its Commander*
> ... There are a company of valiant men
> Who bring the sun with them to their battles,
> A sun out of the heart of the dawn,
> Their bayonets reflect its rays,
> They fly the flags of battles.

It is the Thaelmann Battalion. . . .
No drum came to summon them,
No rifles pointed at their doors,
But there's no drum or threat
Stronger than conscience;
Conscience aroused by bloodshed,
By the tongues of a thousand bells:
To arms! To arms!
The traitors are already on the march,
Their guns are blazing!
Their cannons are booming!
To arms! To arms!
With sickles, with knives,
With pitchforks, with muskets,
With teeth, with nails,
If there are no bullets, with stones,
If there are no rifles, with sticks,
If there are no barricades,
The bodies of our fallen comrades
Will build the first one.
Alien metal
Shatters our streets
And bloodies our fields.
Cast out the traitor
Who dares rise against Spain.
They cross Villalba among the junipers,
Tall oaks, gray stones;
They climb to Navacerrada;
There Bárzana waits;
And Modesto too is there,
Man of iron and stone,
Tender as a child,
A tiger in his strength.
Peguerinos, comrades,
Was taken, it is no longer ours!
And below, there's Talavera,
Menaced by the Moors.
Rise up, Thaelmann Battalion!
To the attack! We must surround it!

May our red star
Free Madrid
And stick like a spur
In the flanks of fascism
To drive it from our land.
You'll do it, comrades,
All Spain counts on you.
Good Communist Modesto,
Whose words proclaim the truth,
Modesto, my commander,
Father of iron and stone,
I know your militiamen
And the faith that drives them.
Now, in your new brigade,
The leaven rises
For the good bread of victory,
Made by the Thaelmann Battalion!

Miguel Hernández, the shepherd poet and soldier, killed by pain
and despair in a Franquist prison, persecuted by the hate of the
Falangists, who did not forgive him for his loyalty to the people,
wrote some 1,000 poems dedicated to the soldiers of the Republic.
The following poem vividly expresses his feelings toward the heroes
of the International Brigades, who fought and died for the liberty of
Spain.

If there are men with souls transcending borders,
With the broad brows of universal brothers,
With visions of horizons, ships and mountains,
Of sand and snow, you are such men.
Your native lands called you waving all their flags,
Your life's breath will bless the earth with monuments.
You came to stop the blood thirst of the panthers
Full tilt you hurled yourself against their fangs.
With the ardor of all the suns and all the seas,
Spain holds you close because you showed
The tree-like strength which spans the continents.
The olive trees will grow up through your bones,
And send down through the earth their firmest roots,
For you are universal men faithful to Man.

During the days of the defense of Madrid, popular songs wei
dedicated to the Communist Party and to the Fifth Regiment. Her
is a song first sung in the trenches of Madrid, later in all Loyalis
Spain:

> The Communist Party,
> First in battle,
> Formed the Fifth Regiment
> To defend Spain.
>
> The flower of Spain,
> The reddest flower of the people,
> Are with the four batallions
> Defending Madrid.
>
> Mother, mother,
> Look this way!
> Singing, our regiment
> Marches off.

## [29]

## Delegation to Paris

> *If there is a tree in Spain tinged with blood,*
> *It is the tree of liberty.*
> *If there is one mouth left to speak in Spain,*
> *It speaks of liberty.*
> —PAUL ELUARI

Because of the nonintervention policy, which was so damaging to
the Republican cause, the Popular Front named a committee which
was to journey to France to solicit aid from the various parties composing the French Popular Front and from the French government
itself.

Members of the delegation were José Salmerón, Marcelino Domingo, Recaséns Siches and myself. Señor Lara and, for part of the time, Señor Jiménez de Asúa, joined us in Paris.

We left Madrid at the end of August. This journey to the France of the Rights of Man, the France of the Revolution of 1848 and the Commune, was full of surprises; some agreeable, others—well, why speak of human weaknesses?

The trip to Barcelona through Valencia was uneventful. In the Catalan capital we stayed at the Hotel Colón, which was in the hands of the UGT's Hotel Union.

Shortly after our arrival, we paid a visit to the President of the Generalitat, Luis Companys. Valdés, secretary of organization of the PSUC, accompanied us. Companys received us cordially. We explained the object of our trip, and he wished us success in our mission.

We told him how surprised and troubled we were by the situation in Barcelona, where we saw no flags in the streets except the FAI's red and black banners; and also our concern about the persecution of Socialist and other left-wing workers who refused to accept Anarchist rule in Catalonia.

Companys agreed with our observations and reacted strongly: "What you say is true! But what do you want me to do? I'm surrounded by cowards who've joined the CNT because they're afraid. The FAI militia meddles in everything. I have to control the situation all by myself! And I can't go on much longer!"

One of our colleagues from the PSUC reminded him that he wasn't alone, that on his side were the PSUC and the UGT, willing to help him establish and maintain order.

Companys agreed that he did have the aid of the United Socialist Party of Catalonia and the UGT. He was an ardent patriot, a Catalan with a deep love for his people and his land. He warmly praised the Catalan workers and peasants. He told us of the conversion of Catalonia's industry to war production and the notable results produced in a relatively short time.

With his habitual nervousness, Companys opened a drawer and took out a small bottle of yellowish liquid. Holding it in his hand like a trophy, he said: "See for yourselves how much progress we've made in manufacturing war products. This is *trilita!*"

My colleagues looked at the bottle uneasily, perhaps confusing

"*trilita*" with nitroglycerine. Salmerón, a little hard of hearing, didn'
understand and nudged me with his elbow.

"What's he saying?"

"That's *trilita!*" I told him.

"Trilita?"

"Yes, *trilita!*"

It meant nothing to Salmerón. Companys put the bottle back i
the drawer. An air of calm settled on us all.

We said goodbye warmly and returned to the hotel. There w
found a surprise no less unpleasant than our first one. When we lef
Madrid, the Minister of State had given us diplomatic passport
But in Catalonia in 1936, there was no such thing as diplomati
courtesy. Our passports were worthless pieces of paper.

The FAI militia were in command in Barcelona, headed by th
Anarchist Escorza. This man, a hunchback and paralyzed, was
physical ruin. The only thing alive in him was his hatred of norma
persons. He would have liked to see all humanity deformed an
paralyzed like himself.

Doctor Trabal, a Catalan deputy, who was perpetually switchin
from the Right to the Left, and vice versa, came to tell us that w
had to send our passports to the FAI militia for our visas.

"The Anarchist militia issuing visas for diplomatic passports?"
asked astounded. "Why? Doesn't the Generalitat have its officials
Doesn't Catalonia have a government? Don't you see how absurd i
all is? We're going to France to tell the world that there is a legit
mate government in Spain, exercising its full powers, and we ou
selves negate it by carrying in our passports authorization to leav
issued by the FAI militia. I'm going to talk to the PSUC first."

My companions weren't in agreement. They were very nervous an
wanted to leave at any cost, even if it meant humiliation. Alone,
went to see the officials of the PSUC. They advised me to send m
passport to the FAI to avoid any problems, since the most importan
thing was to leave and to publicize abroad the nature of our struggl

A policeman took all our passports to the FAI's "diplomatic" de
partment. Within approximately one hour, Aurelio Fernández cam
to the hotel, accompanied by his "palace" guards. He was in charg
of the militia's Department of Investigation. He entered the smal
room where we were waiting for our passports as if it were his ow
home.

He looked at us with the air of a bully. "So you're going to Paris, eh?" he said.

My companions were silent. I answered for them: "Yes, to Paris. What of it?"

"Nothing, but it seems that there'll be some difficulty."

"Who'll make the difficulty, you?"

He didn't answer.

"Will we be able to leave the country or not?" I insisted.

"I don't know," he replied. "I only know that they keep a close watch on the border and inspect everyone's luggage very thoroughly."

"Everyone's?" I asked.

"Everyone's!" he said.

"Including those who leave to be on the safe side?" I insisted.

"What do you mean by that?" he asked uneasily.

"You know very well what I mean." I answered. No one else was speaking. Our dialogue was steeped in controlled hostility and must have sounded disastrous to my colleagues.

Fernández left a fat envelope on the table. "Here are your passports. I hope, friend Pasionaria," he said very slowly, savoring his words, "that we can continue our discussion when you return."

"Of course," I said, "we'll continue it, and we'll talk about the FAI's dictatorship, about the workers of the UGT Transport Union who are taken from their homes and killed, just as in the good old days of Bravo Portillo."

"Can you prove that workers of the UGT were assassinated?"

"I certainly can, and the families of those men can prove it even better than I."

He looked at me with murder in his eyes. He left with his guards, who looked as if they would have enjoyed taking me for a "ride."

"Why do you pay attention to those people?" said Marcelino Domingo. "We thought they wouldn't let us go. We'd better let Madrid know what happened."

"Don't worry," I assured him, "we'll leave."

Meanwhile, Fernández had notified the border police that we were coming and had given the order not to let us leave the country.

However, things turned out differently than he had planned. When our train arrived at the border station, we were met by railroad employees and workers, comrades from the PSUC, and other people who had learned of our arrival. Everyone came to the train to greet us, to tell us of their confidence in victory and to wish us success in our mission.

After talking a long time with the people in the station, we told them that we were worried lest the authorities wouldn't let us enter France. "Don't worry," everyone told us, "if necessary we'll get you a special train so you can arrive on time." With warm words, the workers shouted their faith in the triumph of the Republic, in the triumph of the people.

Finally, we left. Long live the Republic! Long live Catalonia! Long live the Popular Front! These were the last words we heard as we left Catalonia on our way to Paris.

Our arrival in the French capital caused some excitement. The press controlled by the "two hundred families" demanded our expulsion. The hatred of all the right-wing newspapers was especially aimed at me.

We were in our hotel only two days when the owner threw us out. It's true he did it courteously, begging a thousand pardons, but, he told us, *La Croix du Feu* (Cross of Fire, French fascists) had threatened to attack the hotel and ruin him. He was terribly sorry for "*madame*" (me) but he had no other choice.

We moved to a hotel near the Spanish Embassy. That same day I received a warning from *La Croix du Feu* ordering me to leave France. "If you don't," the note said, "we have ways to stop you from making propaganda for Republican Spain in France."

I showed the note to our comrades of the French Communist Party, who denounced the incident in the pages of *l'Humanité*. They also protested to the Minister of Interior and intensified their campaign in favor of the Spanish Republic.

At that time, the Spanish Ambassador in France was the "jurist" Alvaro de Albornoz, who had been a candidate for election with me in Asturias. I never really knew how Spain's diplomats functioned abroad. I must admit I was deeply disillusioned when I saw our ambassador in action. He was more a decorative figurehead than a representative of a people at war.

With Albornoz was Fernando de los Ríos, a former Socialist minister. He and Otero, also a Socialist deputy, were in charge of purchasing arms and equipment for the Republic.

As de los Rios stroked his seraphic beard with his right hand and hooked the thumb of his left hand in the armhole of his vest, he lamented: "Who would have thought that I would be here buying arms so that men can kill each other!"

I stared at him for a long time, not knowing whether to laugh or cry. I thought: "Who was the idiot that gave this job to a sister of charity?"

The switchboard operator of the Spanish Embassy in Paris had worked for the Monarchist Ambassador Quiñones de León. Thus, every communication to and from the embassy was known by the enemy long before it reached the Republican government, or the ambassador himself. The person in charge of sending and receiving coded messages, that is, the man who had all the government instructions, all the embassy secrets, in his hands, was also a monarchist.

And if it was not bad enough to have enemies working in the embassy, it was even worse to have an ambassador who hadn't the slightest idea of his duties as a representative of a people and a country engaged in a terrible war to prevent the spread of fascism in Europe. His face was a sight to behold when we suggested that the embassy carry on propaganda work for the cause of the Republic. Alvaro's opinion was that the ambassador could not "intervene in these matters. Like the President of the Republic, the ambassador is to a certain extent a moderating power above all partisan strife."

With such an idea of his role as a representative of a country at war and a war as special as ours, enemies were completely free to attack the Republic in most of the French press without opposition, except for the ardent defense of the Spanish people in the pages of l'Humanité, the organ of the French Communist Party.

Two days after our arrival in Paris, our French comrades and representatives of other popular organizations organized a mass meeting in the Winter Velodrome so that the members of our committee could inform the French people of the true situation in Spain and the nature of our battle.

As it turned out, the members of our delegation were extremely "sensitive" persons. In a previous meeting with the French comrades, our own committee members had suggested organizing some public appearances. Everyone agreed. But—those accursed "buts" that blight our lives—our French comrades hadn't realized that there were "important personalities" in our committee and that they had to "invite" them to speak in a demonstration in favor of the Republic. They assumed that our mutual conversation was enough invitation. But they forgot protocol!

Tens of thousands of people came to the first meeting. And the men that the Popular Front of Spain had sent to France to enlist aid in defense of the Republic refused to speak because they had not been officially invited!

The meeting was an impressive demonstration of the solidarity of the French people with their fellowmen in Spain. Without bothering about the protocol that so worried my traveling companions, I spoke, if not in the name of the committee, then in the name of those we had left fighting in Somosierra and Guadarrama, in the name of all who were sincerely fighting to prevent the enthronement of fascism in Spain.

And the Paris of the workers, democratic Paris, the Paris of the Commune and the Popular Front—the Paris where, inspired by our close comrade Maurice Thorez, who was always on our side ready to help us, groups of volunteers left France to fight in Spain against fascism, which also threatened their country—this Paris rose like one person, with one will and one demand: "Cannons and airplanes for Spain!"

After the meeting that shout extended in a wave of solidarity through all France: "Cannons and airplanes for Spain!"

The next day, when the other members of the committee read in all the newspapers of the success of the meeting, they were terribly unhappy. They hadn't realized how intense and warm were the feelings of the French people for Spain! They had refused to participate in the meeting because deep inside they thought that this first demonstration would be a failure!

They never had a chance to participate in any further mass meetings afterwards because the French reactionaries were so frightened by the success of the French people's first public demonstration of solidarity and their clamorous demands for cannons and airplanes, that we were unable to organize another meeting.

We visited many people and were received cordially by all. Practical results? None.

After many attempts by Jiménez de Asúa, our committee was finally received by the Social-Democrat Léon Blum, prime minister of the French government. I have never had a feeling so strange as that which came over me when I met Blum, the most important

man in the French Socialist Party. I felt a moral and physical revulsion, an instinctive class shudder at the thought that this was the
man who represented the French working class which had written
the immortal pages of the Commune.

With a languid voice, as if it were an effort to speak, he asked us
the object of our visit. Marcelino Domingo gave him an accurate
general idea of the Republic's situation. Jiménez de Asúa told him of
the importance of the struggle in Spain.

Blum began to speak in a hesitant voice: He wanted to help
Spain . . . but he couldn't. . . . It would mean war. . . . He was a
pacifist. . . . Nothing could be done. . . . He was suffering. . . . Besides, the war in Spain was a civil war. . . . France couldn't intervene.
. . . France would get into difficulties.

I answered him sharply: "Our war, Mr. Blum, is not a simple civil
war, but a war in defense of the peace and liberty of Europe. If you
refuse to aid Spain, if you let the Spanish people suffer defeat, France
will have to face war under the worst of conditions."

Blum sighed. He covered his eyes with his long spindly fingers.
Was he crying? With an elegant silk handkerchief he dried an im-
aginary tear. We rose to leave. We couldn't expect anything from the
French Socialists nor from the government. Marcelino Domingo
turned to me silently. I understood him.

In our attempt to do the best job of publicizing our resistance
movement, we decided to travel to Brussels, where we expected to
find at least the Socialist Party supporting our battle. We were too
naive; we didn't know what size hats the leaders of the Belgian
Socialist Party were wearing.

We were an official delegation of the Spanish government. But, oh!
these ghosts of Socialists, servants of the Belgian monarchy and
bourgeoisie! The Republican government represented the Spanish
people, it was a plebeian government with no famous corporation
lawyers, no representatives of the landed aristocracy. The aristocracy
were on the side of Franco, so were the big bourgeoisie, the Church,
Hitler and Mussolini, the petroleum magnates, the British and
Americans. What status did we miserable beings have, who dared
incur the wrath of the great powers by attempting to stop fascism
when it tried to force our people to their knees and make Europe a
base for Hitler's dreams of power?

The Belgian Socialists received us courteously but coldly, making it plain that we had no business in their country.

Nevertheless, they could not openly flout the feelings of the Belgian working class, which with all its heart was on the side of the Spanish people. To close the Conference for Universal Peace, a huge meeting was organized in the Brussels Stadium. We were invited to attend, and one of our committee was asked to speak. A sizeable delegation from the Belgian Socialist Party, headed by the apostle Vandervelde, attended.

There is a saying that silence is golden. That's just what we were told in Belgium some moments before the meeting. When the stadium was packed with people, the venerable Socialsit apostle told us, putting his ear trumpet in place to hear our answer, that it would be unnecessary for us to speak that night "since our silence would be much more eloquent than our words."

Marcelino Domingo, who was supposed to speak, didn't know what to say in answer to such an outrageous statement. Our struggle had received a good swift kick from an old mule. This was perhaps the last good turn Vandervelde would be doing for Belgian reaction.

After the meeting, the apostle invited us to take tea in his elegant apartment together with a group of his friends, where we proceeded to make a huge social blunder. We greeted his wife who was 40 years younger than he as his daughter. And we greeted his mother-in-law as his wife. I still laugh when I remember the confusion it produced.

"Mais non, mais non! Celle-ci c'est ma femme, celle-là ma belle-mère."

As our knowledge of French was less than elementary, although our delegation included a university professor, a teacher and a lawyer, Vandervelde's wife served as interpretor. She had lived many years in Argentina, where she had learned Spanish. She was most cordial and affectionate with us, as if wanting to make up for her husband's attitude.

Before leaving Belgium, the French Communist Party told me that Vicente Uribe had called from Madrid to inform me that a new government had been formed under Largo Caballero. The Communist Party had two ministers in the new cabinet. Knowing the party's opinion on this matter, I realized how grave the situation must be if our comrades had agreed to participate in the government.

Uneasy, I tried to persuade the delegation to end the trip. They insisted on going to England, New Zealand, the United States—anywhere but Spain.

Finally, one morning I said goodbye to them and returned to Madrid alone. Salmerón returned a few days later. Lara remained in Paris. Marcelino Domingo and Recaséns Siches went to America. Domingo died in exile still dreaming of Spain.

[30]

# Why the Communists Entered the Government

So many lies have been perpetrated about the events in Spain before and after the military fascist rebellion; by force of repetition the lies have too often been accepted as truths.

Did the Communist Party want to participate in the Largo Caballero government in the beginning of September 1936?

Decidedly not. At the time of the Popular Front victory in the elections of February 1936 the party was in favor of forming a government which would include representatives of all the political parties in the Popular Front; after the uprising, all the efforts of the Communists were directed to supporting the Republican government and to stopping the political machinations of its enemies.

The position taken by the Communist Party was fundamentally different from that adopted by the Socialist Party. After the electoral victory of the Popular Front, the Socialists under Largo Caballero, who never forgave the Republicans for ousting the Socialists in 1933, opposed the formation of a Popular Front government. Largo was hoping that Republican governments would fail—a very real possibility, if they lacked the support of the various working-class parties —and that the President would ask the Socialists to form a government.

Out of Republican defeat the Socialist Party expected to realize its dream of forming a basically Socialist government or one led by the Socialists, with a Socialist majority. This was what happened in

September 1936, at the beginning of the war. The Socialists themselves forced the issue by threatening the President: "Either you ask the Socialist Party to form a new government or the Socialists will withdraw from the Popular Front."

In spite of the decision of the Socialists, the Communist Party maintained its position of supporting the authority of the government, putting all the instrumentalities of action into its hands and ending the duplication of efforts and waste of resources which inevitably resulted when organizations and parties were each a small government in themselves.

To resolve the dilemma posed by the Socialist leaders, and to prevent even the hint of a split in the Republican camp, the Communists reluctantly agreed to participate in the government. At the same time, it would continue its fight against the untenable positions and extravagant concepts which were causing great damage to the Republic and making it very difficult to carry on the resistance movement.

For example: The fact that the militia had stopped the advance of the insurgents on Madrid led many people, including Largo Caballero himself, to conclude that a Republican army was unnecessary. They overlooked the fact that this had happened not only because of the heroism of the militiamen, but also because of the enemy's weaknesses at the time. They opposed the organization of a regular army (although officially there was a decree authorizing its establishment) using arguments that were extremely oversimplified, such as that Spain was a nation of guerrillas; that it was with guerrillas and militiamen, not with a regular army, that Spain could defeat an insurgent army even when it was re-enforced with Italian military units and German technicians and supplies.

In the event of an invasion, guerrillas, supported by a national army, can play an important role, although not a decisive one. In the conditions of Spain in 1936, Spain's first and most urgent need was to organize its combat forces and create a regular army.

One day at the front would be enough to convince anyone of the need for a regular army. Every militiaman, every Republican soldier, occupied the post he thought most useful to the resistance, and abandoned his post when he thought that it wasn't the best place to be in, or when his ammunition ran out, or when enemy bullets put him out of combat.

Those who opposed the creation of an army refused to see that the lack of experienced commanders and technical material was handicapping the inexpert militia units. Their determination and heroism were not enough to enable them to withstand the severe blows of the enemy. Little by little they were ceding ground and abandoning their positions. The Republican successes in the first weeks of fighting conclusively showed the need for an army, since "miracles" could not go on happening indefinitely, especially with an enemy who could keep renewing his troops and supplies.

The formation of a new government in September 1936, with the participation of the Communist Party, was greeted enthusiastically by the people, particularly by the combatants. They viewed Communist participation as a guarantee that their efforts and sacrifices would not be in vain.

The Largo Caballero government had aroused great expectations in the masses. Were these to be illusory?

The situation grew more tense every day. Badajoz was lost to the enemy, and the insurgents were marching on Talavera under the command of Colonel Yagüe. They received scant resistance from the militia, who were demoralized by the lack of adequate arms in the face of the enemy's technical and military superiority.

Under the Giral government, the militia had been able to check the insurgent's advance on the capital from the north, when the rebels were marching through Alto de León, Somosierra and Navacerrada. Now the Largo Caballero government had to confront the enemy offensive in the south. This time the enemy was better prepared, with fresh and experienced troops, in high spirits because of their victories in Badajoz and Mérida—achieved with the aid of Portugal.

The resistance in Talavera was broken, and the enemy marched through the streets of Oropesa. They surrounded a church where a group of United Socialist Youth militiamen, led by Andrés Martín, held out to the last man, turning the church into the scene of their heroism and loyalty to the Republic—and their tomb.

The loss of Talavera and Oropesa was aggravated by the situation in Toledo. When the insurgents in Toledo found they couldn't resist the onslaught of the people, they had sought refuge in the Alcázar, taking along with them hundreds of hostages, many of them women and children.

The Republican government undertook to negotiate with the rebels in the fortress for the safe release of the hostages. Colonel Moscardó, who was in command of the Alcázar and who maintained radio communication with the rebel army advancing from the south, refused to let anyone leave the fortress. He prolonged the negotiations, stalling for time to give his friends a chance to arrive and extricate him. In its efforts to end the siege of the Alcázar, the Republican government used Colonel Moscardó's son, who was said to have been taken prisoner. This attempt, like the others, failed.

What happened to Moscardó's son? Who arrested him? Who was responsible for his disappearance? The answers to these questions were not clear at the time and they still remain a mystery. As on other occasions, attempts were made to blame the Communists for deeds which others had engineered. Communists are revolutionaries and not criminals.

The FAI militia were having a "camping party" in Toledo instead of trying to eliminate the resistance of the rebels in the Alcazar. Under the black-and-red banners flying over Toledo's marvellous monuments and buildings, the Anarchists had turned the city into a cross between Sodom and Gomorrha, practicing the so-called libertarian communism which the Anarchists offered Spanish workers as a foretaste of the "ideal" future society.

In the middle of September the situation in Toledo was critical. The loss of Toledo, so near the capital, was one of the hardest blows which could have hit the Republic at that moment.

On behalf of the Communist Party, José Díaz and Enrique Líster asked Largo Caballero to order the Fifth Regiment to defend the historic city in order to end the situation created there by the Anarchists and to protect Madrid from the danger which the loss of Toledo would entail.

Largo flatly refused. Only in extremis, when the enemy was at Toledo's doors and it was lost to the Republic, were some forces of the Fifth Regiment sent in. Their first concern was the evacuation of the wounded. There was no transportation available. The FAI heroes had taken all the cars and trucks with them in their flight from the enemy.

Hundreds of wounded who had been taken to Toledo from other places were evacuated to Levante and other provinces in whatever transportation could be found. Under these conditions the most seriously wounded could not be moved. Adequate transportation was promised but it never arrived.

When the Moroccan army entered Toledo a short while later, the wounded and all medical personnel were knifed to death. Toledo lived days of horror and bloodshed, days when human ferocity had no limit. The rebels in the Alcazar, released from the weeks of anguish and fear in the fortress, wreaked bloody vengeance on the defenseless population for their defeat in the first days of the war.

Old differences over the basic problems of a democratic revolution dissolved in the heat of the war. The centuries-old conflict between feudal and democratic Spain was in process of being resolved as the new government began to function.

If the achievements of the Popular Front government, led by Largo Caballero, with Communist participation, had been fully realized in 1931, the fascist rising would never have taken place.

The Basque Country was granted its autonomy. For the first time, Euzkadi had its own government. And also for the first time in traditional and uncompromising Spain, Catholic forces such as the Basque Nationalists collaborated with left-wing elements to form a government led by the Nationalists with the participation of Republicans and Communists.

The granting of autonomy to Euzkadi, while failing to satisfy all the national political aspirations of the Basque people, was nevertheless a great step forward in that direction. It also assured the Republic the political support of the Basques, as well as contributions from its iron and steel industry to the Republic's war needs.

The most crucial of all Spain's problems, which preceding Republican governments had failed to solve both in 1931 and 1933, was that of land. Agrarian reform which would eliminate the huge feudal estates and give the land to those who worked it was imperative. This would guarantee the country's food supply and create a solid base for the domestic market.

The Largo Caballero government had hardly taken office when, in a cabinet meeting, Vicente Uribe presented a proposal based on the needs of the peasants and the country. Strong opposition within the cabinet to the Communist minister's proposal obliged us to modify the original plan. But even in this form it constituted a great democratic and revolutionary advance in the solution of Spain's agrarian problem.

The agrarian reform gave the land of the large landowners involved in the fascist conspiracy to the peasants in permanent usufruct. At the same time, the Minister of Education presented another proposal, which opened the institutes and universities to workers. Under this program, the government helped the workers finance their studies.

These measures were approved without any objections by President Azaña. This proved that even the ideas of men who are most strongly against radical reforms in the country's political and economic structures can evolve and change when the masses' demands are sufficiently loud to be heard.

In keeping with its position of defending the Republic and democracy, the Communist Party had from the start of the war firmly opposed the distortion of the nature of the war by the Trotskyite and FAIist groups. With the support of the peasants, the party fought against the pseudorevolutionary projects of those who took the peasants' land and belongings and forcibly herded them into Anarchist cooperatives. The agrarian reform, based on the proposal of the Communist Party and signed by the President of the Republic, brought to an end many of the abuses of the unprincipled libertarian experiments of revolutionary adventurers at large in the Spanish countryside.

A battle against illiteracy was launched by Comrade Wenceslao Roces, Under-secretary of Education. Volunteer militiamen taught the illiterate peasants in their batallions how to read and write. Measures were taken to protect small businessmen and to eliminate the system of taxes imposed by the Anarchist "caudillos."

For the first time, and on a mass scale, children and nursing mothers received medical attention and services under a program organized by Comrade Juan Planelles, Under-secretary of Health.

The Spanish Republic, which at the beginning of the war was a democratic bourgeois republic, in the course of the war was transformed into a popular democratic republic of a new kind. Conserving private property, the state took over the direction of the great industrial companies, the banks and transportation in all Spain, except in the Basque Country. It confiscated the lands of the large landowners supporting Franco and formed voluntary cooperatives and associations of workers and peasants supported by the state.

# Freedom of Conscience

In keeping with its political position and its stand on the nature of the war, the Communist Party attempted, insofar as was possible, to uphold freedom of religion and to refute the absurd idea that everyone who was a Catholic was *ipso facto* a fascist. Thus the Communist Party did everything it could to normalize the life of the people, even if it meant incurring the wrath of the charlatan Trotskyites and FAIists.

The party did what others had failed to do. It worked to protect the nuns who, for one reason or another, were undergoing hardship in our zone. There were more than a hundred nuns in the Madrid women's prison who were more "retained" than detained and lived under penurious conditions.

They had been taken from their convents to the prison, in some cases as a security measure to prevent rash actions, and in others because the convents had been taken under the protection of the state or of Popular Front organizations. For the most part, the nuns did not have families or friends in Madrid, and if they had, they were probably not in any condition to come to their rescue. The Communists took the initiative of ending that situation, offering these women an opportunity to lead a normal existence in which they could continue their religious activities.

The party leaders decided to entrust me with this task. With the Justice Ministry's authorization for their release, I went to the prison. The head matron gave me permission to speak with the sisters, who were assembled in a large room. When I appeared in the doorway, they thought I was a new prisoner and began to lament my arrest and to console me.

Gently I explained that I wasn't a prisoner. I asked them to move to a larger hall where I could speak more freely and propose something of interest to them. They did as I asked, not very willingly, since my request must have seemed strange. I began by introducing myself. I never imagined that my name would produce such an impression on those nuns. What tremendous lies about Communists, especially about me, had they been told to make these poor women feel their last hour had come?

Calming them, I explained our plans, which were to release them from prison and take them to the huge empty Augustine convent. There, each community could establish itself independently, and live according to the rules of their respective orders. If they wished, the nuns could embroider or make articles of clothing for the children and families evacuated from rebel-held zones. With the aid of the government we promised to guarantee them food and their safety. A guard would be stationed in the convent to prevent anyone from bothering them.

They hesitated a long time, until three of them decided: "We'll go with you," they said.

I assured them that nothing untoward would happen, and we left the prison. They were cloistered nuns. Since entering the convent, they had never seen the outside world. Everything surprised them. As we were driving through Madrid, I commented on each of the places we passed and explained the causes and origin of the war that was ravaging our country.

We arrived at the Augustine convent and explored it from basement to attic, inspecting the kitchens, dormitories, libraries and studies. The church was just as its former occupants had left it. Nothing broken, no litter; obviously, the FAI had not passed through there.

Later, I took them to see the palace of the Dukes of Alba, which had been taken over by the Fifth Regiment. The palace servants had remained to take care of the building, so everything was spotless and intact. The staff remained there until fascist airplanes destroyed the magnificent building.

The nuns picked some flowers, after I had convinced them that it wasn't a sin and that we had the permission of the palace employees. We returned to the prison so they could describe our excursion to the other nuns of their order, who were waiting anxiously, fearing that I had kidnapped or mistreated them.

I returned to party headquarters and informed our comrades of what had happened. Everyone was satisfied with the outcome of my mission. We invited the Basque delegation to discuss the problem of supplying household linen and all the other items that a group of nuns belonging to different orders with different rules and ways of life would need. The next day, in the party headquarters which was now in the former office of Popular Action, we discussed practical ways to help the nuns, many of whom were aged and unable to work.

Because of the deterioration in Madrid's situation, I had to divert my energies to other aspects of the war. I left the task of taking care of the nuns to the Basque Nationalists. "God knows," as the saying goes, we did everything we could to help them.

This was not the first time that the Communists had aided the nuns, despite the party's reputation for being "priest-killers"—one of the many slanders invented by the reactionaries.

One day in September, a group from the Fifth Regiment which was looking for a building in the Salamanca district to set up its headquarters discovered that a religious community was hiding in one of the houses. They were leading a terrible existence, caught between the hope of survival and the fear of being condemned to a horrible death if they were discovered—which, according to fascist propaganda, was what would be in store for them.

The women were stunned when they opened the door and saw the men of the Fifth Regiment. The soldiers tried to convince the nuns that they weren't looking for them, that they had run into them by chance and that their lives were in no danger. The men put a notice on the door declaring that the house was under the protection of the Fifth Regiment.

They told me of the encounter and asked me to visit the nuns so that we could help them and allay their fears. The next day, I and another comrade knocked at the door with a document that guaranteed the occupants against molestation from the FAI or the notorious "dawn brigades," about which certain respectable Socialist gentlemen might be able to testify.

A modestly dressed woman about 50 years old opened the door. When we asked if this was the place where a religious community was living, the poor woman shook visibly. To end her uneasiness, we told her we came in behalf of the Fifth Regiment. She let us into an utterly bare room. Not one chair, no pictures, nothing to indicate the presence of a religious community. I asked her to call the rest of the nuns. They came quickly, all fearful at the unexpected visit. There were 20 to 25 women of different ages, all dressed shabbily.

"Forgive us for the intrusion," I said. "We've come to help you. I think we should introduce ourselves first. Although it may sound vain, I'm sure you've all heard of me and I'm sure that from all the stories you've heard of how evil I am, you all think I'm the devil himself. But please be calm, nothing will happen to you. I'm La Pasionaria."

The nuns looked at me horror-stricken, trembling as if an electric current had passed through the room. La Pasionaria!—that symbol of all horrors, all abominations!

"Let's forget about the stupid stories you've heard and talk like normal people. Since yesterday you have been under the protection of the Fifth Regiment, which means that no one will dare harm you. However, I would like to make the proposal that you all work, do something useful, that you help us in some way that is not opposed to your religious sentiments."

A woman, apparently the Mother Superior, spoke: "We could work in the hospitals caring for the sick and wounded."

"I'm sorry, sister, but you can't work in the hospitals. The wounded soldiers wouldn't accept it."

"Then we can look after the children."

"Not that either, because mothers wouldn't trust you with their children."

"Well, what can we do then?"

"Something much simpler, which will keep you together and help you through your difficulties. You can make clothes, little jackets, bonnets and shoes for evacuated children, for the orphans and the abandoned children, right here in this house. We'll come to pick up the clothes and help you get all the material you need so you won't have to go and walk around the city."

They all agreed, and asked when they could start working.

"Tomorrow. I'll bring you everything you need to start."

Before going, I asked them: "Don't you have any statues or crucifixes? I'm sure there are sisters here who are devotees of the Sorrowful Virgin, the Virgin of Carmen or the Miraculous Virgin. How would you like it if I also bring you some pictures and a crucifix tomorrow?"

They looked at me not knowing what to answer. They thought I was mocking them or preparing some diabolical scheme.

"As you like," the Mother Superior finally answered.

We left, positive that the women had not believed a word we said and were still terrified as they waited to see what would happen to them the following day.

We spent the morning in the shops buying wool, percale and white cotton fabrics. In a children's asylum on a nearby street which had been bombed, we found a beautiful crucifix and several religious images. We took them, carefully packed, to our new acquaintances.

Surprise took their breath away. When they unwrapped the crucifix and gave it to the Mother Superior, she looked at it with eyes full of tears, kissed the image's feet and passed it around to the other nuns. "God bless you!" she said as we left.

We promised to call for the finished work when they notified us. We gave them the address and telephone number of one of the party offices, in case they should ever need us in some emergency or difficulty. More than once they came to us for aid and they always found our comrades respectful and cordial.

While I was busy with the task of easing life for hundreds of nuns, the fascist Parisian newspaper *Gringoire*, on September 19, 1936, among other sensational "news," published a biography of me that made Frankenstein sound like a good-natured, innocent child.

"La Pasionaria," said *Gringoire*, "although of Spanish blood, is nevertheless an unspeakable person. A former nun, she married an unfrocked monk. Hence her hatred for all religious orders. She is famous for having leaped on an unfortunate priest in broad daylight and having torn open his jugular vein with her teeth."

This was the way the history of our war and of Communist activities in particular was written and is still written today by certain corrupt historians peddling baseless slanders.

Naturally, I ignored these filthy attacks. Every time I received the brutal insults of some silk- or burlap-clad boor—and these were not infrequent—I remembered the words of Turgenev, a great Russian novelist:

"The insults of swine's feet," he wrote referring to the kicks inflicted on Don Quixote by a herd of pigs, "occur in the lives of all Quixotes precisely before they come to their end. This is the last tribute they must receive from the casual gross remark, from the outrageous or insensitive lack of comprehension. It is the pharisee's blow. After this, the Quixotes can die peacefully."

During those first days of the war, one of the convents that aroused our curiosity because of the social service it performed was the Convent of Domestic Service, founded for "the protection of girls who arrived in the capital looking for work."

When I discovered that the nuns of this convent had fled after the rising, and that the militia had occupied the buildings, we went there to see if they could be used for the temporary housing of families deprived of homes by the war. When we arrived we found that a small group of girls had remained behind.

At first the girls were reticent and reserved. But when they saw we were friendly, they opened up and talked of their sad lives, devoid of illusion and hope, eternally chained to the convent which gave them work and showed them the way to "paradise." They spoke of the cruelty of some nuns, the kindness of others, and the employment of some girls in some sort of work—what it was they didn't know.

They told us of one girl, whom they depicted as a terrible person, who was treated with much consideration by the nuns and visitors to the convent. No one knew where she worked. It seemed it was at some kind of an office where, they were told, other girls could also have jobs and enjoy a secure future if they proved themselves to be docile, faithful and willing to study and work.

As we were speaking, the girl they had spoken of appeared in the doorway. She turned away abruptly when she saw us and realized we recognized her.

"Impossible! We know that girl. She's a student?" we asked.

"Yes, a student like ourselves. A domestic service student. There's her bed and her closet," the girls said, pointing to a corner of the room.

The girl was pale and nervous.

"Are the girls telling the truth? Do you live here?"

"I'll tell you the truth. Is it so impossible to be a student and live here in the convent?"

"Of course, it's possible. What we're interested in is what you are giving in return. Perhaps you were hiding something behind your disguise as a student?"

We certainly did know that "student." But we knew her not as a domestic service girl, but as a Communist. We discovered that she had enrolled in the university with false papers, with the help of a professor.

Her admission to the university was the first act in the tragicomedy she was forced to play. The girl, of humble origin, was led to believe that she soon would become a Spanish Joan of Arc. To show that she was doing her job of infiltrating the communist organization, she took the brother of the founder of the Falange, Fernando Primo de Rivera, whom no one knew, to the office of the Madrid provincial committee, where she had worked after she left the "university." Accompanied by the "Communist" student, young Primo de Rivera had free access to all the party offices as a "comrade."

When they planted their "student" in the party organization, the fascists not only wanted to know the party's inside activities, they were also preparing attempts against the lives of Communist leaders. According to her own confession, the fascists had considered "eliminating" me on several occasions. But assassinating a woman, even if she were a Communist, was too risky a business even for gentlemen who understood only "the dialectics of the pistol."

However, if the assassination were committed by a woman, then everything was permissible, even the most flagrant acts. As a matter of fact, without knowing it, I had foiled their first attempt against my life. It happened at the funeral of Lieutenant Castillo, who was murdered by the Falangists.

A group of comrades and I were waiting for the arrival of the funeral cortège when the girl "student," carrying her inseparable handbag, came over to us. After exchanging a few words, she suggested I take a car, since we had to walk a long way in the stifling heat. I refused her suggestion. "I have good feet," I told her, "and the heat doesn't bother me."

When we began to walk, I lost sight of her in the crowd. Very shortly thereafter, I noticed two women behind me. They were two plain, robust women, with a determined air and firm gait. At first, I attached no importance to them. But then I noticed that when I walked fast, they also walked fast; when I turned to the left, they were right behind me; and when I went to the right, there they were again! If they hadn't been obviously humble women, I certainly wouldn't have tolerated their "company." Nevertheless, I was getting more suspicious with each moment.

We left the cemetery, and they continued right behind me. At this point the "student" appeared again, repeating her invitation.

"Let's take a car, Dolores, you're tired."

"I'm used to walking," I said. "I don't need a car. I'll go with the comrades."

"And you're doing the right thing," said a voice behind me. "You're one of ours and you'll walk with us."

I turned and my leaping heart subsided. My two shadows greeted me warmly.

"You were worried about us walking behind you, weren't you?"

"Yes! I don't understand why you never left me for one second."

"Very simple," said one of them. "There are a lot of good-for-nothings here and we wanted to protect your back. If anyone had come near you to try something, he'd never live to regret it. Look!" she took a knife from her pocket, one of those weapons well-known for inflicting mortal wounds.

"Don't think I'm joking. I've spent three years in the Alcala prison for cracking the head of an uncle of mine who thought he could enjoy himself at my expense when I was down and out." She told me her sad story, which was like that of so many women in our country.

I thanked the women for their protection. They gave me their address and I promised to visit them. The next morning, with two other comrades, I went to their house. They were fish vendors, whose life was hard and rough. They scarcely made enough to live on. The house, if you could call that hovel with a tinsheet roof and walls made of crates a house, belonged to them, as well as the burro they used to carry their fish to other districts, a goat and some rabbits. This was their whole fortune, which they promptly offered to us.

"If the party needs it, we'll give everything we own. We can do without these things."

"We thank you very much, but the party doesn't demand unnecessary sacrifices."

"Ah! but we'll not only give these, we'll give our lives for the party if necessary."

The sincerity of those two simple women determined to make any sacrifice for the party was impressive.

When we were leaving, they asked us to go with them to see a friend of theirs who lived in the same neighborhood. They told us why on the way. They wanted to get even with some anti-Communists who lived in that district by showing them how Communist deputies went to the homes of workers, while their own deputies, after asking for their votes, never remembered them. We laughed at their ingenuousness and after visiting their friend, we said good-bye.

"Come back soon," they said. "We'll go to all the party meetings and we'll be near you always."

And so they were. At all the party activities, there they were in the first row, firm, attentive and alert, accompanying me at every moment.

[32]

# The Defense of Madrid

With Talavera and Toledo lost, the only possible points of resistance to the enemy advance on the capital were the towns near Madrid. The militiamen were not equipped to handle the defense of these points. The Moroccan cavalry, far outnumbering them, committed atrocities and razed the towns and fields.

Our party leaders met to discuss the grave matter of the defense of Madrid. Come what might, at any cost, Madrid must be defended. Madrid was not to fall into the hands of the insurgents. It was clear to all of us that the key to victory for the Republic was in the defense of Madrid. And we put all our efforts in explaining this to the people and the government.

The people understood and supported our efforts. In the face of the delays and vacillations of those who believed it was impossible to defend an open city like Madrid, we called on the people to build barricades. Setting the example, we were the first to wield the picks and shovels and surround Madrid with a belt of barricades. Every day thousands of men and women, young and old, even children, joined us in digging trenches and antitank ditches, building a defensive belt around our beloved Madrid. The Fifth Regiment acted as the party's right hand in organizing the defense of the capital.

But defending Madrid would be no easy task without an army and adequate weapons to face up to one of the best equipped armies in Europe. Only the will of the people, the decision and determination of the masses to defend the capital to the last stone, to the last man, could save the city.

The Communist Party and the Fifth Regiment put all their efforts into kindling the will to fight and the spirit of sacrifice in the combatants, transmitting to them our own determination. The United Socialist Youth joined us in these efforts and out of their ranks came countless fighting heroes.

The enemy circle was tightening around Madrid. There was fighting in University City; part of the Clinical Hospital was held by the militia and part by the insurgents. The Casa de Velázquez, which had been set on fire during the fighting, fell into enemy hands. The militiamen blew it up, thus destroying a rebel vantage point in Madrid.

The trenches and barricades that the Ministry of War and its advisers had refused to build because they considered trench-fighting "unmilitary" now had to be constructed in a hurry and under the fire of enemy artillery and machine guns.

Commenting on the government's blindness to the need for digging trenches and continuing to engage in the type of fighting carried on in the Middle Ages—face-to-face with the visor up—an antifascist combatant, a former officer of the German Army, the writer Ludwig Renn, wrote to the militiamen in the columns of *Mundo Obrero*, October 26, 1936: "The soldier in a trench need not fear enemy airplanes or cavalry. A tank can hardly harm you if you're in a trench. It is not cowardly to throw yourself on the ground in the heat of battle. A good soldier must guard his life well, since only live men can continue fighting."

Thousands of women and children were evacuated from Madrid to Levante. They were a source of constant worry to the authorities and to the combatants since they would be the first victims in case the situation deteriorated.

During the entire month of October, the Fifth Regiment was feverishly organizing the defense of the city. On October 9, in a speech made to the commissars of the Fifth Regiment to prepare them politically for the resistance, Líster called on the people to defend the capital:

"We must organize the defense of Madrid, make Madrid the tomb of fascism and the beginning of a great general offensive of our forces against the insurgents in all Spain." He called for "the strictest iron discipline. Lack of discipline leads to retreat, to breaks in the ranks. It engenders cowardice; it is the cause of defeat. Whoever breaks discipline is a provocateur in the service of the enemy. He is a traitor who eases the work of the fifth column. All the people of Madrid should take part in the fortification of the city. The Fifth Regiment will occupy the positions of greatest danger. Fascism shall not pass!"

Each day the Fifth Regiment's newspaper, Popular Militia, published more urgent appeals to the populace: "Every house a fortress! Every street a trench! Every neighborhood a wall of iron and combatants!"

On November 2, 1936, in view of the gravity of the situation, the Communist Party published a manifesto calling on combatants and the people in general to give their utmost in defense of Madrid, now "the most coveted prey of the enemy" and "the heart of Republican Spain." It called upon the Communists especially: "To the front lines to defend Madrid! We, more than anyone else, Comrades, are duty-bound to be the first in every effort and sacrifice, in shedding our last drop of blood in defense of the cause of liberty, the cause of the people." It urged nationwide aid to Madrid: "Let us save Madrid and we shall save Spain. . . . Madrid will be invincible, because its men and its women will make it so!"

The enemy was tightening its net around Madrid. The militiamen never showed the least sign of wavering. In three months of resistance, the Spanish people had matured politically. New values emerged and great figures that the revolutionary surge had carried into the limelight of the political scene in 1931 could now be recognized in their true stature.

Because of the imminent attack on the capital, the government moved to Valencia, leaving behind a Junta of Defense with General Miaja as president. Participating in the new junta were the representatives of all Popular Front parties and organizations. The Communist Party constituted the backbone of the junta, and was represented by Antonio Mije, Diéguez and Yagüe; Santiago Carrillo and José Cazorla represented the Socialist Youth, acting in coordination with the Fifth Regiment.

The junta was in charge of evacuating persons and the nation's art treasures. Thanks to its activities, many priceless objects in the Prado Museum were saved from the incendiary bombs which had already seriously damaged the art collections.

In addition to the thousands of women and children who were evacuated from Madrid by the party and the Fifth Regiment, the most outstanding intellectuals of Spain were also helped to leave Madrid and go to Levante or even to other countries. Some of them, by their conduct, showed little understanding of the immensity of the sacrifice made by the people to prevent the victory of fascism. Others, such as the great physicist, Arturo Duperier, a world-renowned scientist, remained a true democrat both during the long years of exile and after his return to Spain. (The Franco dictatorship confined him to his residence and refused to give him the necessary cooperation to carry on his studies in nuclear physics. It was only after his death that Franco's journalists remembered that Arturo Duperier had been a great scientist.)

Among others whom the Fifth Regiment helped to leave Madrid were Dr. Marañón, Antonio Machado, Pío del Río Hortega, Dr. Sánchez Covisa, Enrique Moles, Antonio Madinaveitia, Dr. Sacristán, José Moreno Villa and many others. As their farewell to Madrid, these men, the pride of Spain's scientific and intellectual life, figures of international fame, made the following declaration:

"We professors and scholars, poets and scientists, holding university titles from Spain and abroad, have never felt so profoundly attached to this land, our country, as we do now. We have never felt so Spanish as at this moment when the people of Madrid, who defend the liberty of Spain, have insisted on our leaving Madrid so that our work may continue unhampered by the bombings suffered by the civilian population of Spain. We have never felt so Spanish as when we saw how, in order to save our artistic and scientific treasures, the militiamen, who risk their lives for Spain's welfare, have taken time to save the books in our libraries and the equipment in our laboratories from the incendiary bombs being hurled by foreign airplanes on our buildings of culture.

"We want to say that these deeds honor us as men, as scientists, as Spaniards, before all the world and all of civilization."

Those moments of tension and anguish were described by the United States poet Norman Rosten in the following emotional lines:

> Spain, the body.
> And in its center,
> Beating calmly
> Its great heart, Madrid.
> Weep, women, for the children have gone.
> The houses have gone,
> But the heart keeps beating.
> Madrid! Burning by night;
> Bleeding by day,
> But on her feet!
> The heart of a people
> May bleed,
> But not to death,
> Never to death!

Madrid began to feel the horrors of the enemy siege. The first trenches were opened on the outskirts of the city. The enemy was at Madrid's doors, and fascist propaganda was announcing the imminent fall of the capital.

The district of Carabanchel became the front battle line. The last occupants of the district departed under the shrieking of howitzers and bombs. The last trolley cars which linked Carabanchel to the center of Madrid were leaving, loaded with the humble belongings of the people. The sight of women carrying babies in their arms and urging on their older children in their flight from death was one of unforgettable anguish.

On November 5, the first enemy tanks arrived in Carabanchel. The Moroccan army was already occupying the first houses. At breakneck speed, the militiamen dug ditches in the streets to stop the tanks. The militiamen fought the Moroccans over every house—with bullets, or dynamite or knives—to the death. New batallions of militia arrived to replace the men who, exhausted from long hours of vigilance, had never thought of sleeping or eating.

The odds were heartbreakingly unequal. Only the heroic determination of the militiamen to die before letting the enemy pass could bring about a miracle. The breach opened toward the center of Madrid by the concentration of enemy troops in Carabanchel was closed by the militiamen, united in one patriotic resolution, to prevent the fall of Madrid.

In the front lines were the members of the Central Committee of the Madrid Communist party, inspiring the combatants, fighting side by side with them. All Communists were in the front lines, ready to defend Madrid. With them were the men of all the anti-fascist organizations.

With the rebel advance on Carabanchel checked, Franco divided his troops into two long arms, one reaching toward the Usera district and the other toward the highway going to Estremadura.

The history of the Moroccan Army ended in Carabanchel and Usera. They had been used by Franco as a psychological weapon because of the ill fame they had won by razing towns and committing every kind of atrocity on the defenseless civilian population.

When Getafe was lost on November 5, Usera became the enemy's chief target. But here, as in Carabanchel, the militiamen were determined to stop the enemy. Combatants of the United Socialist Youth organized all the people of Usera. Ditches were dug, barbed-wire fences were put up, parapets made of sand bags were built, which provided a minimum of protection, all along the Prado Longa, the Zofio, Cerro Blanco and Cerro Negro. The real resistance, however, the effective, unbreakable resistance, was not in stones and cement. It lay in the hearts and the will of the people of Madrid.

Dynamiters bringing the experience acquired in Carabanchel sped to the rescue of Usera. The Princess Bridge was mined to blow up the enemy, should it manage to pass beyond the first battle lines. As in Carabanchel, the men of the Fifth Regiment were there. The Moroccan cavalry attempted several times to surround Usera, but each time it was repulsed. After a long prelude of artillery fire aimed at the fragile defenses of the militiamen, the insurgents unleashed their tanks.

Six Italian tanks headed for the Cerro Blanco, which was defended by a company of sailors. Days before, in the capital, the sailors had seen a Soviet movie called "The Sailors of Kronstadt" and had learned how to attack the tanks. They fired their rifles ceaselessly, without abandoning their positions.

One sailor, Antonio Coll, left the trenches and went to meet the enemy. With a grenade he put the first tank out of combat. A moment of hesitation on the part of the tank drivers gave Coll the chance to throw a second grenade and temporarily halt the advance of the tanks. It has his last feat of bravery. Machine-gun fire mowed him down. All the combatants, moved by his example, left the trenches to help Coll as the tanks retreated. The fascists were held at bay in Usera, where they remained until the end of the war unable to advance beyond the positions occupied in the first days of their offensive against the capital.

The name of Antonio Coll became a symbol. Antitank brigades were organized on all the fronts in the determination to live up to the bravery of the hero who with his sacrifice had pointed the way to honor.

The great sculptor, Victorio Macho, deeply moved by Coll's deed, wrote the director of La Voz, a Madrid newspaper, the following letter offering his talents to perpetuate Coll's heroism in a monument:

"Last night I read in this newspaper that the popular municipal government of this invincible city will begin a public fund-raising drive for a monument honoring the heroic sailor Antonio Coll, whose magnificent feat of bravery and boldness has already won him immortality.

"Such a feat, which will be sung of in our popular songs and stories deserves to be perpetuated, as La Voz has said, so that it may endure through the ages. Certainly, the sculptor will find his task easy, because we can say that the sailor Antonio Coll was himself made of the purest Iberian bronze ever alloyed in the fertile womb of this immortal race, whom no one and nothing can keep from carrying out its historic destiny.

"Antonio Coll was made of bronze, golden-hued from the sun of victory and with whole-hearted enthusiasm we will raise a monument to him on a pedestal of mountain granite.

"Therefore, there is no need to begin a fund-raising drive, since there is no more worthwhile, beautiful and rewarding compensation for a sculptor who profoundly feels, understands and loves the sovereign people than to entrust him with this artistic mission in the service of the Republic and in memory of one of its heroes."

# Unforgettable Moments

Madrid feels the foul breath of the beast in its face, the beast which advances closer, ready to deal a deathblow to the popular resistance on this day, November 7, 1936, the anniversary of the October Revolution of 1917.

With a violent thrust which would open the way to the heart of the city and force Republican Spain to its knees, the insurgents hope to triumph and to wipe out the memory of that immortal date from the peoples' consciousness.

In raging battles, the militiamen defeat the first rebel attempts to take the capital; nevertheless, the insurgents manage to gain ground.

Wounded Madrid, bleeding from the thrusts of metal, seals its outer ring of streets with antitank trenches, with crenellated walls and barbed wire.

The shriek of the sirens breaks the silence of the city and warns the population of the approaching danger.

Artillery projectiles from the Cerro de los Angeles and bombs dropped by the rebel airplanes tear into the city's tallest buildings, explode in their entrails and destroy centuries-old monuments, priceless art treasures and thousands of lives.

The Prado Museum is bombed and the palace of the Duke of Alba burns to the ground, with all the historic and artistic treasures that our militiamen had so carefully watched over. The occupants of the streets under artillery fire move to less dangerous spots. The population crowds into the still intact districts.

The loudspeakers of the Fifth Regiment intermittently give instructions to the people about the precautions they should take. They warn the people of Madrid of a new enemy attack which is being organized openly and which must be repelled. Madrid is no longer the open and free city of yesterday. Today, it is a besieged fortress. Its children, its sick and aged, have been taken to open-armed Levante.

The men and women remaining in the capital are determined to write another chapter in the glorious history of Madrid, to defend their beloved city, street by street, house by house, stone by stone.

The approaching enemy attack keeps the population alert and prepared. Estimates are made, possibilities are weighed. Hours pass and the tension is unbearable. With clenched fists, with alert ears and steady eyes on the places where the enemy lurks, where the enemy bares its teeth, where the enemy searches for a weak spot through which to send its hordes to the attack, the people of Madrid wait. . . .

Wait. In the silence heavy with threats, dangers and bloody surprises, we begin to hear a monotonous, rhythmic sound, the pounding of firm steps which grows louder, comes nearer. . . . Now we can hear the thud of iron-clad boots on the pavement.

There is a moment of uncertainty, of indecision. Who is coming? Who are these men who on November 7, 1936, march through the streets of our Madrid, silent, erect, severe, with rifles on their shoulders and their bayonets fixed, making the earth tremble under their feet?

Behind the windows, eyes anxiously follow the steps of the marchers, who grasp cocked guns and bombs ready to be thrown. In despair, the women turn to the men: "They've come! What are we waiting for?"

We hear a command given in a strange tongue cutting the air like a whiplash. Then we hear the first stanzas of a beloved hymn, accompanied by the rhythmic movement of the unknown marchers. The air fills with vibrant sounds and words, sending a thrill down the spines of the people of Madrid.

"Good God! Is this a dream?" ask the women, sobbing.

The men marching through the streets of besieged Madrid sing the International in French and Italian, in German and Polish, in Hungarian and Rumanian!

They are the volunteers of the International Brigade who answered the call of the Comintern and have come to our country ready to fight, perhaps to die, along with us.

The people of Madrid rush into the streets to welcome these men. They now know these are their friends. Men and women in a surge of uncontrollable emotions cry and embrace the combatants of the International Brigades.

Their ranks are broken. Everyone wants to make a gift of the best thing he has to the "Internationals." Every person in Madrid wants to take one of those men or all of them to his house. The enemy siege is forgotten, danger is forgotten. Suddenly, drowning out the shouts and exclamations of happiness and enthusiasm filling the streets, we hear a hum of motors in the distance.

There is a moment of panic. "Airplanes! Airplanes! Airplanes!" everyone screams.

A few black dots grow larger, take shape and come nearer, flying low. They are not Messers or Savoys. Unknown airplanes are in our skies, coming towards us. But they're not shooting. They're not dropping bombs. What are they?

A squadron of I-15's and I-16's, which later the people would affectionately nickname "Flies" and "Snubnoses," move rapidly across Madrid's skies, saluting the truly astonished population. As the airplanes dip, in homage to the combatants, we can see the Republican flag on their wings.

It is an undescribable moment. An immense shout of joy, of gratitude, of relief, from thousands of throats, rises to the heavens, meets and accompanies the first Soviet airplanes in the skies of our country.

"They're Soviet airplanes! They're ours . . . ours . . . ours!"

In one instant, that distant Socialist country comes so close to the hearts of our combatants, of our women and men, that there never will be any borders, seas, mountains, terror or prisons that can separate the people of Spain from the people of the Soviet Union now or in the future. They are united forever in battle, in heroism, in sacrifice.

A feeling of identification with the men of the Soviet Union whose participation in our war contributed the blood and heroism of some of their best stimulates the fighting spirit and unity of our forces.

Madrid has regained its strength. It feels unconquerable. The insurgent attacks, with all their troops and war equipment, have been repelled again. And they will be repelled a hundred times.

The victory the enemy could not achieve in the first days of November, would not be attained until 1939, when treason opened the doors of the unconquerable capital.

There is a new morale, the morale of the offensive. The morale of a people willing to undergo the supreme sacrifice, a people that feels it is not alone in the fight; the morale which drives an army to the highest peaks of heroism.

The Fifth Regiment and the Defense Junta have fulfilled their mission. The names of their men shine in the skies of Spain and live in the hearts of the people. It will do no harm to repeat their names: Antonio Mije, Santiago Carrillo, Enrique Líster, Juan Modesto, Isidoro Diéguez, Commander Carlos, Daniel Ortega, Márquez, Francisco Antón, Domingo Girón, Yagüe, José Cazorla, Edmundo Domínguez Heredia, Arellano, Barceló, Ascanio and Mesón; the combatants of the United Socialist Youth and the United Socialist Party of Catalonia, and later those of Durruti.*

And above all, the simple men, the mass of anonymous heroes, the combatants who never retreated, who with their bodies closed the gaps opened by the enemy artillery in the walls and parapets from which they defended the city.

And those of the Sierra who broke the enemy troop concentrations and stopped their advance, who fought while behind them Madrid lay in flames—but a Madrid which had nailed the enemy at its doors, forbidding it to pass. The will of the people was stronger than the desperate fury of the enemy.

The combatants of the International Brigades hold a place of honor in the defense of Madrid. Several groups of foreign volunteers arrived in Albacete in the middle of October. They were swiftly organized into three batallions: German, French, and Italian; a short while later, Polish volunteers formed the Dombrowski Battalion.‡ On the first of November, they were officially baptized with the name of the XI International Brigade.

The first battalion of the Brigade was sent to the vicinity of Madrid on November 6 as a reserve force. The German Battalion, Edgar André, named after the worker leader executed in Germany, arrived at the Atocha Station on November 8 and joined the battalions formed by French, Italian and Polish volunteers.

* Durruti, Buenaventura (1896–1936), Anarchist leader, hero of the Aragón front. He was killed in action at the head of his Catalonian column in defense of Madrid.
‡ Named for Jan Henryk Dombrowski, or Dabrowski (1775–1818), patriotic Polish general and leader of anti-Tsarist insurrections.—Ed.

These were the men who had marched through Madrid when the city felt the dagger of the siege at its throat. The enthusiasm and the combativity of the people grew so great that Madrid, defended by its men and women together with the brigades, united for a common cause, became unconquerable.

The Edgar André battalion arrived in University City with the order to close the way to West Park, where the enemy was trying to break through. On November 9, the Battalion received its baptism of blood on Spanish soil. While the Edgar André Battalion advanced its positions, the Dombrowski Battalion stopped the fascist attack on the Casa de Campo. The French Battalion, led by Colonel Dumont, resisted enemy pressure without breaking its lines.

Here the song of Thaelmann was born. It was sung by the German fighters in battle and in death; today, the people of Germany still sing it, proud of their sons' participation in the Spanish war.

> Spanish heavens spread their brilliant starlight
> High above our trenches in the plain.
> Then early morning comes to greet us,
> Calling us to battle once again.
> Far off is our land.
> Yet ready we stand.
> We're fighting and winning
> For you: FREEDOM.

In University City, in the Casa de Campo, in West Park, in Frenchmen's Bridge, in Humera and Aravaca, the battalions of the XI International Brigade fought tirelessly to defend Madrid, united in battle and in death with the Spanish Republican combatants.

Singing the glories of the men of the International Brigade, Alberti wrote:

> You come from afar . . . But what does distance
> Mean to your blood, which sings without borders:
> Death may call your name any day;
> Who knows where, in what cities, fields or roads?
> Whether it be this country or that, whether it be large or small,
> Whether it be colored pastel on the map,
> The people spring from the same roots, the same dream.
> Anonymous, speaking simply, you have come.

You don't even know the color of the walls
In houses you have pledged to guard.
The earth now covering you was what you loved.
Ready for battle, accepting the bullets of death.
Stay—the trees, the plains wish it,
The particles of light that radiate
From the one song the sea roars out: Brothers!
Madrid grows greater and brightens with your names.

The fascist rising which was devastating our country like a cataclysm, tearing up the very roots of Spain, and the peoples' heroic resistance engaged the attention of the world. There were no neutral opinions on our struggle—you were with us or against. Indifference in matters of peace or war, democracy or fascism, always favors the aggressors.

Acting on the fraternal sentiments that people all over the world were expressing, the Comintern called upon all democrats and antifascists to help the Spanish people. It urged them to form brigades of volunteers to fight for their own countries' liberty on Spanish soil.

The first to answer the call were the French, Germans, Italians and Poles. Leading the first International Brigade, came the Hungarian Communist, General Emil Kléber, to help us defend Madrid.

From Germany, enslaved by the Nazi beast, came antifascist fighters and Communists, ardent defenders of revolutionary ideals which Hitler could not altogether destroy, outstanding combatants such as Franz Dahlem, Hans Beimler, Heinrich Rau, Gustav Szinda, Heinz Hoffmann, Luis Schuster, Ludwig Renn.

From the Bulgaria of Dimitrov, great challenger of Hitlerism, glorious son and revolutionary leader of the Bulgarian people, came hundreds of workers, peasants and intellectuals, bringing their heroism and revolutionary experience to Spain. Among them were Ruben Abramov, Damianov, Dichev, Lukanov, Petrov and dozens of other enthusiastic and heroic fighters.

From Italy came the experienced antifascist combatants Luigi Longo, D'Onoffrio, Nino Nanetti, De Vittorio, Pietro Nenni, Antonio Roasio, Vittorio Vidali—our "Commander Carlos"—Pacciardi, Barontii, Roselli.

From France, so close to the heart of Spaniards, came thousands of fighters—the French group was the most numerous—men who had received their baptism of fire in World War I fighting against the Germans, men like Commander Fort, Dumont, Andre Marty, Dr. Rouques, the great surgeon Doumanski-Dubois, as well as Colonel Fabien, Roll Tanguy and Pierre Rebière, who would later become heroes of the French resistance.

Leading the French and German volunteers who marched through the streets of Madrid in the first days of November 1936, were two men who had become symbols: Hans Kahle, a former officer of the German Army during World War I, and Dumont, also a former officer, of the French Army. Eighteen years earlier these men had fought each other from opposite trenches. Today, they were in Spain, united in the common cause against fascism, fighting together to defend liberty and democracy.

From the Poland of the big landowners and from the Polish emigrés living in France, came thousands of men who formed the Dombrowski Batallion, which would later receive the Medal of Bravery for its heroism. Among the Polish heroes who fought in Spain were the already legendary Karol Swierczewski (Walter), Jaszunski, Salomon, Kochanek, Antoni, Szyr, Eugeniusz, Komas Waclaw, Korczynski, Grzegorz.

From the country of the Magyars, Hungary, bled white by the violence with which Hungarian reaction crushed the first Soviet Republic in that country, came groups of antifascist fighters who had already felt in their own flesh what fascism meant to the working masses. Among them were Ferencz Münnich, the present-day President of the Hungarian government, the poet Mate Zalka (Lukacz), Szanto Rezso, Mezo Imre and Csebi Lajos.

From Rumania, subjugated under the sceptre of a foreign monarchy, under a regime of terror maintained by the Iron Guards in the service of the boyars and the capitalists, came hundreds of men. Noted for their heroism were Commander Borila, later a member of Rumanian Workers' Party national leadership, and Comrades Walter, Burca, Galia, Stoica, Florescu, as well as other glorious fighters inspired by the example of those self-sacrificing leaders of the Rumanian working-class, Gheorghiu Dej and Chivu Stoica, who were imprisoned for their revolutionary activities in the sinister Doftana.

From Czechoslovakia came Lastoviska; Svoboda; Bubenicek Alexander, killed in Morella; Cerni Jan, shot by the Nazis in 1944; Majek

Jozko, President of the Catholic Youth in Slovakia, killed in Madrid in November 1936.

From north and south, Americans, British, Belgians, Norwegians, Finns, Danes, Swedes, Austrians, Swiss, Albanians, Yugoslavs—volunteers from 54 countries—fought the war in Spain, shedding their blood unhesitatingly in deeds of inspiring bravery.

Today a worldwide movement of solidarity with revolutionary Spain exists. Far from being a Communist conspiracy, as claimed in Franco's propaganda, the cause of liberty for Spain is alive in all countries because democrats from nearly all of them established ties of blood with the people of Spain which can never be destroyed no matter how much the spawn of Hitlerism rage and rant.

The International Brigades, small in number, immense in historic importance, brought us their own native peoples' traditional love of liberty to merge with the similar traditions of the Spanish people in heroic fraternalism.

Langston Hughes wrote these lines to the American heroes of the International Brigades who died in Spain:

> I came
> Crossing an Ocean,
> And half a continent.
> Borders
> And mountains, as high as the heavens,
> And governments who told me: NO!
> YOU CANNOT GO!
> I came.
> In the luminous frontiers of tomorrow
> I put the strength and wisdom
> Of my years,
> Not much,
> Since I am young.
> (I should have said, was young,
> Because I'm dead).
>
> I've given what I wanted to
> And what I had to give
> So that others would live.
> And when the bullets

Stopped my heart
And the blood
Flooded my throat,
I didn't know if it was blood,
Or a red flame?
Or simply my death
Become life?

It's all the same:
Our dream!
My death!
Your life!
Our blood!
A flame!
It's all the same.

[34]

# Soviet Aid

It is impossible to speak of the defense of Madrid without mentioning the extraordinary role played by the tank drivers and aviators
of the Republic who by sheer audacity, effort and courage made up
for the shortage of equipment.

In November 1936, when Franco thought he could successfully
assault the city, he began to prepare the way by intense bombing
raids which resulted in enormous damage and thousands of civilian
victims. The Republic's Air Force, consisting of some 20 planes, at
the cost of heroic and superhuman efforts managed to defend Madrid
from fascist air attacks and to instill terror in the ranks of the enemy
pilots.

The Air Force gave rise to its own legion of heroes, men like
Domingo Bonilla, Fernando Blanco, Paredes, Zarauza, Antonio Arias,
Morquilla, Orozco, Llorente, Gisbert, Puig and others, many of

whom were killed in battle. Many others received the Medal of Bravery for their heroism.

The Republic's aviators counted on the invaluable aid of Soviet pilots, as well as the dedication of General Hidalgo de Cisneros, who was constantly concerned with training new pilots for the Republic, Hernández Franch, Ignacio Aguinaga and other expert, selfless aviators.

The defense of Madrid would have been impossible without airplanes and tanks. The few airplanes at the disposal of the Popular Army were up in the air practically around the clock, to the confusion of the enemy, who never imagined that the miracle of defending the skies of Madrid was the work of just one group of planes and pilots.

It was the same with the tanks. The tank drivers fought all day, surprising the enemy, destroying its artillery and spreading panic in its ranks, most of the time without infantry support since our commanders had not yet learned to use the tanks rationally.

During the day, the tanks protected the accesses to the city. They returned at nightfall. The tanks would be repaired during the night and then, against all technical and human norms for the stamina of men and equipment, they were back in combat the following morning.

Many of these heroes were Soviet tank drivers and pilots who fought with the Spanish combatants, forgetting the long hours of fatigue, their wounds and even their lives. They came as volunteers to fight and die by our side—generous and heroic men, trained and tempered in the splendid school of Soviet life.

The German General Sperrle later wrote in the Spanish edition of *Die Wehrmacht*, commenting on the operations in Madrid: "Our bombers had the mission of opening a route to Madrid and demoralizing the city so that Franco's troops could enter. But the troops found it impossible to follow the route we had traced for them."

What the Nazi General's cardboard brain couldn't understand was why neither German artillery nor its aviation could achieve their objectives. In much the same way, they were to fail years later in the Soviet Union.

In the titanic task of defending Madrid, which Hitler's generals believed to be undefendable, Soviet volunteers, tank drivers and aviators cooperated valiantly with their Spanish comrades. Among those who were distinguished in courage, self-abnegation and devotion were Anatoli Serov, "the ace of the night flights," and his companions Nikifor Balanov, Piotr Desnitski, all Heroes of the Soviet Union; Alexander Minaev, killed in the defense of Madrid; Fiodor Oproschenko; Mikhail Polivalov; Pavel Richagov, Hero of the Soviet Union; Grigori Tjor; Piotr Ugrovatov; Anastas Yarkovoi; Victor Yolsunov and Boris Smirnov, both Heroes of the Soviet Union, as well as many others.

Among the most noted tank drivers was the group under Major Paul Adman, and the tank drivers, Semion Krivoshein, Victor Novikov, Pavel Tsaplin and Mikhail Yudin, Heroes of the Soviet Union, outstanding not only in the fulfillment of their dangerous missions, but also in the comradely and generous cooperation they displayed in the training of tank drivers and aviators for the Republican Army.

In the dark hours when the help we needed from other countries was denied us, a group of heroic Soviet soldiers came to Spain as volunteers. Their names are now forever part of the history of the Spanish peoples' epic battle for national liberty and independence, for democracy and the Republic.

Glorious men and names, those of Rodion Malinovski, Kiril Meretskov, Alexander Rodimtsev, Nikolai Voronov, Grigori Stern, Yakov Smushkevich, Dimitri Pavlov, Nikolai Kusnetsov, Gorev, who left their countries, their families and homes to bring us their invaluable experience and knowledge, their blood and their lives. They will always live in our memory and our gratitude.

The people of Spain will never forget the generous and unconditional aid received from the Soviet Union in those desperate moments.

Our situation was serious. The enemy had already begun to ring the bells of victory. The Spanish government had with extreme difficulty managed to purchase a few thousand rifles in Mexico. The attitude of the Mexican government, especially that of General Lazaro Cardenas, a great friend of Spain, was fully appreciated by our combatants. Although the purchase took care of only a minimal part of our needs, it was a very different stand from that of the British, French and other so-called democratic governments.

At the beginning of the war, the Soviet government joined the Nonintervention Committee, founded in London, believing that its participation would help end the war rapidly in favor of the Republic.

When the Soviet Union saw that in practice the Nonintervention Committee, engineered by British perfidy and initiated by the Socialist Léon Blum, prime minister of France, was not aiding the Republic; that, on the contrary, it was a cover for activities of the fascist and "democratic" powers in favor of the insurgents, the Soviet Union declared on October 7, 1937, that it would withdraw its participation in the Nonintervention Committee. At the same time, it announced its intention of aiding the Republican government and the Spanish people in their heroic resistance against fascist aggression.

In keeping with its position and as a pledge and encouragement to the popular resistance, Stalin, on behalf of the Central Committee of the Soviet Communist Party, sent a historic telegram to José Díaz on October 16:

"The workers of the Soviet Union, aiding the revolutionary people of Spain in every possible way, do more than fulfill their duty. They know that to free Spain from the oppression of the fascist reactionaries is not a private concern of the Spaniards, but the common cause of all advanced and progressive humanity."

Very soon Spain, engaged in a struggle for its liberty, began to feel the warm, fraternal solidarity of the Soviet people and government.

The women workers of the Moscow textile mill, "The Three Mountains," sent clothing, food and medicine to the women and children of Spain. Their example was followed by many of the Soviet people. In October 1936, Soviet ships began to ply the seas between Spain and the Soviet Union. Two months later, the Spanish government received the first shipments of aid, valued at nearly 60 million rubles, from the workers of the Soviet Union.

The *Sirianin*, the first Soviet ship to arrive in Barcelona, the *Neva* and the *Turksib*, brought the fraternal aid of the Soviet Union to our shores. These ships, manned by sailors who were genuine sea wolves, not only brought cotton, butter, sugar and flour but also carried airplanes, tanks, cannons, machine guns and men who knew how to operate them and who would teach our own combatants.

Madrid could never have been defended without Soviet tanks and airplanes. The fact that the people of Madrid hung pictures of Soviet leaders in the balconies and streets of the besieged capital, which produced so much fury on the part of the rebels, was no strange or extraordinary thing. The people looked on these men as their leaders also, since without them and their aid the fascists would have swiftly realized their plans.

From devoted interpreters such as Maria Fortus, Tatiana Ivanova, Elena Lebedieva, the sisters Adeline and Pauline Abramson, Nora Chegodaieva, Saitseva and many others who accompanied the advisers and specialists to the fronts, up to the Soviet Commercial Attaché in Spain, Marchenko, and his wife Teodora Feder—all worked tirelessly to help our people and government.

In all the fields where the cause of Republican Spain could be defended through political and diplomatic channels, in the meetings of the Nonintervention Committee and the League of Nations, Soviet representatives firmly and tenaciously supported the right of the Spanish people and government to receive aid for the undertaking of stopping the march of fascism in Europe, of muzzling the instigators of war.

Indalecio Prieto, minister of the navy and armed forces, expressed the gratitude of our people and leaders in these deeply felt words during a luncheon tendered by the Soviet adviser on aviation, on January 3, 1937:

"The Soviet Union has come to the aid of Spain in a direct and simple manner, giving all that it can for the triumph of Spain's legal government, while other democratic countries in Europe where Socialist parties influence or largely constitute their governments have given us, at best, absolutely inadequate aid, and have even on several occasions raised obstacles to purchases of war equipment that the Republic is legally entitled to transact. And one day Spain's Socialist Party will have to admit this publicly, not in formal acknowledgement, but as an expression of sincere conviction."

# 35

# Friends

Many visitors came to the Republican zone during the war. Many, like Nehru, Branting and Krishna Menon, came as friends; others, like Attlee, Olenhauer and other Social-Democrats, as observers; and still others were just curious.

Paul Robeson visited our country and went to the front to greet a small group of his compatriots, among whom was the Negro Oliver Law, a former corporal of the U.S. Army and now a captain in the Peoples' Army of Spain.

When an American colonel visited the Lincoln Brigade and saw the Negro captain, he haughtily asked Law: "How dare you wear a captain's uniform?"

"Because I am a captain," Law replied. "In the United States I could only be a corporal because I was a Negro. Here, we get our stripes not because of our color but because we earn them."

This brave captain is buried in Spain. He was killed in the battle of Brunete.

Paul Robeson sang for the combatants. The magic of his voice brought his fellow-Americans, fighting in Spain for liberty and justice, the memory of their own distant land, whose democratic traditions were being daily trampled upon by the capitalists who had turned the United States into the incarnation of the gold madness.

Mr. Nehru's visit was immensely important for all of us. He came as the representative of the Indian people, who were struggling to free their country from the oppression of British imperialism. We openly discussed our ideals and aspirations with him. He came as a friend and left as one, wishing for our victory, which he considered not only just and possible but also of great consequence for all the democratic countries in the world.

Among the representatives of Great Britain frequently visiting us in 1937 was the Duchess of Atholl. She paid me a visit, which we spent pleasantly. I thought I would never see her again, but later in Paris in 1938 I met her again during the Spanish Aid Conference organized by the Universal Peace Committee. Here the Duchess was very enthusiastically endorsing policies that were contrary to the people's interest. In Paris she was no longer my guest, but an individual who was advocating a policy that I considered harmful to our cause. Very respectfully but firmly I opposed her proposals. Yet in all honesty I must say that aside from some of her political opinions, the Duchess of Atholl in her attitude to the Spanish people and their struggle against fascism was much better than many who politically passed as democrats or even Social-Democrats.

During the Paris Conference Mr. Nehru, also a participant, and his beautiful daughter Indira backed my position protesting against the conduct of those who were presiding over the meeting that day and who had threatened to suspend the session if I spoke. The Laborite Elena Wilkinson also condemned the incomprehensible attitude of the committee's chairman.

United States trusts supplied Franco with all the petroleum the insurgents needed to keep their war machine going. But the progressive people of the United States were on the side of the Spanish Republic, rejoicing in its victories and suffering with its defeats. In 1938, the President of the League of American Writers, Donald Ogden Stewart, organized a survey in the United States. In answer to the questions: Are you for or against Franco and fascism? Are you for or against the legitimate government of the Spanish Republic? the League received 418 replies. Of these, 410 were in favor of the Republic, 7 were neutral and only one was in favor of fascism.

On November 28, 1936, the well-known writer Romain Rolland called on all the French people and men of good will everywhere to come to the aid of Republican Spain: "Come to the aid of Spain! Come to our aid, to your aid! Remain silent and tomorrow it will be our sons who perish!"

Later, in July 1937, the International Congress of Antifascist Writers met in Valencia to reiterate its support of the Republic and pass important resolutions in defense of culture. Romain Rolland sent the congress the following message:

"To my fellow writers meeting in Valencia, Madrid and Barcelona, I send my most ardent greetings. In these moments, the civilization of the entire world is united in these capitals; a world menaced by the airplanes and bombs of the fascist barbarians, as it was in antiquity by the barbarian invasions. . . .

"It is with fervor that we show solidarity to our brothers and fellow combatants in Spain.

"Glory to this nation of heroes, to these knights of the spirit, to this alliance of two forces—the power of the popular masses and their elected leaders! May this alliance serve as an example to the great democracies of Europe and America! May this alliance, strengthened in combat, safeguard the progress and liberty of the world!"

Participating in this historic congress, which opened new perspectives to all intellectuals worthy of the name, were Pablo Neruda, César Vallejo, Huidobro, José Mancisidor, Octavio Paz, Pablo Rojas, Raúl Gonzáles Tuñón, Amparo Mon, Juan Marinello and Nicolás Guillén from Latin America; Teodoro Balk from Yugoslavia; Ludwig Renn and Anna Seghers, Willi Bredel, Erich Weinert, from Germany; Kristo Beleev, Ludmila Litvanova, from Bulgaria; Tse-Hu from China; Julien Benda, André Malraux, Tristan Tzara and Leon Moussinac, Jean Richard Bloch, from France; Alexei Tolstoy, Alejandro Fadeiev, V. Stavski, Vishnevski, Ilya Ehrenburg, Savich, Kelin, Mikhail Koltsov, from the Soviet Union; Gerde from Poland; Egon Erwin Kisch from Czechoslovakia; Donini from Italy; Spender from England; John dos Passos and Ernest Hemingway from the United States; Andersen Nexö from Denmark, as well as many others. Among those representing the intellectuals of Spain were Rafael Alberti, José Bergamín, Alvarez del Vayo, Wenceslao Roces, César Arconada, Margarita Nelken, Constancia de la Mora, Antonio Machado, Corpus Barga, Pla y Beltrán, and a large group representing the combatants of the various fronts.

Among the hundreds of messages sent to the congress was one from the scientist Albert Einstein. Moved by the peoples' resistance against fascist aggression, he declared his opposition to the great powers who were trying to asphyxiate Republican Spain: "Under the circumstances of our era, the heroic struggle of the Spanish people for human liberty and dignity is the only thing that can keep alive in us the hope for better times."

Many of these intellectuals, stirred by the heroic grandeur of the Spanish people in their fight against the fascist imperialist coalition, remained in Spain and fought with us. They were caught up in the wave of the ardor and determination of our combatants who would rather die fighting for liberty than live abjectly under the yoke of fascism.

At the end of 1936, the well-known British writer Ralph Fox met a heroic death on the Cordoba front. He was commissar of the 14th International Brigade and shed his blood for his democratic convictions and the cause of the Spanish people. Also giving his life, at the age of 29, was Christopher Caudwell, the brilliant British Marxist, in the battle of Jarama. One year later, in the battle of the Ebro, James Lardner, son of the American writer Ring Lardner, was killed.

The Mexican painter David Alfaro Siqueiros also fought in the ranks of the Popular Army. The Cuban writer Pablo de la Torriente, who came to Spain to aid the cause of the Republic together with a numerous group of Cubans led by comrade Joaquín Ordoqui, was killed on the Madrid front, as well as the young student Alberto Sánchez and Comrade Candón. All of these names and lives will remain models of valorous youth for all time.

Many Socialist and even labor leaders in various countries personally sympathized with the Republican cause. But in practice they failed to do all they could have done to aid the Spanish people in their fight against fascism. This does not in any way lessen the political and historic importance of the contributions of men of all political shades from many countries who were sincerely on our side, among them Senator Branting of Sweden, Camilo Huysmans and Isabel Blume of Belgium.

And although their views differed from our own, we cannot help remembering with emotion and gratitude the participation in the International Brigades of Social-Democratic leaders such as the Austrian Julius Deutsch; Pietro Nenni, commissar; and other anti-fascists like the Italian Pacciardi of the Garibaldi Brigade and André Malraux, the present Minister of Culture in France, who was an aviator in the first days of our war.

In spite of its broad international basis, solidarity with Spain was obviously not extensive enough. Dimitrov, the great antifascist fighter and secretary of the Comintern, rightly said when he wrote an appeal to the international Socialist movement:

"The international proletariat is completely on the side of the Spanish people and against the fascist rebels and invaders. It has shown and continues to show its solidarity with the combatants. It has not limited itself to giving material aid and sending food and ambulances; it has sent its best sons to fight on the fronts of Madrid, Guadalajara, in the ranks of the Republican Army.

"But all this is not enough. The international workers' movement, its labor and political organizations, must not think that they have fulfilled their duty until Republican Spain's international rights are recognized and guaranteed and the fascist intervention in Spain halted."

In order to create an international single front in defense of Republican Spain, the Comintern proposed the following basic points:

"Immediate withdrawal of Italian and German troops from Spain.

"Cessation of the blockade of Republican Spain.

"Recognition of all the international rights of the legal Republican Government.

"Application of the statutes of the League of Nations against the fascist aggressors who have attacked the Spanish people."

The Comintern's efforts bore fruit. Although the Spanish Republic and its people did not receive all that it deserved and needed, a resolution was approved by the representatives of both Internationals in Annemasse on June 21, 1937. Adler and De Brouckère signed for the Socialist International, while José Díaz, Maurice Thorez, Cachin, Luigi Longo, Franz Dahlem and Pedro Checa represented the Communist International. The resolution stated:

"1. On the question of Spain, both Internationals have essentially similar objectives.

"2. Both parties agree that they should increase their efforts to obtain common actions favorable to the Spanish people wherever possible.

"3. The delegates agree to hold further meetings within a short time to study in more detail concrete ways to aid Spain, both materially and morally." (This was the main point of the resolution.)

Unfortunately, these resolutions were never put into practice, because the labor leaders refused to recognize the authority of De Brouckère and Adler to act, since the Socialist International supported the policies of the Nonintervention Agreement.

# 36

# Difficult Moments

The year 1936 was drawing to a close. January 1937 arrived full of predictions and painful question marks. After the first victories, the Republican cause had suffered serious setbacks. Toledo, Talavera and many other cities had been lost. Oviedo was still ridden with enemy troops who held critical positions and tied down important militia units which could have been fighting elsewhere.

The fronts in the North were stationary. The enemy's chief concern was the Center and South of Spain, since the insurgents did not receive aid from the North.

At the beginning of the new year, I spoke on Radio Madrid explaining the party's policies in light of the new situation and the measures that the Communists considered necessary for victory. The latter I summed up as follows:

"1. A government, such as the present one, composed of the representatives of all the forces expressing the opinions of our popular masses must have full authority. Everyone, individuals and organizations, must respect and obey it, carry out its decisions and those of its officials.

"2. Military conscription should be started immediately as the only rapid way to create a great peoples' army, duly organized and disciplined to ensure military effectiveness. This army should have both civilian and military commanders, loyal to the Republic and its people. The army and its commanders must be respected and their orders obeyed without discussion. We must create a general staff and a single command for the armies operating in the different fronts. This general staff and single command should be composed of the best and ablest soldiers, as well as the best representatives of those parties and trade-union organizations that enjoy the confidence of the people. Their orders must be obeyed without discussion.

"3. The strictest discipline in the rear guard to be achieved by means of an educational campaign on the nature of this war, to end the simplistic and dangerous idea that the war concerns only those regions in which it is fought rather than the people in every region of the country. The sacrifices and shortages due to the war should be shared by all the inhabitants of loyalist Spain.

"4. Our basic industries should be reorganized and nationalized, primarily the war industries, in order to satisfy the needs of our combatants and civilians. All the trade unions, political parties and individuals loyal to the popular cause should strive to impress upon the population the importance of one single concern and goal, that of producing more goods of better quality in order to speed our triumph.

"5. A coordinating board should be created to regulate industry and the general economy. Board members should be the representatives of all the technicians and specialists of the Popular Front to ensure that this important state agency may guide and direct production. Their decisions must be carried out by all.

"6. Production should be controlled by the workers, but the organisms entrusted with applying this control must act in accordance with the plans outlined by the coordinating board.

"7. Our agricultural zones should produce all that is necessary for the battle and home fronts. This should be achieved on the basis of a plan established by the representatives of the peasants' associations and Popular Front organizations and parties. The peasants should be assured the ownership of their produce whether it be produced individually or collectively. Agricultural producers should be guaranteed national and international markets and a fair price for their products.

"8. Agricultural production should be coordinated with that of industry and both should have the same objective: To win the war.

"We must end the war rapidly. Let us show the people who are suffering under fascist tyranny that fascism is not invincible, that we can fight against fascism, that we can triumph over fascism!"

Four months had passed since Largo Caballero had formed his government and assumed the post of minister of war. Carlos Asensio Cabanillas, whom he had promoted to general, was his under-secretary, adviser in military matters and confidential adviser.

Even for a man experienced in politics and of solid ideological foundation, the direction of a government like that of the Popular Front in a country divided by a war of such special characteristics would have been an extraordinarily thorny task, one beset with difficulties capable of being resolved only by the participation and cooperation of all the forces represented in the government.

Largo Caballero, badly advised by persons with ulterior motives and dubious Socialist convictions, failed to overcome those difficulties. During the moments in which the fate of Spain was being decided, he had by his side only one military adviser, General Asensio, whose dislike for the combatants of the Republic was obvious. The political advisers who surrounded Largo were irresponsible flatterers such as Baraibar, Aguirre, Llopis and Araquistain. These characters pushed him toward the precipice of an insensate, subjective policy which brought him into conflict with his own party and with all the other Popular Front parties—a policy that was carrying the people to disaster.

I find it necessary to recall all these circumstances because with time many things are forgotten. And without knowing our internal difficulties, the new generations will find it impossible to understand some of the factors that weakened the popular resistance and brought about the defeat of the Republic.

If at times my criticism of attitudes seems incorrect or over emotional, I can never, on the other hand, be accused of deliberately false or malicious interpretations, since the criterion in all my judgments has always been whether or not the interests of the people, the interests of Spain, were being defended.

I use the same criterion today in assessing the political and military activities of men and parties, and in forming my own opinions. My views may be controversial, but they are based on real experience and facts which were well known during our national revolutionary war against fascism—facts which many people have tried to twist or forget.

At the end of January 1937, Comrade Bolivar, the commissar of Málaga, arrived in Valencia. He had come to tell Largo Caballero of the critical situation on the Málaga front created by the lack of arms and ammunition. At the same time, he protested against the attitude of the Anarchists who refused to join the Peoples' Army and insisted on keeping their own independent militia units.

After his visit to the Minister of War, Bolivar, a Communist deputy and member of the party's Central Committee, went to party headquarters to ask our national leaders to help him overcome the resistance of Largo, who had refused to send arms to Málaga.

"Not one rifle, not one penny more for Málaga!" Largo had replied to Bolivar's requests. All our pleas and explanations about the gravity of the situation and the enormous enemy pressure on Málaga were of no avail.

We couldn't budge him from his stubborn stand, nor could we overcome the resistance of Asensio. Largo showed us the famous notebook in which he kept a list of all the arms sent to the various fronts. Asensio insisted that there were already more than enough arms in Malaga for its defense, and Largo Caballero believed it because he believed in Asensio.

Asensio was deliberately lying. Bolivar returned to Málaga heartbroken but determined to help the people of Málaga defend the city as best they could. But it was impossible, the insurgents reinforced with numerous Italian troop units steadily advanced by land and sea.

While the most tragic retreat of our war was taking place in Málaga, while women carrying babies in their arms fled from the Italian army by the only road that still remained open, and were being strafed by Italian airplanes, General Asensio was proclaiming to our people's astonishment that the loss of Málaga had no importance within the general plan of "his personal strategy."

Another general, Cabrera, the "hero" of Guadarrama, declared that "the loss of Málaga was an advantage, because now we had fewer fronts to worry about," a declaration which fully warranted a court-martial.

In those moments of national anguish, when the fate of a Spanish city and of thousands of men and women hung in the balance, the government, at the demand of the Anarchist ministers and against the protest of the Communist ministers, spent four hours deliberating whether it should or should not destroy empty glass bottles to stimulate the production of a trade-union glass cooperative directed by the Anarchist Peiro. That day the Communist ministers went to party headquarters and asked our leaders to approve their resignations because they couldn't answer for themselves any longer!

The Anarchist militia continued its refusal to join the regular army, and the government never took steps to correct the situation. The Anarchist press called our demands for a general mobilization, military discipline and conscription counterrevolutionary.

On February 11, 1937, the Communist Party published a document which stated:

"We must transform the militia into a regular army because what happened in Malaga can happen on other fronts if we fail to take the necessary measures. We can vacillate no longer. We can no longer allow the gangrene of the enemy's actions to eat at our own vitals. War cannot be waged according to the likes or dislikes of one party or organization, or to satisfy the members of this or that association. Let us be implacable with traitors and spies. Our important posts should be held by civilians, by men loyal to the popular cause in close collaboration with military commanders capable of taking the military and political reins of the war in their hands.

"We must thoroughly review all our high and important posts, in order to weed out doubtful and suspicious elements or those who because of inertia or ineptitude play into the hands of the enemy."

Stifling our own indignation, we defended the government of Largo Caballero and silenced the protests that were arriving from the front, because we knew that every fissure opened in the Popular Front was a gap through which the enemy would crawl. We did our best to convince Largo Caballero of the necessity for purging the ranks of the military, which were teeming with our enemies, for changing his policies, and for waging the war with total commitment.

In the belief that the Communists were trying to undermine his authority, Largo Caballero took offense because we refused to be the naive tools of his disastrous policies. The Communists' conviction that his policies and the persons he had placed in the War Ministry would lead to the Republic's defeat was shared by Socialists, including Indalecio Prieto, who at times supported the Communist proposals in cabinet meetings.

The loss of Málaga, a painful defeat for the Republic, once again showed in all its tragic reality the terrible damage that the lack of a regular army was inflicting. Moreover, the existence of numerous independent regions, with their diversity of objectives and interests, was plunging the Republican camp into a suicidal situation.

The Minister of War knew that an attack on Málaga was imminent. Instead of ordering the nearby forces and even the distant ones to move to the north, he allowed the fronts to follow their own wishes. And what they wished was to defend their own sector if attacked, without heeding the necessity for coordination and planned actions, since the government itself lacked a general plan of action. Even though some groups of Asturians went to the Basque Country and some Basques, under the leadership of our unforgettable Larrañaga, fought in Asturias during the difficult moments, the plain truth was—even though we hate to admit it—that every militia unit preferred to fight in its own region.

Therefore, to speak of our Northern Army was a euphemism. Instead we had the militia of Asturias, the militia of Santander and the militia of the Basque Country, each of which, acted, by and large, under its own commanders. Largo Caballero sent General Llano de la Encomienda to Asturias as Chief of Staff of the Northern Army, but Llano soon discovered that his services were not really required. Vested interests refused to tolerate any intrusion or meddling in "family" affairs, even if this kind of egoistic, provincial mentality might carry them all to catastrophe and prepare the way for the defeat of the Republic.

When the Basque government learned that General Llano de la Encomienda had arrived to take charge of the Northern Army, that is, the Basque, Asturian and Santander forces, President José Antonio de Aguirre sent the general the following communiqué:

In a meeting held on the 13th of this month, the Council of Ministers of the Basque Government discussed two matters:

1. The relations between the General Staff of the Northern Army and the Basque government;

2. A reply to the letter sent by the General Staff of the Northern Army, in which a series of questions is raised.

Concerning the matter of military action, the Basque government has agreed to continue the policy it has been following up to now.

After this decision, unanimously approved by all the ministers, it was decided to answer the letter of the Commander of the Northern Army, as follows:

All matters concerning the war, the utilization of human and material resources within the territory of Euzcadi, except for the command of military operations, are the exclusive jurisdiction of the Government of Euzcadi and its Minister of War.

This does not weaken the necessary coordination of military activities or the joint actions of the Santander and Asturian forces, which together with those of Euzcadi, form the Northern Army.

In keeping with Your Excellency's request, the Government of Euzcadi will continue, as far as it is able, to supply material and other aid to the other units of the Northern Army, those of Santander and Asturias, as it has done in the past.

Bilbao, January 13, 1937
José A. DE AGUIRRE.

General Llano de la Encomienda sent a reply insisting that he take full command of the Northern Army as he had been expressly ordered to do by Largo Caballero. President Aguirre in turn replied:

The ministers of the Basque Country who have been in Valencia discussed with the Republican Government the question, among others, of the relationship of the Northern Army and its arbitrarily created General Staff with the Basque Government.

The clear and categorical declaration of Largo Caballero that the Northern Army and its General Staff do not exist in fact has led us to the conclusion that any arbitrarily created institution lacks juridical power as far as the Basque Government and the military units exclusively depending on it are concerned.

Therefore, the Basque Government, according to its agreement with the Minister of War and the President of the Republic, plans to send the President a proposal providing for the coordination of the military forces of Asturias, Santander and Vizcaya. This proposal, after being discussed and unanimously approved by the Council of Ministers of the Basque Government, will be transmitted to the President of the Spanish Republic.

We communicate this to Your Excellency and inform you that until the new organization of all forces, institutions and material situated in Basque territory is approved, they will remain within the exclusive jurisdiction of the Minister of War of the Basque Government. Therefore, any other power or institution should refrain from issuing any order until the new organization comes into effect.

Your Excellency is also informed that this communication is in reply to all the letters sent by you in the last few days concerning planned military operations, all orders given by you to various institutions in Basque territory and all the questions sent to the High Command of the military forces operating in Euzcadi.

Bilbao, January 28, 1937

JOSÉ A. DE AGUIRRE.

General Llano de la Encomienda sent the following telegram to Largo Caballero the same day:

TELEGRAM NO. 80 FROM CHIEF OF NORTHERN ARMY, LLANO DE LA ENCOMIENDA, TO THE MINISTER OF WAR OF THE REPUBLICAN GOVERNMENT.

The Basque Government informs me that the Minister of War, Largo Caballero, has declared clearly and categorically that the Northern Army and its General Staff do not exist; therefore, the Government of Euzcadi intends to propose a plan to coordinate military actions in Santander and Asturias, which it will remit to Valencia. Meanwhile all armed forces in Basque territory remain under the exclusive jurisdiction of the

Government of Euzcadi, consequently I have been requested to refrain from issuing any orders.

This was the answer I received from the Basque Government to my request for support of the military operations I am planning in Asturias.

I have communicated to the Basque Government that pending orders from the Government of the Republic, I have moved my General Staff Headquarters to Santander.

I request Your Excellency to inform me whether the army which I have the honor to command exists or not—a command given me according to the order published in Official Gazette No. 239, with all the juridical powers inherent therein.

The loss of Málaga was the drop that caused the Communists' cup of patience to spill over. All the more when all the persons directly responsible for Málaga's defeat tried to put the blame on Bolívar. A cowardly and arbitrary accusation was made that he had abandoned his post when, immediately before the attack, he had come to Valencia to inform the Prime Minister of the situation and request aid to defend the city.

The anticommunism of certain social classes is understandable, and it neither disturbs nor surprises us. We consider it a natural phenomenon, one of the political expressions of the class struggle. But the anticommunism of those who call themselves revolutionary and pretend to be the priests of democracy is a policy that debases those who practice it, if they weren't already debased before they became anticommunists.

In a cabinet meeting, the Communist ministers energetically raised the question of responsibility for the loss of Málaga. The finger of suspicion was automatically pointed at the Under-Secretary of War. The Communists demanded his resignation and an investigation of the Republic's defeat in Málaga.

Largo Caballero, indignant because his right-hand man was being accused, asked for proof.

"Proof?" replied one of the Communist ministers. "What better proof is there than what happened in Málaga?"

"That's not enough," answered Largo. "I want more proof."

In spite of Largo's attitude, the ministers unanimously agreed to start an investigation and expose those responsible for the defeat. It was agreed to name a committee of two ministers, García Oliver, an Anarchist, and Vicente Uribe, a Communist, to go to the Málaga front and make an on-the-spot study of the situation. It was also agreed that two other ministers, a Socialist and a Communist, would attend the meetings of the Central General Staff.

The Communist Party could not resign itself to the fact that the post of maximum reponsibility after that of prime minister was occupied by a man who, if not an enemy agent himself, was certainly aiding and abetting enemy agents. Neither could it resign itself to the fact that General Asensio continued to direct the war. His policies were resulting in tragic defeats and the loss of important cities at a time when the Republic's militia possessed the means of defense which had been so sorely lacking at the beginning of the war.

The government had to change its policies. After its victory in Málaga, the enemy began to put strong pressure on Euzcadi and once again had its eye on Madrid.

The loss of Málaga affected people's emotions so strongly that the UGT organized a mass meeting to demand that the government take energetic steps to reorganize the conduct of the war and the defense of the Republic. Since the meeting was arranged by the trade-union organization which he controlled, Largo Caballero thought that it was a demonstration of unconditional support of his policies. Carried away by his imagined success, he refused to take any measure that would throw light on what happened in Málaga, or to purge the military apparatus.

The Communist Party organized a meeting in Valencia where we denounced those guilty of the defeat in Málaga. I spoke in the name of the party's Central Committee, informing the people of the true situation on the fronts and explaining the significance of the mass demonstration held a few days earlier. I strongly insisted on the necessity for creating a regular army, one cleansed of traitors and enemy agents.

"We want an army," I said, "where there are no generals who revel at brothels while our people and soldiers fight heroically, while our women and children are machine-gunned by fascist airplanes on the roads of Málaga. . . . We, the women of Spain, are determined to make any sacrifice, but we will not let our sons be ordered into battle by generals who are indifferent to our cause, the cause of liberty and independence for Spain."

That night General Asensio resigned. Just as the arrival of the dawn is welcomed after a nightmare, so was his departure from office greeted throughout the country.

The loss of Málaga had aggravated the political situation both at home and in the battlefields. Civilians and combatants alike demanded a change of policy.

Cabinet meetings became more unpleasant each day because of Largo's attitude. He had hit upon the idea, which he thought would be easy to put in practice, of pushing the Communists and Republicans out of the government and forming a so-called trade-union government, with the collaboration of the Anarchists. The Anarchists supported and encouraged him in this plan. They already had visions of themselves deciding the destiny of Spain and destroying, not the insurgents but the Communists who were the core of the resistance movement.

In reply to a survey taken by *Mundo Obrero* on the plans for a UGT-CNT government then being hatched in febrile brains, I gave the party's opinion on the matter, writing the following:

"When we must concentrate all our efforts on the waging of a war so vital for Spain, experiments in trade-union governments seem to me a grave error. Should this plan materialize, it would lead to the disintegration of antifascist unity and accelerate the triumph of fascism.

"The trade unions are already represented in the government and enjoy ample freedom to act. We suspect this plan is nothing but a maneuver to push the Republican parties out of the government, and the Communist Party firmly opposes it.

"With the Popular Front we won in February and with the Popular Front government, which gives proportional representation to all antifascist forces in the country, we shall win the war.

"I would like to make one thing clear: Communists will oppose everything and everyone that serves to break the unity of the Spanish people as expressed in the Popular Front government. The Communist Party will defend this policy as the only one which in present circumstances can lead the people to victory."

The capture of Málaga gave the enemy more freedom of action. Now the insurgents were planning a demolishing attack from the south to cut the communications between Madrid and Valencia. Early in February we knew that the enemy was concentrating its troops in the Jarama sector either to block the road to Valencia or to reinforce its right flank.

The enemy began a new offensive in the direction of Vaciamadrid on February 6, 1937. It attacked continuously, with the object of bringing the road to Levante under fire. On February 12, enemy troops crossed the Jarama River, thus creating a point of support for the next offensive on the east bank.

The enemy once again was favored by the fact that we had no reserve troops in Jarama and they easily captured our positions.

The insurgents prepared a new attack on the capital in the direction of Guadalajara and sent several Italian divisions to that zone. To block the attack, on which the enemy had placed high hopes, two brigades of the troops under Líster, one International Brigade and two supplementary brigades to act as reserves, were stationed in vulnerable spots.

The weight of the battle against the Italian divisions in Guadalajara was born by the combatants who had attended the military school in Madrid during the unforgettable month of November. Once again Republican combatants and the men of the International Brigades showed their heroic mettle and will to victory.

The hordes of Mussolini, drunk from their bloody victory in Málaga, had especially asked Franco for her "honor" of fighting this battle, since they wanted the capture of Madrid to go down in history as an Italian victory. But the Blackshirts never managed to reach Madrid through Guadalajara. Instead they left thousands of dead and hundreds of prisoners in the battlefields. Under the pressure of our militia, they did more than retreat; they literally fled in panic, abandoning tanks, cannons and all their war equipment. With the enemy offensive destroyed, Madrid once again seemed invincible as the bastion of popular resistance.

Our victory in Guadalajara, which ought to have encouraged Largo to take additional steps to convert the militia into a regular army, on the contrary convinced him that the militia was sufficient to handle any job. The Communist Party insisted on this action, but Largo refused to hear us. He ignored the fact that the men with whom he shared the responsibility for leading the country represented different sectors of opinion and forces, large and small, outside his own Socialist Party, and that without these forces he could not wage the war.

Largo Caballero, normally a difficult and temperamental man, was now even more so because of Asensio's resignation. His hostility toward the Communists who bore the brunt of the struggle grew to proportions that were absurd and completely out of place for a man leading a country engaged in war.

This only served to aggravate the already latent government crisis. In cabinet meetings it became increasingly more difficult to discuss the situation of the battlefronts and to reach agreements about problems relating to the war.

When the Communist Party decided to participate in the government, it did so without renouncing its right to criticize policies it thought erroneous and to inform the workers of its opinions on war problems and on social changes taking place during the conflict. Largo Caballero could not accept this, perhaps assuming that in order to keep its two ministers in the government, the Communists would compromise their principles and patiently tolerate his temper tantrums and excesses.

[37]

# Counterrevolution in Catalonia

In the heat of the war, when the North was in the middle of an enemy offensive, when Málaga was a bleeding wound in the side of the Republican resistance movement, the FAI and POUM (the Trotskyite party) rebelled in Barcelona on May 3, presenting an ultimatum to the Generalitat of Catalonia which in effect was a demand for power.

The ultimatum presented to the Catalán President on the points of Trotskyite and FAIist bayonets demanded the following: "The Ministry of War; the Ministries of Industry, Transportation, Trade, Finances, Agriculture; the posts of Chief of Police, Police Commissar of Barcelona and all other important police posts, in addition to the participation of the Anarchists and Trotskyites as undersecretaries in those ministries which were left to other parties, and half of all subordinate posts in all the ministries."

If they won their demands in Catalonia, the Anarcho-Trotskyites would be in a position to make the same demands of the Republican government on the threat of starting a new civil war in the Republican camp.

Franco's General Staff was hardly averse to this possibility, as shown in a report which Faupel, the German ambassador who maintained close contact with Franco, sent to Hitler about the counterrevolution in Catalonia. Dated May 11, 1937, Faupel, among other things, wrote:

"Concerning the disorders in Barcelona, Franco has told me that the street fighting was provoked by his agents. Nicholás Franco has confirmed this report, informing me that they have a total of 13 agents in Barcelona. Some time ago one of them had reported that the tension between Anarchists and Communists in Barcelona was so great that it could well end in street fighting. The Generalissimo told me that at first he doubted this agent's reports, but later they were confirmed by other agents. Originally he didn't intend to take advantage of this possibility until military operations had been established in Catalonia. But since the Reds had recently attacked Teruel to aid the Government of Euzcadi, he thought the time was right for the outbreak of disorders in Barcelona. In fact, a few days after he had received the order, the agent in question with three or four of his men succeeded in provoking shooting in the streets which later led to the desired results."

Isn't there a close connection between Faupel's report to Hitler and the cynical declarations of Diego Abad de Santillán, the FAI leader, in his book *Por qué Perdimos la Guerra* (Why We Lost the War, Buenos Aires, 1940) in which he admits his tie with José Antonio Primo de Rivera, the founder of the Falange?

The instigators of the counterrevolution in Barcelona overestimated their power and underestimated that of the Popular Front parties and organizations fighting for the victory of the Republic. If in the first weeks of the fascist rising the Anarchists dominated the scene in Catalonia, this situation didn't last long. It is by now an established truth that Catalonia's Communist Party, the then recently created United Socialist Party and the UGT played major roles during the struggle to check the rebels.

The Anarcho-Trotskyites felt the strength of these organizations when their counterrevolutionary putsch, encouraged by the fascist radio, ended in defeat. The leaders of the counterrevolution found themselves alone. The workers of Catalonia, even the federalists, refused to support the movement. When a few factories stopped production, it was not because the workers wanted to join the rebels but because their lives had been threatened.

The war irretrievably discredited Anarchist tactics and methods and their use of violence. The failure of the May putsch showed the Anarchist leaders that they had to contend with an authentic national revolutionary movement led by the Communist Party which would always oppose political adventurism and pseudorevolutionary demagogues whose activities serve fascism and reaction.

Just as Largo Caballero never abandoned the idea of heading a Socialist government as the culmination of Spain's revolutionary process, so too the Anarchists never renounced the plan to establish "libertarian communism" and took advantage of the war situation to make such an attempt.

As a pretext for their rebellion in May, the Anarchists claimed that the revolution was failing. In order to save it, they alleged, it was necessary to socialize and collectivize the entire country, a process they aimed to start in Catalonia. The Anarchists were in a hurry. Events were taking place rapidly, and before the rug was pulled out from under their feet, they had to try their strength. And their strength failed them.

The peasants, among whom they had considerable influence, started to break away from the Anarchists because of their violent methods and taxes levied by the notorious FAI "committees." They forced the peasants into cooperatives and took away their possessions not for the benefit of society in general, but for the benefit of the committees themselves—which the peasants came to fear more than they did the rebels.

While it is true that the Anarchists had a powerful following among the Catalán factory workers, their influence in this sector was not as strong as it had been before the war. In spite of their depleted membership, however, the Catalán Anarchists still controlled the railroad, transport and building unions as well as 50 per cent of the textile, food and chemical products unions.

But it was a different story on the battlefronts. Only on the Aragón front did their red-and-black banner wave above some of the combatants—combatants who never went into battle. The Aragón front had remained frozen for many long months. Since it was stationary, the insurgents frequently withdrew their troops and used them in other places, That's how positive they were that the Anarcho-Trotskyite front wouldn't budge an inch in their absence!

For example: The rebels took two brigades from Aragón to reinforce the Italian attack on Madrid through Guadalajara. The Anarchist commanders never took advantage of this circumstance to launch military operations that could have stopped the fascists in Aragón.

When the Anarchists were reproached about the immobility of the Aragón front, they replied that they had no arms, which was not true; in fact, they had more arms than did many other fronts. At the beginning of the war they had captured most of the arms in the Barcelona fortress. Moreover, until the Negrín government later established state control over them, the factories in Barcelona worked for the Anarchists and no one ever objected to this arrangement. They also had at their disposal a complete network of international brokers who purchased arms for them in France and other countries with the foreign exchange the Anarchists obtained in their own fashion inside Spain.

What they didn't have and what they were constantly demanding were airplanes and tanks. And they didn't have them because the Republic government didn't have them either, except for those it received as aid from the Soviet Union—in spite of the obstacles the French government put in the way of letting Soviet material pass through France.

The real reason for the immobility of the Aragón front stemmed from the policies of the FAIist-Trotskyite group, led by Abad de Santillán and his crew, which were all slanted in one direction, namely, "Don't waste your strength fighting." And not because "first comes the revolution, and then the war," as they affirmed; rather because they needed to keep their forces intact as a means of pressure on the Popular Front and as a bulwark for their plans to seize power and rule the country.

The Civil War was waged with a minimum of Anarchist participation. An exception was the case of Durruti, after the insurgents had already been repulsed at the doors of Madrid. The Anarchists jealously preserved their troops, but their prestige was dwindling, while the authority and influence of those who marched in the first ranks and unhesitatingly occupied the most dangerous positions was, in spite of tragic losses, growing stronger.

The conservative policies of the Anarchist leaders were at sharp variance with the desires of the workers in their ranks, who wanted to fight to win the war and wipe out fascism. And indeed, there were individual anarchist combatants in units led by the Communists who fought magnificently, shoulder-to-shoulder with the Communists. The natural and logical result, so feared by the FAI and POUM, frequently took place. After living and fighting together with the Communists, the Anarchists would join the party.

Opposing the efforts of sensible men to organize a regular army, the Anarchists distributed the following propaganda piece among the Anarchist militia in Aragón: "We do not accept militarization because it would lead to an obvious danger. We do not recognize military formations because that is the negation of Anarchism. Winning the war does not mean winning the revolution. Technology and strategy are important in the present war, not discipline which presupposes a negation of the personality."

The Anarcho-Trotskyite putsch of May, which was inevitably to lead to a crisis in the Largo Caballero government, had been in the making for months. The time for the outbreak was not chosen in Catalonia, but in the General Staff offices of Franco, as proved by the document already quoted from German Ambassador Faupel, which gives testimony of the ties of the POUM and FAI with the enemy.

And if they bloodied the streets of Barcelona with a criminal revolt, it was because neither the Catalán nor Madrid governments wanted, for different reasons, to end the shameful, violent provocation.

On April 29, 1937, after the loss of Málaga, and when the situation in the Basque Country and consequently in all the North was extremely serious, men and arms were withdrawn from Aragon by order of the Anarcho-Trotskyite command and transferred to Barcelona.

During the first and second of May, the Anarcho-Trotskyites attempted to cut rail, telephone and telegraph communications in Barcelona. The Catalán Government then ordered its troops to occupy the *Telefónica* and to disarm all persons in the street carrying arms without the required authorization.

The rebels replied with more violence. While fighting was going on in the streets of Barcelona, the Anarchist rebels demanded that the Catalán government step down and forthwith disband all its armed forces.

On May 3, the Anarchists captured and disarmed the Alpine

Batallion barracks. The Trotskyites took control of all communications in the city and its outskirts. Meanwhile, the government failed to take any measures to end the situation. The new rebels attempted to assault the offices of Catalonia's United Socialist Party and were repulsed by a strong volley of rifle and machine-gun fire.

The announcement that the Republican government was sending a squadron of airplanes and tanks to crush the uprising considerably cooled the enthusiasm of the rebels, who already saw themselves in the presidential palace of Catalonia, giving orders to the Madrid government and making pacts with Franco.

All during the uprising the Franquist radio was constantly inciting the rebels and trying to direct their activities. Their plans turned to ashes, but not without some tragic losses to the Republic. Several of our comrades of the United Socialist Party were killed during the putsch, among them Antonio Sesé, General Secretary of the Catalán UGT, murdered by a cowardly shot in the back as he was walking to the presidential palace.

The counterrevolution in Catalonia was dying of itself. Failing to enlist the popular support they had expected, its leaders found themselves alone. As late as May 6, when negotiations had already been started between the Catalán government and some of the Anarchist ministers who had come from Valencia, two battalions of Ascaso's division and one POUM battalion were ordered to leave the Aragon front and were transported in 45 buses to Barcelona.

When Comrade Reyes, Aragon's chief of aviation, was informed that these troops had abandoned the front, he took a squadron of planes and went in search of them. When he sighted Ascaso's own column, he ordered them to turn back or else be bombed for having deserted. The battalions returned to their units. Only a group of the POUM militia arrived in Barcelona—in time to see the ignominious uprising gasp its last breath.

Combatants of all fronts demanded the punishment of those responsible for the counterrevolutionary movement. The Minister of War refused to take steps against them in order to avoid alienating the FAI and POUM, for he viewed them as useful instruments in his fight against the Communist Party.

Everyone in Spain was outraged. For the Communists, participation in the government was growing more difficult each day.

# 38

# From Largo to Negrín

The news arriving from the Basque Country and Asturias was alarming. Unless the Government radically changed its policies, its localistic military and political approach, a swift defeat was inevitable.

On May 9, 1937, after Largo Caballero had refused to punish those who were playing into the enemy's hands, José Díaz, in a meeting held in Valencia, brought out into the open the country's political problems, which in one way or another had hitherto been kept from the public.

Ten months of war and eight months of the Largo Caballero government had convinced us of the impossibility of continuing along the same path. We had no intention of forcing Largo, who represented the Socialist Party, to resign; instead we wanted to make an attempt to discuss collectively the problems relating to the war, within the framework of the government. It was quite obvious that if the Republic were defeated as a result of the government's policy, the blame would be shared equally by all, whether or not they had participated in drawing up war plans and governing the country.

The Communist Party made public its disagreements with the conduct of the war at this time because the situation in Euzcadi was extremely grave. By this action we hoped to turn the steering wheel in the right direction and head north, with all the means at the government's disposal, to aid the Basque combatants and those in Asturias and Santander, already under the threat of a direct enemy attack. To continue on the road we had started in September 1936, was to dissipate the heroism and fighting spirit of our people, it was to march toward an inevitable defeat, despite our partial victories.

José Díaz's speech evoked an extraordinary response from the people, although he discussed the urgent problems of military and political leadership with the utmost discretion. If the people had been kept in ignorance of what was happening behind government doors, it was they who had suffered the consequences of an erroneous, negative policy in their own flesh.

A cabinet meeting was held the day after the Díaz speech. As if nothing had occurred, Largo Caballero presented the meeting's agenda, in which, as always, questions relating to the war were conspicuous by their absence. One of the Communist ministers rose to say that the party representatives did not approve the agenda. Our ministers demanded that the military and political situation be discussed and that the President state what he intended to do to aid the North.

Largo Caballero refused, declaring that it was he who drew up the agenda and not the Communists. The Communist ministers replied: "You can keep on making the agenda and rule personally if you like, but not with the complicity of the Communist Party. We withdraw from the government as of this moment."

"Then we'll go on without you," coldly answered Largo.

Indalecio Prieto, one of the most greatly esteemed Socialist ministers in the Republic, arose and resolutely told Largo Caballero that without the participation of the Communist Party there could be no government. Largo then held a series of consultative meetings in which his sole supporters were the Anarchists, whom he had rescued from ignominy after the May putsch in Catalonia. The Anarchists agreed to form a syndicalist government if they were given ministries and time—in other words, if the political sense and instinct for self-preservation of the Republican forces would disappear long enough to accept such an extreme proposal.

Largo Caballero found himself in a position where he had no choice but to dissolve his government. He presented his resignation to the President, who asked another Socialist, Dr. Juan Negrín Lopez, to form a new cabinet.

During the nine months of war, the influence of Anarchism had been drastically reduced in the industrial and agricultural regions of our country—Catalonia, Valencia, Aragón and Andalusia—areas where previously it had enjoyed the upper hand. This was not by chance, but the result of a latent process which the war had brought to the surface.

Ever since the Socialists had withdrawn from the Republican government in 1933, changes favoring the Communists within the workers' movements and the political camp in general had been evident. From 1933 to 1936, the Communist Party made great strides, strengthening its ranks by leading the struggle for a popular front, by its participation in the insurrection of October 1934 and by its efforts to create an antifascist block of all democratic-bourgeois and working-class sectors.

Thus a "phenomenon" had taken place that staggered the Socialist and Anarchist leaders, who obstinately refused to admit the Communist Party's influence on the national scene. From 30,000 Communist Party members in January 1936—a figure which the Socialist Party had reached only after 40 years of activity—membership soared to 100,000 in July of the same year.

Though the Communist Party nearly quadrupled its membership from January to June 1936, it had two shortcomings: Its influence was weak in the trade unions, and it lacked a body of Marxist intellectuals. The latter was also the most serious problem of the Socialist Party, despite its many jurists and professors.

If it is curable, a defect that is admitted can be overcome. Unlike the Socialists, the Communists worked to create a core of Marxist working-class intellectuals. It gave to its best and most stalwart workers the solid Marxist theoretical base needed to strengthen the party's ideological backbone. With the invaluable aid of Comrade Codovilla, and later Comrade Togliatti, the Communists organized a group of leaders on national and local levels who, with the cooperation of the teachers, journalists, professors and scientists in our ranks, were the architects of the Communist Party of Spain, the heart of the popular resistance against fascist aggression.

The Socialist Party could not tolerate the existence of a strong, influential Communist Party which seemed capable of walking on the stormy waters of Spanish political life. When concrete facts brought the reality of our strength home to the Socialists, in their resentment they resorted to the shoddy assertion that the "Communist Party grew in the shade of Soviet airplanes." Our Socialist friends in their resentment had to resort to false arguments such as these. As a matter of fact, from April 14, 1931, to July 1936, there was not one Soviet airplane, tank or rifle, not even a Soviet consulate in Spain! The Republican-Socialist government that, de jure, had recognized the Soviet state had not even established normal diplomatic relations with it.

From January to July 1936, when Spain had no relations of any kind with the Soviets, the Communist Party's progress was far greater than that of other left-wing parties. It had become an important national political force while the rest of the political and trade-union organizations of the Republican camp were faced with the dilemma of "renewal or disappearance."

In 1935 when Largo Caballero was forced under pressure from the masses of his own party—especially the Socialist Youth, who were irresistibly drawn to the Soviet Union—to establish relations with the Communist Party, he did so, but with secret reservations and not-so-secret hostility toward the Communists. He saw the Communists not as a revolutionary force on whom he could always count, but as a rival threatening the hegemony of his party in the working-class movement. In order to check what he considered excessive Communist expansion, he made tremendous errors which led him to inflict flagrant injustices on the party and to enforce policies which weakened the resistance and unity of the Republican camp.

Objective observers of the Spanish situation at that time arrived at a similar evaluation. The Catholic journalist, Henry Buckley, of Great Britain, whom no one could accuse of partiality to the Communists, was a correspondent in Madrid for nine years. In his book *Life and Death of the Spanish Republic* (London, 1940), he wrote: "If Largo had been more flexible in his ideas, he could have taken the inevitable in his stride and made a pact with the Communists. In an alliance of the two parties, led by Largo, the Socialist Party could have conserved all of its sober judgment, and taken advantage of the new ideas and useful methods of organization supplied by the younger Communist Party. Instead of this, he chose to fight them."

A new stage in the war began with the Negrín government, one much more difficult than the others. Our superiority of the first weeks with respect to territory had diminished. The enemy's situation was now greatly improved.

The Republican government still had important bases, good human potential and economic resources, but food and war material were scarce. The shrunken territory of Loyalist Spain could not feed its population, especially since tens of thousands of agricultural workers and peasants were now engaged in military activities. The importation of prime commodities and war equipment was becoming increasingly more difficult. The solidarity of democratic men and organizations of all countries, fraternal and impressive though it was, did not fulfill our need for arms and food.

In contrast to the shortage of basic goods, which affected the morale of our civilians and combatants, the insurgent army was excellently supplied with war equipment by the two fascist powers, Italy and Germany.

The political heritage left by Largo Caballero weighed heavily on the life of the nation. There were no Anarchists in the new government. They refused to participate in the Negrín cabinet out of sympathy with Largo Caballero in whom they had found a protector and, because of his anticommunism, their best supporter.

The Negrín government was composed of three Socialists, two Communists, two left-wing Republicans, a representative from Catalonia and one from the Basque Country. Negrín stayed on as Minister of Finance, a post he held since 1936. Another Socialist, Indalecio Prieto, occupied the Ministry of Defense, comprising the war, aviation and navy ministries.

At the time he assumed power Negrín was known only in certain intellectual circles. Because of his determination in waging the war, he soon won the confidence and respect of the people. This made the Anarchists change their minds about participating in the government. In their vanity, the Anarchists had believed that any government formed without them would end in failure. They forgot that much blood had been shed since July 18, and that "this year's birds don't roost in last year's nests." Far from justifying their arrogant approach, the government went on without them, and their absence not only failed to stop the wheels of government but, on the contrary, made them turn faster.

When the Anarchists became convinced that popular support was necessary to carry on any kind of struggle and that this could not be done with leaders who did not have the needed qualifications, they agreed to participate. But they returned to their government seats greatly reduced in size and prestige. They had had four representatives in the Largo Caballero cabinet; now they had only one.

With the putsch of Barcelona, the violence of Ascaso's men in Aragón and the collectivization program in Valencia which had been nullified by the Agrarian Reform decree drawn up the Communist Minister Vicente Uribe, with the aid of the peasants, the FAI ghost was beheaded. It was seen lurking about only where the weakness of other anti-Franco organizations gave it room to reappear.

The new government was determined to hit the enemy in its own territory. One of its first acts was to order the bombing of the port of Iviza, a rebel supply base used by the Italians and Germans. A German ship was sunk during the operation.

This attracted the world's attention to Hitler's participation in the Spanish Civil War. As a retaliatory action, German battleships opened fire on the city of Almería in full daylight, taking a large toll of victims among the civilian population, which included a large number of refugees from Málaga. The people had fled from Italian bombers only to die under the fire of the howitzers of Nazi battleships.

A defenseless Spanish city had been bombed by the navy of a foreign country which had not declared war, indeed, a country that had no dispute with the victimized country. The so-called democratic countries of the world remained silent. Not a protest was heard. France was quiet. Great Britain was mute.

The Socialist-led Scandinavian countries and Belgium considered the moment inopportune to meddle in other peoples' affairs. The United States continued supplying Franco with petroleum and allowing Nazi Germany, which was preparing war against Europe, to test its aviation on the defenseless cities of Spain.

# 39

# The Fall of the North

> Do not weep, Euzcadi,
> Listen to this truthful song
> Whose music tells of
> Something great that I can't express,
> Even though fascism
> Has trodden on your soil . . .
> Our people swore
> Euzcadi will be free,
> For there still are people in Euzcadi
> Who love their country
> And prefer death
> To life with dishonor.
> —Popular Basque Song

The enemy was intensifying its pressure on the North. The rebels needed to destroy the popular resistance in the Basque Country at any cost, since, once this was done, the Asturian and Santander fronts would fall soon after in a chain reaction. The insurgents needed the North's arms industry in Guipúzcoa, the iron and steel works and the explosives factories in Vizcaya, the agricultural and livestock wealth of Santander and Asturia's coal mines.

While a large part of the blame for the fall of the North can be attributed to the policies of the French government under the Socialist Léon Blum, who prevented aid from reaching the Republican combatants defending Irún, we must be absolutely objective in passing judgment on what happened in the North. We must also search inside the Republican camp itself to determine whether a share of the responsibility lies with the men who led the war both in the Basque Country and in Madrid, the men whose differences and conflicts affected the political and military activities of the North.

Undoubtedly, the War Minister's policy of skimping on aid to the

Basques, of refusing this aid at the most critical moments, helped to weaken resistance in this nerve center of the Republican camp.

Considering the enormous industrial importance of the Basque Country, we ask: Was everything possible done to use fully the North's technical and human potentialities? Whose fault was it that Basque industries and their highly skilled workers and technicians were not put on a wartime basis? Had they been converted to war production, they could have supplied not only Euzcadi but all of Republican Spain with basic material to continue the resistance.

And later, when the loss of the heart and pulse of Spain's iron and steel industry was inevitable, why weren't its factories, its blast furnaces, its plants, destroyed, as the patriot Jesús Larrañaga and all the Basque Communists had demanded?

These questions were never brought up for discussion, in order not to offend elements which the Republic wanted to keep friendly.

To silence an error is to leave the way clear for compounding others. Mistakes of tremendous consequences have been piously committed to oblivion, making it impossible to analyze objectively the general reasons for the defeat of the Republic.

Where did the responsibility for the North's collapse lie? In behind-the-scenes rivalries? In suicidal competitions? In fits of vanity on both sides? Did the Prime Minister have sufficient understanding of the nature of the autonomy granted to Euzcadi? On the other hand, wasn't the Basque government making a serious error when it insisted on keeping separate military commands in each region, in each zone? These were to a certain extent independent of the Central General Staff and the Republican government, from whom it demanded complete autonomy, but to whom it ran demanding supplies which could well have been produced in any one of the regions of the North still loyal to the Republic.

Probably there is an element of truth in all of the implications of these questions. At this point let us recall the correspondence between the Basque government and General Llano de la Encomienda, chief of the Northern Army. This correspondence reveals much as to the divergencies within the Republican camp and as to the double-dealing of the War Minister who, on the one hand, gave General Llano de la Encomienda the command of the Northern Army, and on the other (according to the explicit statement of José Antonio de Aguirre, President of the Basque Country), declared that "the General Staff and Northern Army do not exist." Despite the gravity of these implications, they reflected only a small part of the true state of affairs.

If Aguirre's statement was true—and we find it difficult to doubt it, in view of the seriousness of the matter—who was to blame for preventing the coordination of military actions in the North? Who was to blame for ordering a loyal general of the Republic to assume command of an organism whose very existence was later denied by the War Minister himself?

What the Republic failed to do in Euzcadi when it still had the opportunity was done by the insurgents when they conquered the Basque Country. Its industries began to produce feverishly for the war, giving to Franco's Army what it had held back from the defenders of the Republic. This is a fact, and facts are what count in judging the activities of men and parties. Although it may be distressing to recall the tragic pages of history, they are still there. History recalls them for us.

While the ashes of Guernica were still warm, the Communist Party examined in a critical spirit what had happened in the North. It did not exempt from criticism or absolve from responsibility some Basque Communists, in particular Astigarrabía and Urondo, the former a minister, the latter the Director of Public Works in the Basque government. They had done nothing toward converting the militia into a regular army or utilizing the full industrial capacity of the Basque Country. To avoid difficulties, Astigarrabía and Urondo had taken the path of least resistance, adapting themselves to the Nationalist policies, against the opposition of Comrades Ormazábal, Monzón and others.

The loss of Irún on September 4, 1936, aggravated the situation of the Basque Country, since it cut our communications with France and made the resistance more difficult. The Negrín government made great attempts to aid Euzcadi. The best airplanes at its disposal, which were not many, were sent to the North. They were forced to land in quickly improvised landing strips at places whose position was known by the enemy and where movement was difficult. The bases were bombed relentlessly, making it impossible to save Euzcadi.

The terrible destruction of Guernica on April 26, 1937, by rebel airplanes showed to what lengths the insurgents were willing to go to conquer the Basque Country and seize its industries, minerals, ports and economic potential. The Germans who directed the offensive, the Italians who marched with the Requetés, and the Falangists did not hesitate to resort to any method, even if it meant wiping Basque cities and towns from the face of the earth.

The loss of Euzcadi was a step toward the defeat of Santander and the complete surrender of the whole region where the bulk of Nationalist forces were stationed. Euzcadi was the tragic prelude to the fall of Asturias.

All the North fell into the hands of the rebels—men, iron, steel, mineral, coal, wood, heavy industry, precision arms, explosives, electric power plants, meat, milk, hides, fruit, fish . . .

The Republic was losing its territory, and bleeding to death.

As a diversionary maneuver, the Central General Staff organized an offensive against the rebel troops in Brunete in July 1937 and later on the Aragón front. But the shadow of the ideas and spirit of Asensio and Cabrera hovered over the plans of the Defense Ministry.

It was chiefly the men of the Fifth Regiment who carried out the Republican offensive in Brunete. They were already a part of the Peoples' Army organized by Negrín and they brought discipline, fighting spirit and organization to its ranks. Líster and Modesto had the task of putting the General Staff's plan into practice and they did it brilliantly. Had it not been for the sabotage of their operations by Colonel Casado and company, they could have destroyed the entire enemy front in Madrid.

The Peoples' Army swiftly won Brunete but had no chance to put this advantage to use. The army was forced to hold out in Brunete, by now converted into ruins, for almost a month. Enemy aviation bombed the town day and night. Republican forces were powerless to stop the raids partly because of their lack of aviation, but chiefly because the General Staff sabotaged the entire operation. In the heat of combat, Colonel Casado withdrew, claiming an indisposition. Instead of putting him before a firing squad as a traitor, the War Minister played the nursemaid. Casado's real trouble was his heart of mud which quivered with fear lest the Peoples' Army might conquer the rebels.

It was an agonizing sight to watch one wave of enemy airplanes after another raid our positions, wipe out our units, and inflict terrible losses on that legion of heroes. After four long weeks of resistance without water, without most necessary supplies and without reserves to relieve the combatants, the order was given to abandon Brunete.

One month later, in another diversionary movement, the General Staff decided to start a series of operations in Aragón in the direction of Saragossa. The operations were planned by Comrade Cordón, a professional soldier and member of the Communist Party, dedicated heart and soul to the cause of the people. He had been Chief of Staff of the Eastern Army and later Under-Secretary of War, posts to which he brought all his ability and courage.

After a brief rest, the troops that had fought in Brunete were sent to the Aragón front to carry out the planned offensive. The Republic could not rely on the undisciplined FAI militia, much less on the Anarchist militia of Ascaso, to carry out such an important mission.

With the arrival of Líster's troops in Caspe, the FAI's reign in that region of Aragón came to an end. Republican order was established. The Anarchist Ascaso, president of the Council of Aragón, went to France, later to America, taking with him the booty he had extracted from his experiments in "libertarian communism."

The undisciplined militia that had been vegetating in Aragón, against the desires of many soldiers and commanders who honestly wanted to fight, were incorporated into the Peoples' Army. The first objective of the military operations begun at the end of August 1937 was Belchite, stronghold on the road to Saragossa. I arrived there at the height of battle.

House by house, street by street, our soldiers were taking the city, demolishing the desperate resistance of the enemy. A flag was placed in every important spot taken by the Republican combatants. From Modesto's headquarters situated on the side of a small hill outside the city we could see the flags that marked the progress of the battle.

The seminary at the entrance to the city, converted into a fortress by the rebels, was destroyed; the Civil Guard barracks were assaulted. Our job was to win every important building where the enemy was holding out. The church and the town hall were the last two points of enemy resistance. When I entered Belchite fighting was still going on.

While crossing a street through a mountain of smoldering ruins, I came face to face with General Walter, who was preparing his men to take the town hall. He instructed me to turn back and stay out of the city until the enemy was completely routed. There were still many snipers hidden among the ruins.

I returned to Modesto's headquarters and in a short while the first prisoners of war began to arrive, soldiers and civilians along with a group of priests dressed in street clothes. All expected to be shot without mercy now that they were in the hands of the "reds." The stories told about Republican forces by the fascist propaganda would have put to shame the most hair-raising tales about vampires and cannibals.

After the prisoners had eaten and rested, they were permitted to talk with the combatants. They spoke of La Pasionaria with horror, of the crimes she had committed, of her cruelty with prisoners, especially with monks and nuns, of the songs about her heard on Radio Saragossa. After listening to them quietly, I asked:

"What do you think La Pasionaria looks like?"

"Well, we really don't know. But they say she's more like a beast than a woman."

"Something like me?" I asked smiling.

"How can you say such a thing? You're a Spanish woman. They say La Pasionaria isn't Spanish, that she looks like a man."

The physical and moral picture that those poor people painted of me, repeating what the rebel propaganda had fabricated, made me laugh out loud. When they said I looked like a man, they were only being euphemistic. What they really meant to say was another, more colorful, word. But they wouldn't dare repeat all they heard about me; after all, they were prisoners of war in the hands of Republicans.

The reader can imagine the astonishment of those people when I told them who I was.

"It can't be true," they said. "You're joking."

When they were convinced that the flesh-and-blood Pasionaria was standing before them, they looked at me quivering with fear for their lives. I told them that nothing would happen to them, but it was difficult to convince them after the "compliments" they had paid me.

The Aragón offensive could have been started many months earlier had it not been for the policy of tolerance toward the military inactivity of the Anarchist militia. The offensive compelled the fascist commanders to withdraw their forces from other fronts and concentrate them in Belchite to contain the advance of the Peoples' Army.

While this operation, too late, too limited, failed to prevent the fall of the North, it was at least proof that something had changed in the new government's concepts of waging the war, and that the Peoples' Army was able to handle successfully offensive as well as defensive operations.

[40]

# Triumph and Defeat in Teruel

In December 1937, after the fall of the North, the enemy ordered a large part of its troops to the region of Guadalajara in preparation for a new attack on Madrid. To frustrate this plan, the Peoples' Army decided to open an offensive in Teruel. Because of the secrecy with which the preparations had been made and the heroism of our troops, the operation was a complete success. Not expecting a Republican attack from that direction, the enemy was forced to give up its plan of besieging Madrid.

Shortly after Republican troops had liberated Teruel, I was there talking with the combatants and the inhabitants of the "city of lovers." The people—as if they were still living under the nightmare —told us of the horrors of the fascist occupation. The history of Teruel now had a new chapter, one very different from the romantic legend of Isabel and Diego, who are preserved as mummies in the Church of San Pedro. Now there were terrible pages describing the fascist occupation, the horrors of the Plaza del Torico where the so-called ladies of good society made a fiesta out of the executions of Republicans. I often wondered if their dreams were afterwards disturbed by the memory of the crimes sanctioned by their presence, or if they ever told their children what they had seen.

Among the outstanding combatants who fought in the battle of Teruel were our unforgettable Comrade Líster; the Commissars Santiago Alvarez, Barcia, Sevil, Alvaro Carvajosa, and party chiefs Felipe Ortuño, J. Sandoval, Sánchez Vázquez and M. Azcárate.

The bravery of our combatants was almost always nullified by the inept direction of the war. Arbitrary decisions continued to come out of the Ministry of Defense. The military concepts of Indalecio Prieto, the new Defense Minister, were based on an underestimation of the capacity of the Peoples' Army, whose operations, according to the ministry, were capable of only limited objectives. Therefore the operations of other fronts were not coordinated, sufficient troops were not reserved for possible military contingencies, and initial victories were not fully taken advantage of—with predictable physical and moral damage to our troops.

While the enemy was sending some of its most important reserves to reconquer the city, on three different occasions the Republican General Staff thought the battle was over. The Republic's tactical divisions and aviation were ordered to retreat three times, and were ordered back another three times under enemy pressure. As a result of this unnecessary strain on our troops and our failure to take advantage of the demoralization and initial edge we had won over the enemy, we had to abandon Teruel on February 22, 1938, after a two-and-a-half-month battle.

Ever since he had become Minister of Defense, Prieto, like his predecessor, was obsessed with the idea of destroying the Communist Party's influence, even at the cost of weakening the combativity and efficiency of the military and civilian resistance. Prieto did not believe in the military capacity of our nonprofessional commanders. The truth is that he was also wary of the professional soldiers' abilities, but these he at least supported and even protected. On the other hand, he allowed no occasion to slip by to create problems for the militia commanders, especially if they were Communists.

Behind Prieto's attitude there was, apart from his inveterate anti-communism, a fear he never admitted but frequently revealed. He was aware that the army led by men of the people, tempered in battles for the Republic, constituted an immense revolutionary force which could play a decisive role in the organization of Spain's future political system.

Prieto's policy was to weaken this force, to convert the army into an amorphous mass under the leadership of "apolitical" career soldiers, subject to the War Ministry and sharing its opinions, without questioning whether they were just or unjust.

In peacetime, mistaken policies could have been debated. But in wartime these policies were more than debatable, more than counter-revolutionary; they were, to put it plainly, sheer suicide.

On more than one occasion honest military chiefs objected to the Defense Minister's policies because of their demoralizing effect on our troops. They knew that Prieto's policies, which had clearly proven their ineffectuality in the battle of Teruel, endangered the resistance. Before long they were to bring even more disastrous consequences.

On March 9, 1938, the enemy began a general offensive on the Eastern front, managing to break through Republican lines and disperse some units in that sector. Through no fault of its own, the Peoples' Army was forced to retreat. The disaster occurred because the Defense Minister acted against all military logic and common sense. The retreat spurred the defeatists who existed in the government itself into an extremely dangerous enterprise. Rumors of capitulation began to spread through the capital of Catalonia.

The Communist Party mobilized the population of Barcelona and the armed forces who were not willing to lay down their arms to demand that the government continue the resistance and take measures to stop those who advocated surrender. On March 16, 1938, a massive demonstration marched through the principal streets of Barcelona up to the Pedralbes Palace, where the Council of Ministers was in session. There the demonstrators demanded that the resistance continue and that those ministers not willing to defend the Republic be replaced.

A committee was formed with representatives from most of the organizations that wanted to continue the fight against fascism. Representing the UGT was Pretel; the CNT, Mariano R. Vázquez; the PSOE (Socialist Workers Party of Spain), Vidarte; the Socialist Youth, Santiago Carrillo; the United Socialist Party, Sierra Pamies; and the FAI, Guerrero.

I represented the Communist Party in the committee. In our interview with Negrín, he tried to attach no importance to the rumors about capitulation and promised to continue the war as long as it was possible to do so.

The demonstrators disbanded, some going to the center of the city and others, the majority, to their homes.

Then a shocking thing happened, something strongly indicating that within government circles there was someone who was passing information to the enemy, someone who had warned the enemy of a possible government crisis which would lead to capitulation if it materialized.

When there was no sign of the Republic's surrender, and before the thousands of workers who had taken part in the demonstration could reach their homes, Franco ordered the major part of his bombers to raid Barcelona. Hundreds of civilians perished. The fascists savagely bombed Barcelona for several days in the attempt to break the morale of the people and force the government to surrender.

A crisis did take place but not with the results desired by the enemy and its agents in the Republican camp. The Minister of Defense resigned. Representatives of Spain's two trade-union organizations entered the government: Ramón González Peña, of the UGT, and Segundo Blanco, of the CNT.

The Communist Party did everything it could to keep Prieto in the government at the head of a ministry other than that of defense, but he refused all the proposals offered him. In order to expedite the formation of the new Negrín cabinet, which had to have the participation of the most diverse political parties and continue the war, the Communist Party withdrew one of its own ministers.

On April 6, 1938, a communiqué published by the Politburo of the Spanish Communist Party gave full approval to "the changes which have transformed the government of the Republic into a *War and National Unity Government*," and welcomed the presence of the trade-union organizations in the government as "an expression of unity in this supreme moment of our fight which will mobilize everyone to the last able man, achieve the maximum industrial production, put the whole country on a war footing so that we may regain our fronts and fight until the end for the liberty and independence of Spain."

Dr. Negrín substituted for Prieto as Minister of Defense. By this time the fascists were waging their great offensive on the Eastern front and had reached Lérida. Further south the insurgents were advancing toward the Mediterranean with the aim of cutting the Republican zone in two—which they proceeded to do.

In spite of the difficult situation, Negrín was determined to face it, and he called upon the people to show themselves worthy of the combatants. He declared that resistance now would mean the first step toward victory.

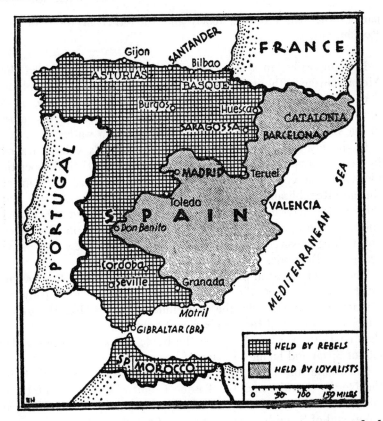

*Spain in February 1938, two months before Italian troops reached Vinoroz on the coast, midway between Barcelona and Valencia.*

On April 15, a little more than a week after Prieto had resigned, Italian troops reached Vinaroz, isolating Catalonia from the rest of the peninsula. The insurgent General Staff had planned a double offensive which was to start in Vinaroz and go north toward Barcelona and south to Valencia. If they succeeded in capturing Valencia, Madrid would be isolated and the enemy could wipe out Republican resistance.

The insurgents did not have complete success in their plans. The Republican Army, in a heroic effort, managed to stop the enemy offensive north of Valencia and in Tortosa, which was cut in two, one part in the hands of the rebels and the other in those of the Republicans.

It is impossible to speak of the arrival of Franco's army in the Mediterranean without mentioning the activities of the Republican fleet. What was wrong with the fleet? While our soldiers were fighting for every inch of national territory against the insurgents, most of our ships remained safe and snug in Republican waters.

In the first days of the uprising, the battlefleet's sailors, headed by a small group of corporals and officers known for their democratic ideas, kept the fleet loyal to the Republic and frustrated the plans of the anti-Republican, reactionary officers who wanted to put our ships at the service of Franco. A large number of the officers involved in the uprising abandoned ship and remained in Cartagena, not waiting passively for the war to end, but actively conspiring against the Republic.

The lack of a general plan of operations on the part of the government kept most of the fleet inactive, anchored principally in Cartagena. Consequently, the most militant sailors, like the group under Coll, preferred to disembark and fight with the soldiers rather than continue passively to watch the battle which was deciding the fate of Spain and taking so many of our peoples' lives.

Small naval units were stationed in different ports, particularly in the North—Asturias and the Basque Country. Every one of these sailors was a hero who continued the glorious tradition of the Basque sailors and of Spanish sailors in general. One of the men who played an important role in keeping the fleet loyal to the Republic was Pedro Prados, commander of the *Méndez Núñez*, who later became chief of staff of the navy.

Some of the most heroic sailors of the fleet were serving on the destroyer *José Luis Díez* and provided an admirable example of the decisive role that the fleet might have played in the war, if it had not been for the sabotage of the reactionary commanders who were reinstated on their ships, and the incompetence, or perhaps something worse, of those who planned the Republic's military operations on land and sea.

The destroyer *José Luis Díez* gave battle to several enemy ships in the Straits of Gibraltar. After a savage battle to escape from enemy encirclement and in the face of the military superiority of the enemy, the crew foundered the ship in Gibraltar rather than let it be captured. On board were Commander José Antonio Castro; Hernandorena, captain of the Merchant Marine and lieutenant of the Naval Reserve, who served in the Republic's submarine fleet; Rafael Menchaca, captain of the Merchant Marine and of the Naval Reserve.

There were many other heroic sailors, some Communist, others firm democrats, who showed their loyalty to the Republic and proved that there were men in the fleet on whom the people could count for their defense in any circumstance. Nothing was done to give these men adequate opportunity to help the war effort. On the other hand, in the name of an antirevolutionary eclecticism, the government was very considerate with the commanders and technicians who were enemies of the Republic. After the first violent outbreak, they were gradually given back their posts and supplied with documents testifying to their "loyalty." They later proved themselves to be not as inactive as their ships.

The navy lacked leadership. The Socialist-Anarchist policy of keeping the armed forces "apolitical" was bearing fruit. The fleet was a deadweight in the peoples' great fight against fascist reaction. The Communists in both the Largo Caballero and Negrin governments proposed an infinite number of times, to no avail, that the fleet be reorganized and that an investigation be ordered to find out what was going on in the naval base at Cartagena. Our officers there were more than a little suspicious of foul play.

It was not by chance that the fleet was inactive. After the fall of Catalonia, the fleet mutinied in Cartagena and sailed to Bizerte, the French base in North Africa, leaving the Republic without a navy. The rebellious officers and technicians were outspoken in their allegiance to Franco when the Franco-French committee arrived in Bizerte to take charge of the fleet.

The Republican fleet was much stronger than Franco's. It could have prevented the transport of men and material from Africa to Spain. In the North, when the battle was raging in the Basque Country, the fleet could have paralyzed enemy action by sea and checked the enemy advance by land. The fleet could have attacked ships that were transporting war material for Franco in the Mediterranean and in the Atlantic. It could have prevented rebel ships from attacking friendly vessels carrying war material for the Republic. Far from doing so, the fleet allowed them to sink, like the Soviet ship *Komsomol*, or let them be captured by the enemy, like the *Mar Cantábrico*, which was carrying airplanes.

The fleet could have prevented the Republican zone from being cut in half by attacking Franco's troops advancing to the Mediterranean coast through Vinaroz. It could have saved Majorca and kept the Balearic Islands loyal to the Republic. It could have acted to prevent the fall of Málaga. The fleet could have aided the destroyer *José Luis Díez* in its heroic battle against the rebel fleet. It did none of these things.

After the fall of Catalonia, the fleet could have given decisive aid to the army in the Central-South zone by helping to organize the resistance or by rescuing tens of thousands of combatants. But under the leadership of a Socialist commissar, Bruno Alonso, it chose to abandon the Spanish coast and defect to the enemy side.

The General Staff of the navy had nothing to do with the sinking of the *Baleares*, according to the admission of its officers. It was sunk because the commander of the ship brought it within firing range twice. The first time, the fascist officers who had infiltrated the fleet managed to prevent a direct hit. The second time, the sailors without waiting for orders, fired and sank it.

By order of the Navy General Staff, the *Jaime I* was sabotaged and sunk in order to destroy the important nucleus of Communists who were serving on this ship. The *Jaime I* was a perpetual thorn in the side of an officers' corps that wrote the most shameful page in the history of the Navy during the war.

This was the sad balance sheet presented by the officers and technicians of the Republic's fleet to the Franco-French Committee in Bizerte. Although they catalogued their failures, it is not difficult to imagine how many truths lay behind these confessions. Now we can understand why, despite the fact that the sailors were mostly of Republican persuasion who had conducted themselves heroically in the beginning of the war, the fleet became an important foothold enabling the fascists to climb to victory, and this was one of our own greatest weaknesses. Absorbed in the problems of the war on land, we failed to give adequate attention to the fleet, leaving the way free for the Socialists to apply their policies, with results that should have been foreseen.

# The Thirteen Points

> The Italian flags have fallen and sunk into
> the Ebro,
> And only the flags of the Republic wave on
> the bridges.
>
> —Popular Song

In answer to those who were advocating unconditional surrender
and to refute foreign propaganda to the effect that Communism was
the issue being fought in Spain, the Prime Minister published a
document on April 30, 1938, which held out the possibility of
negotiations with the enemy to end the terrible war that had taken
so many lives.

In this document the Republican government put forth a program
known as the "Thirteen Points." The Communist Party fully supported it, once more showing that it would remain faithful to its
obligations and the cause of democracy. Enemy propaganda grossly
distorted the party's support of the program, accusing Communists
of Machiavellian motives.

In brief, the Thirteen Points of Negrin's program were the
following:

The independence and integrity of the Spanish state; withdrawal of all
foreign troops from national territory and cessation of all foreign intervention.

A plebiscite at the war's end to decide the form of Spain's future
government; development of national liberties within a framework of
national unity; the right of all citizens to all social and civic rights, including freedom of religion.

Protection of property and the means of production, but control over
abuses existing in the accumulation of wealth and the exploitation of
man; agrarian reform; renunciation of war; social legislation guarantee-
ing the rights of workers; the cultural, physical and moral development
of the nation.

An army in the service of the people; the renunciation of war as an instrument of national policy and loyalty to the League of Nations Pact.

Amnesty for all Spaniards willing to cooperate and help rebuild the country, including the members of the insurgent army.

The Thirteen-Point program was not meant for consideration in the Republican zone alone. It was in a large part aimed at the Nationalist camp, where the prolongation of the war and the growing intervention of Italians and Germans in political and economic life as well as in military operations was producing great discontent among the civilian population and permanent friction between Franco and his generals. Von Stohrer, the German Ambassador, wrote the following in a report dated July 1, 1938:

According to the Reds, the reign of terror presently being conducted in the Nationalist zone by Police Minister Martinez Anido, and the dictatorial methods of the state are completely unacceptable. The aim of this propaganda, which is closely tied up with their campaign against the influence of Germany and Italy, is very clear: To undermine Franco's authority and present his methods of government as an obstacle to the cessation of hostilities. In view of the slow progress of the war and the unrest prevalent in the Nationalist zone, this propaganda has not been entirely ineffective. Voices are being heard, even in Nationalist Spain, asking for an end to the war.

In view of the present equilibrium of forces and the resulting discontent and unrest in the Nationalist zone, this propaganda could be dangerous, particularly since there is already much discontent in Falangist circles with the clerical policies of Franco and Súñer. Moreover, it is becoming increasingly more evident that General Martinez's regime is intolerable and that his methods, which many Nationalists consider to be unbearable, must be changed. The Falange has recently asked Franco for the Ministry of Interior and also that Martinez Anido be transferred to a Ministry of Public Health, to be especially created for this purpose.

I have learned from generally well-informed sources that even the high military commands of the Nationalist Army have raised strong objections to continuing the war, which is advancing slowly and taking its toll in human lives and goods. They have expressed the hope that a formula can be found to end hostilities. . . .

On the other hand, if the war continues much longer, if Franco insists on unconditional surrender of the enemy, and in the event that Franco does not win new and important victories soon, it is not altogether impossible that events will develop in such a way as to oust Franco and bring internal political conflicts which in turn would touch off serious new strife.

As we see, Negrín's attitude and that of his supporters was entirely correct. While the Thirteen-Point program was greeted with open hostility by those Republicans who were intellectually on the side of the enemy, our combatants on the fronts who were facing death daily and the people in general supported it enthusiastically. The people and the combatants now knew that they were fighting not only because there was no other way out, but because the government was seeking the means of ending the war honorably in the belief that the road was open to a compromise solution which would save lives and guarantee the right of the people to express their will in democratic fashion.

Resistance became stronger, more solid. The victories later won by the Republican Army showed to what degree our people backed Negrín's government, which stood as a symbol of resistance. Nevertheless, those who were preparing the Republic's surrender continued with their plans. This was the contradictory situation in which we had to act.

Searching for support, those who wanted to capitulate collaborated with the worst elements in Spanish politics, the instigators of the May 1937 putsch in Catalonia. They intended to give a "proletarian" coating to their plans of handing Spain over to fascism.

In a document which was a monument of anticommunist lies and other infamies, they appealed to the Prime Minister with spurious reasons for disagreeing with his policy. They violently attacked the policy of national unity. They demanded that Communists be removed from the army and state institutions, that the government resign, that war commissars be abolished and that the army be reorganized under professional commanders.

The document was not in vain. It was the rationalization of treason to the Republic and to the people that was being hatched.

At a meeting of the Socialist Party leaders held in Barcelona in November 1938, Julián Besteiro stated that "without the participation of the Communists, there was no possibility of winning the war; but if the war was won, Spain would be Communist." Since this was under no circumstances permissible, the conclusion was logical: "Let's lose the war, so the Communists won't win." These were the lengths to which the anticommunist folly was carried by the "honorable" professor of logic, today considered one of the saints of the Socialist Party.

Besteiro and other Socialists, followers of Largo Caballero, chan-
neled all their activities and influence in this patricidal, counterrevolutionary and anti-Spain direction, culminating in the treacherous
junta under Colonel Casado, who delivered Spain to Franco.

When the Republican zone was cut in two by the rebel offensive
toward the Mediterranean which separated Catalonia from the rest
of Loyalist Spain, the Communist Party spoke to the people. It did
not hide the gravity of the situation created by the arrival of the
insurgents in the Mediterranean. This event lowered the morale of
many people, including sincere antifascists, and encouraged the
defeatists who were now appearing in various sectors of the Republican camp.

In a meeting of the Central Committee held in Madrid, May 1938,
I delivered the political report and showed how, in spite of our recent
defeats, resistance was still possible.

"The military defeats of recent months," I said in my report, "have
created a situation in which the liberty and independence of our
country are in greater danger than ever before.

"We report that Spain's situation is most serious. We are not
alarmists, but must speak the truth no matter how painful it may be
for us. . . .

"The lack of land communications between the Center and
Catalonia has created a situation that cannot be ignored, one that
must be examined in order that we may draw the correct conclusions.
It is most important that we keep in mind that the enemy has occupied
much of our territory (Spain is not a large country like China or the
Soviet Union), that we are in a position today where losing more
territory could be disastrous, since enemy troops are nearing our vital
centers. . . .

"We should recall the case of Euzcadi and Asturias, where separation from the rest of Spain brought in its wake serious political disorder along with manifestations of separatism and narrow localism—
all of which contributed to the fall of all the North. We cannot be
certain that this won't happen again. . . .

"We must defend and reaffirm by every means possible the
authority of the only legitimate government of the Republic. If we
forget what type of enemy we have before us, and occupy ourselves
with creating governments and defense committees in each region,

violating the unity of our country, we will be doing a great service to the enemy.

"The army's resistance is the beginning of a new situation, a fact we should not forget. Under terrible conditions, under the crushing weight of enormous material superiority, our army has resisted heroically. And along with the army, our people have resisted the pressure of those preaching surrender. Faced with our resistance, the enemy, even though still gaining important objectives, has failed to realize its plans completely.

"While our resistance has given the world additional proof of our vitality, of our fighting spirit and organization, of our heroism and self-confidence, we now have the beginning of a new situation in the interior of the country. The indispensable condition for this new start must be the unity of all antifascist forces around the Government of National Unity.

"This situation is signalized in the creation of the second Negrín government as the Government of National Unity. It is characterized by the defeat of those planning surrender and by the strengthening of the unity of the popular forces, a unity which will make it possible before long to pass from resistance to a new phase of offensive."

While the Popular Front had provided the foundation for the unity of all democratic forces against the fascist threat, the necessity for unity in facing the armies of two foreign powers who were occupying national territory led us to revise our policies in accordance with the facts. The second Negrín government with its Thirteen-Point program was a Government of National Unity. The Negrín program had as its objectives the establishment of this unity and the elimination of all regional tendencies.

"The unity we need today," I continued in my report, "is a new unity, larger in scope, more solid, effective and efficient than the unity we have had until now. We should have national unity, that is, the unity of a single program adopted by all antifascists under the leadership of the government, a unity that will permit us to mobilize, organize and send into battle new groups of people, new popular forces."

The Communist Party's confidence in the people and in the fighting spirit of our magnificent Popular Army was soon confirmed by events.

After Franco's forces had reached the Mediterranean, those who hoped for his victory and even many friends of the Republic thought that popular resistance would inevitably crumble. They were wrong for they did not really know our people. In the middle of July, the news from Republican Spain astonished them.

The Ebro Army, led by the two popular military chiefs, Lieutenant Colonels Modesto and Líster, with the help of Communist commanders, Socialists, party commissars and instructors, crossed the Ebro and waged the most important battle of the war, to the amazement of all who thought that the Republic could not possibly continue the war under the onerous conditions facing its army. More than 200 miles on the right bank of the Ebro were occupied by our army after an audacious crossing of one of Spain's most important rivers.

The crossing of the Ebro marked the beginning of a difficult battle which demonstrated the offensive capacity of the Peoples' Army, forged in two years of unequal combat with the enemy.

The ground our army won in less than a week, Franco's Army recovered only after more than four months of hard battle and with an enormous accumulation of men and war material that the Republican Army could not match. For the first time, as the German generals who participated in the war confessed later, an artillery barrage had to be employed to stop the advance of an army. This made any movement of our troops completely impossible, and we were unable to return a counter-barrage greater than that of the enemy.

All the reserve troops that the Republican Army had in Catalonia were used in the Ebro operation. Casualties among the veterans of the Fifth Regiment, the shock troops of all our important battles, were mounting, as they persisted in the difficult effort to open with their blood and their lives the road to victory for democratic Spain.

The troops who retreated in the Ebro, decimated, wounded, but with their spirits intact, were the men who had defended Madrid, the men who had been victorious in Guadalajara, Brunete and Belchite. They had borne on their shoulders the hardest part of the war, while the militia and later, brigades, divisions and armies, had remained paralyzed in the North for one reason or another. Later, in the Central-South zone, troops were not moved because of the sabotage of Casado's General Staff and Miaja, who opposed mobilizing even a single unit—even when the rebel offensive was bearing down on Catalonia with the bulk of its army and the best of its war equipment.

If the Communists had sought personal profit from the war, as claimed by the rats who dared not lift their snouts from the holes where they were hiding and trembling in fear, at that moment—the most agonizing of the entire war, when all the weight of the enemy offensive was on our men—we could have refused to continue sacrificing more lives, while others conspired against the Republic and in favor of the insurgents.

We did not refuse, but continued to send our men to defend Catalonia, since it was a question of life or death from both the politico-military and human viewpoints.

The battle of the Ebro was raging to a close. When misfortune comes it rarely rains but it pours! At the time the General Staff was ordering the retreat, Negrín announced his decision to withdraw the International Brigades, a total of approximately 6,000 men who had shared our battles and fate. The government was forced to take this extreme step to prevent France and England from recognizing Franco's belligerent rights.

Spain's parting with the heroes of the International Brigades was as sad and bitter as it was magnificent. Our hearts were heavy as we watched those heroes march through Barcelona's main thoroughfare, where the people's farewell had been organized. We thought of our own destiny and that of these men, many of whom could not return to their own countries because they were under fascist dictatorships.*

* At the parade of farewell to the Brigades in Barcelona on November 15, 1938, Negrín and La Pasionaria spoke words of thanks. First, she addressed the women of Barcelona: "Mothers! Women! When the years pass by and the wounds of war are staunched; when the cloudy memory of the sorrowful, bloody days returns in a present of freedom, love and well-being; when the feelings of rancour are dying away and when pride in a free country is felt equally by all Spaniards—then speak to your children. Tell them of the International Brigades. Tell them how, coming over seas and mountains, crossing frontiers bristling with bayonets, and watched for by ravening dogs thirsty to tear at their flesh, these men reached our country as Crusaders for freedom. They gave up everything, their homes, their country, home and fortune—fathers, mothers, wives, brothers, sisters and children, and they came and told us: 'We are here, your cause, Spain's cause, is ours. It is the cause of all advanced and progressive mankind.' Today they are going away. Many of them, thousands

For their participation in the Spanish war, nonintervention diplomacy treated these heroes as lepers. They were persecuted, hunted like criminals, confined in special camps and handed over to Hitler and Mussolini.

Those who imprisoned the men of the International Brigades in concentration camps could not know that many of them would soon become resistance leaders against fascism in their own countries.

[42]

## Capitulation Makes Headway

During those hard, bitter days for Spain's popular resistance, full of ominous portents for the peace of the world, the English and French governments, with the resigned approval of the government of Czechoslovakia, signed the shameful Munich treaty. Czechoslovakia was given to Hitler. A new focus of war was created in Europe, the many repercussions of which dealt a severe blow to the resistance in Spain.

A growing atmosphere in favor of surrender, the result of the intensified work of the enemies of resistance, mainly characterized the situation in Republican Spain after Munich, from September 1938 on. Those advocating surrender found fertile ground for their activities in the war weariness of the people, and this was reflected in the weaknesses and vacillations of the Negrín government itself.

---

of them, are staying here with the Spanish earth for their shroud, and all Spaniards remember them with the deepest feeling."

Then she addressed the members of the Brigades: "Comrades of the International Brigades! Political reasons, reasons of State, the welfare of that same cause for which you offered your blood with boundless generosity, are sending you back, some of you to your own countries and others to forced exile. You can go proudly. You are history. You are legend. You are the heroic example of democracy's solidarity and universality. We shall not forget you, and when the olive tree of peace puts forth its leaves again, mingled with the laurels of the Spanish Republic's victory—come back!"—Ed.

Although the second Negrín government had adopted many important political and military measures, it lacked homogeneity and an immediate program of action. The common cohesive factor—the will and decision to win the war—was frequently diluted, and indeed sometimes disappeared among the rivalries and antagonisms of the various political parties and the personal ambitions of their leaders.

The undermining political activity of the forces favoring capitulation was daily becoming more apparent. Mountains of calumny were being reared against the Communists in an attempt to discredit them before the combatants and the people. As the anticommunist offensive, wherein one could easily see the work of Franco's agents, steadily mounted, the fight against the Negrín government also increased in intensity and finally culminated in the crisis of August 1938.

Irujo and Aiguadé, who represented the Basque Nationalists and the Esquerra* of Catalonia, left the government. This was a serious blow to Negrín who was able to avert the ensuing crisis only because of the determined stand of the Communist Party, which advised him not to dissolve the government but instead to replace the ministers who had resigned. This was precisely what Negrín did. Bilbao, of the Basque left-wing Nationalists, and Moix, representing the United Socialist Party of Catalonia, entered the government, thus upsetting the applecart of all those who had expected a mortal crisis.

The worse the Republic's situation grew, the more the ministers opposed Negrín's decisions. Negrín's reaction was not that of a revolutionary leader determined to achieve victory at any cost. Instead, he put his efforts into resolving the immediate disputes of the day and in making ill-advised political concessions to those who refused to compromise for the sake of the Republic's victory. This was the reason why the wheels of government turned so slowly, the reason for the enormous delay in making decisions, the reason why solutions of many vital questions were postponed indefinitely and why so many incorrect policies were put into practice.

Negrín was well aware of the deficiencies and gaps in his governmental machine, but erroneously attributed these to the "party system." Consequently, on December 2, 1938, he proposed the forma-

---

* Lower middle-class party in Catalonia, whose name was the Catalán word for 'Left'.

tion of a National Front which would merge all Spanish parties. He thought this measure would guarantee the possibility of governing without being forced at every step of the way to make allowances for the demands and threats of each of the various political groups. The Communists advised him against this idea on the ground that instead of bringing the desired results, it would open the way for a dangerous personal dictatorship.

While the chief concern of the Communist Party at all times, apart from winning the war, was to maintain the Popular Front, in this period of gloom, conspiracies and intrigues, the Communists channelled all their energies more than ever into preventing a break in the antifascist bloc.

But now the party had to work under more difficult circumstances. Its influence in Madrid had been considerably reduced. The transfer of national party headquarters to Catalonia, near the government, although it was necessary in some respects, in general did us more harm than good. All the work of organization and propaganda in the Central-South zone, particularly in Madrid, was greatly weakened, and our political enemies took advantage of this deficiency to reinforce their own positions.

It was a well-known fact that the party's main strength lay in the fronts, especially the active fronts, which meant that the Communists incurred the major part of the losses.

An important point in evaluating the damaging activity of those who wanted to capitulate is the fact that with the loss of Catalonia, the best and the most combative units, in which Communist influence was the strongest, found themselves virtually outside the territory of Loyalist Spain.

In the military units of the Central zone, we had important groups of Communists and excellent comrades who showed their loyalty to the Republic and their revolutionary firmness. Nevertheless, their inactivity had affected their fighting spirit.

Moreover, there were deficiencies in the political activities of the party organization in Madrid, as borne out in the conference held in February 1939. In general, the party's work with the masses was inadequate, since we stressed the importance of the fronts to the neglect of the work in the rear. The results of these deficiencies was felt sorely in the period of capitulation and later in clandestine work.

Our relations with the Socialist Party were becoming increasingly difficult. The Socialist leaders, even those who were more open to Communist viewpoints, systematically refused to attend meetings of the Coordinating Committee of both parties. Relations with the Socialist leaders were reduced to a few conversations with Lamoneda, secretary of the Socialist Party, who, on various pretexts, avoided any joint action.

At a meeting of the Socialist National Committee in August 1938, open anticommunists became members of the Executive Council, among them Lucio Martinez, a high-ranking Mason, Besteiro, Largo Caballero and Zabalza. Lamoneda justified this move by claiming it was made in defense of Socialist unity. But, in actuality, it led to the immediate cessation of all activities of the Socialist and Communist coordinating committees and an attempt to create a split in the youth organization. At the same time, the new Socialist leaders' hostility toward Negrín became more open and they constantly threatened him with withdrawing their support from the government.

Our relations with the Socialist local organizations varied in direct relation to what was happening in the Socialist leadership. Generally, the most important leaders spent all their time trying to undo what we had done in respect to unity. In spite of all this, there were long periods of joint Communist and Socialist activities, especially in Valencia and other provinces. This, however, was not the case in Madrid, where in general no work of any sort was carried on in common despite moments of occasional good relations.

This situation between the two working-class parties affected the Popular Front negatively and helped to hamper its activities. Nevertheless, it was of great political importance that in this situation of defeatism and intrigue, the Popular Front never openly opposed the government, although some efforts were made along these lines by the Republican left-wing party, under the pressure of Azaña and the Anarchists.

The Popular Front committees were very active in the provinces, so much so that they tended to assume governmental functions. In behalf of the Communist Party, I spoke against these tendencies in a plenary meeting of the committees in Madrid, since these activities could only further provincial policies and increase the general disorder.

Of all the Republican parties, the left-wing branch was most opposed to the participation of the popular masses, especially that of the Communists, in governing the country. Under Azaña's influence, the Republican left-wing party, maintaining itself within the framework of the Popular Front, demanded power under the slogan: "Let the Republicans govern the Republic."

The influence of the Communist Party in the large trade-union organizations was strengthened during the course of the war, at least in the UGT, which played an important role in solving many specific war problems and in supporting government policies. The Communists controlled some trade unions and were supported in their work by a group of unity-minded Socialists, such as Amaro del Rosal, Virgilio Llanos and many others. Nevertheless, our political activities in the UGT were in no small measure nullified by the fact that followers of Largo Caballero controlled the leadership of the organization's three most important unions, Metallurgy, Transport and the Agricultural Workers.

This situation could have been changed had we worked more actively with the unions. For example, in spite of the enormous influence the Communist Party had in the rural zones, our work was extremely weak in the Agricultural Workers' Union, which was the most important member of the UGT and was led by Zabalza, a follower of Largo Caballero. We had missed our opportunity to organize in spite of the discontent of the peasants caused by the enforced collectivization policies carried on by the Socialists in competition with the Anarchists, and also by the fact that peasants who had joined the union since 1936 had no vote.

The Communists could not aid the partisans of unity within the CNT because none of our members could be persuaded to join Anarchist trade unions since they thought, erroneously, that our work would have no effect there.

Such were the conditions and the difficulties facing the government and the Communists, who were the mainstay of the resistance. In view of all these things, we can easily understand what happened in Catalonia after its fronts were broken, and what happened in Madrid when Catalonia was lost.

The enemy knew how to take advantage of its initial victories in the Ebro counteroffensive and how to broaden the scope of its attacks so as to shut off the Republic from all communication with the outside world.

If the General Staff and the Generalitat itself organized Catalonia's defense poorly, the way they virtually abandoned the Central Army fighting in Catalan territory was even more lamentable.

Ever since operations in the Ebro had begun, operations which prevented the fall of Valencia in July 1938, the Catalan Army had not received any effective aid from the armies in the Central-South zone. And not because they couldn't provide this aid, but because General Miaja opposed moving any soldiers from the Madrid front, and the Center's high commands were unwilling to take any risks.

Catalonia could have been helped in either of two ways—by the organization of important operations in the Central zone or by sending one or two army units from the Central zone to Catalonia. The Republican General Staff chose the first. An offensive of great magnitude was planned, which was to be opened in the southerly fronts (Estremadura, Andalusia and the Mediterranean coast). If successful, this operation would change the course of the war.

Essentially the plan was a repetition under different conditions of what had happened in the battle of Teruel, that is, an attempt to blunt the enemy offensive by a surprise attack and to nullify the plans of the rebel General Staff. The navy was supposed to aid in the attack and disembark in the direction of Motril between the 8th and 11th of December. This was to be followed by a heavy attack through Estremadura in the direction of Zafra, to cut off the road between Seville and Badajoz and divide enemy territory in two.

The Motril operation never took place. The troops boarded ship in the port of Almería and were ordered to turn back while they were at sea.

Looking back, we can see this incident as an open-and-shut case of sabotage and treason on the part of Miaja's General Staff or even perhaps higher up. We should have gone into the matter at the time to search for the guilty ones, but we didn't because, among other reasons, the party was misinformed, and belatedly at that, as to the facts surrounding these murky events.

The Estremadura operation was fixed for December 18, 1938. When the troops were all brought together for the attack, the Central General Staff changed the plan and decided to attack in the direction of Granada, which meant that an entire army had to be rapidly transported through impassable roads from one front to another.

When everything was ready for the attack on Granada, the Central General Staff again decided to suspend the operation, telling the Central-South General Staff to operate wherever they thought it would be most effective. Since they thought it convenient to attack through Estremadura, the troops were once again brought back to their original positions, in unheard-of disorder. The attack did not begin until January 5, 1939, that is, 13 days after the break in the Segre front and after the enemy had already made all-important gains in Catalonia.

Despite the chaos and delay, we still managed to surprise the enemy. The operation would have had tremendous repercussions if, after the break in the enemy front, the General Staff had used a little boldness and ordered our troops into the newly created gap, as the fascists had done in Catalonia in an unfortified and weakly defended region. If we had done that, we would have threatened Seville on one side and the road to Badajoz on the other. The Estremadura operation was one of the greatest lost opportunities for the Republican army to give a serious setback to the enemy, but because of the way the operation was handled it had no effect at all on the insurgents' activities in Catalonia.

The Politburo sent me to the Estremadura front with Comrade Girón to see if the situation could be remedied, but it was already too late to do anything. The disorder we found at the front was appalling. Operations had been suspended because rain made it difficult to move the artillery. Meanwhile the soldiers were wandering about without anything to do, and the peasants were lolling about the fields, apparently waiting for "better times."

When we asked Lieutenant Colonel Ibarrola, chief of operations, and one of the few men we could trust, why the army was inactive, he told us it was because of the bad roads. When I demurred and suggested that the roads could be quickly repaired with the aid of the peasants, he answered—and perhaps he was right from the standpoint of the old rules book—"Since there was no state of war, he could not, nor did he have the right to, mobilize the civilian population for military purposes."

When I went to General Staff headquarters I found General Miaja well under the influence of Bacchus, while Franco's agents, Muedra and Garijo, General Staff chiefs, looked on complacently—to the despair of Commissar Ossorio y Tafall, who was completely at a loss as to what to do about the situation. I informed Ossorio that when the government declared a general mobilization, the Republican left-wing party announced its decision to prohibit its members of military age to join the army. Ossorio immediately left for Madrid to see what he could do about making the government decree for mobilization respected.

[43]

# Catalonia Abandoned

After the retreat of our armies from the left bank of the Ebro, the situation of our troops was desperate. The men were exhausted after four months of tenacious resistance. There were no relief troops in sight, because we didn't have reserves.

Catalonia couldn't spare any more men in spite of the efforts of the United Socialist Party and the Communists to mobilize the whole population. The enemy's superiority in men, artillery, aviation and rapidity of movement was crushing. Our army retreated from Catalonia completely routed.

Possibly Barcelona could have resisted had the Catalán authorities been willing to defend their territory at any cost, as were the men of the PSUC and the Communist Party. But there is no doubt that everyone was tired of the war and that the nerves of the Catalans were near the breaking point as a result of the food shortages and the never-ending bombing raids.

The defeatist attitudes of the authorities inevitably affected the people and served to put a damper on their activities. Moreover, the leaders of the different parties refused any kind of joint action.

Ten days before the fall of Catalonia, efforts were still being made to provoke a crisis in the Generalit. Barcelona's municipal council has long since given up meetings but it suddenly decided to hold one when Italian troops were already approaching the city. When they met, the only members present were those from the PSUC and four Catalan councilmen. All the others had already fled the city. The Anarchist leaders had been the first to go.

Since the Communist Party did not have its own organization in the city, it worked together with the United Socialist Party of Catalonia, putting its most trusted men at the disposal of the PSUC organizations and sending the majority of our comrades to the front. But despite our efforts and especially those of the Barcelona Committee under Muní, who kept to their posts until Italian tanks were actually passing through the city, we did not achieve much.

Why wasn't Barcelona defended?

One of the most incomprehensible aspects of the resistance in Catalonia was the total absence of fortifications not only on the main fronts but in Barcelona itself. A plan for such fortifications had been drawn up in August, but nothing had been done to put it into practice. While it is true that the enemy surrounded Barcelona with deadly swiftness, it is also true that the city had not organized any sort of defense. Worse still, it was actually prepared to surrender.

The General Staff had appointed General Hernández Saravia, obviously a complete incompetent, to take charge of Barcelona's defense. It had also instructed the battle-proven Fifth Army Corps under Líster, which was under the orders of Saravia while in the zone of Barcelona, "not to concern itself" with the defense of the Catalán capital. The defense instructions given by Saravia on December 25 presupposed evacuation of the city before any defensive action was even attempted.

That night, 2,000 Assault Guards, well armed with rifles, machine guns and armored cars, were ordered by Paulino Gómez, Minister of the Interior, to abandon the city. This only served to demoralize and panic the inhabitants.

In the midst of appalling confusion, with the roads jammed with people fleeing from the enemy advance, the Fifth Army Corps maintained resistance at several points. It retreated in relatively good order, systematically carrying out its plan of blowing up bridges, roads and arms depots, thus permitting the civilian population, and later most of the arms in Barcelona, to be evacuated into France.

Distressed by events, Negrín called for a meeting of the ministers on January 30 to ask for a vote of confidence authorizing him to determine at what moment the government would move to the Central-South zone. The President of the Republic, all the ministers (with the exception of Comrades Uribe and Moix) and all the party leaders asked Negrín to give up the resistance and accept the mediation of France and England to obtain "honorable" conditions from Franco. No one ever specified what these conditions would be.

Both France and England were extremely anxious to act as mediators. France's attitude toward Republican Spain was frankly inimical, as instanced by her retaining Soviet war equipment in its territory to prevent it from reaching the Republican Army. On the other hand, the Soviet Union, in spite of increasing difficulties, continued to send aid to Spain.

Ignacio Hidalgo de Cisneros, a Republican air force general who had won the respect of the combatants, was sent to Moscow by the Republican government to present the Soviet Union with a list of war material urgently needed by the Republic. The Soviet leaders were willing to send Spain all that it asked. Meanwhile, France and England were intensifying their blockade and already rehearsing for the Republic's funeral rites. In June 1938, France had closed its borders with Spain and kept airplanes, artillery and all other Soviet aid from reaching the Spanish combatants. It even threatened to prohibit Loyalist soldiers from retreating into safety in France.

Undoubtedly Negrín had lost his confidence in the resistance during the last battle, but in his declarations he maintained his old line of continuing the war.

In this difficult situation, the parliament met on February 1, 1939 in the Castle of Figueras and approved a minimum program of three points, as possible conditions for ending the war. They were: (1) The independence of Spain; (2) free self-determination of the Spanish people by plebiscite; (3) abolition of all repressive measures after the war.

Negrín also received a vote of confidence at the same meeting. But something was wrong. Those who supported Negrín's resistance policy and believed in his sincerity voted confidence in him, but those who were in favor of capitulation did the same. The latter supported his three-point program, interpreting it as the first step in the surrender of the Republic, for whose defense they had neither courage nor desire.

President Azaña, as well as certain Republican and Socialist leaders and many professional military men, believed that the three points of Figueras would serve as a basis for Negrín's diplomatic appeal to the French and British governments for their mediatory services. But Negrín refused to be the scapegoat of those advocating surrender and did not accept the suggestion of negotiations which had no real, concrete basis. It was no more than a pure and simple invitation to surrender.

Azaña used Negrín's refusal as a pretext for not going to Madrid. Fifteen days later he declared "that the conditions established between himself and the government had not been respected."

Negrín, whose conduct was incomprehensible, continued to reaffirm his decision to go on resisting, but did nothing to organize the resistance.

To give one example out of the thousands we could cite concerning Negrín's contradictory behavior, when Catalonia was obviously lost to the Republic, Negrín did not order the transfer of war equipment in Catalonia to the Center fronts to reinforce the military capacity of the army in that zone.

In this period of general collapse, the Communist Party worked in Catalonia until the very end, trying to organize a minimum resistance so as to permit the civilian population, soldiers, political and military leaders to reach safe harbor in France.

On January 5, 1939, when the Catalán front was already nonexistent, I left for Madrid with Irene Falcón to organize the preparations for the Fifth Party Congress, which we were planning to hold in 1939. I must admit to a great deal of ingenuousness on our part. Our faith in the people and in our victory, in the possibility of continuing the resistance, was unbreakable and at times blinded us to reality.

# 44

# Heading Toward Disaster

The situation in Madrid was anything but encouraging. The day after my arrival from Catalonia I went to see Colonel Casado, since he was Commander-in-Chief of the Army. By now, General Miaja was completely out of the picture, except for occasional newspaper mention. His military services were reduced to welcoming foreign delegations as the representative of the Loyalist Army.

Casado received me cordially, making a great show of how pleased he was that I had returned to Madrid. He spoke of future military operations which, he said, would be decisive. It is difficult to imagine a slyer, more cowardly old fox than Colonel Segismundo Casado, who headed the junta of capitulation that delivered Spain to fascism. A professional military man, a Mason, Chief of Military Affairs for the President of the Republic, an ambitious politician much admired by Franco's military chiefs, well connected with the Anarchists, he was a continual saboteur of the Republic's military operations and the man to whom Franco owed his victory.

During my meeting with Casado, I asked him to find us a warehouse to store the food products we had in the holds of two ships anchored in the port of Valencia. The food shipments were gifts of aid from different countries sent to us by the antifascist women's organization.

Casado, right then and there, ordered one of his men to find us the buildings and even supply us with a watchman to prevent thefts. He told me of the food shortages in Madrid and I offered to put all the food we had in our possession at his disposal. We were planning to organize in Madrid, as we had done in Barcelona, children's kitchens and dispensaries for nursing mothers, with the aid of Dr. Planelles and other doctors who had been helping us out.

Casado was not only willing to aid us; he even became enthusiastic about our plans. He kept talking about how difficult it was to obtain food for the population, and I kept insisting on our willingness to give him the food and all other goods that our women's organization had received from abroad, including the shipments in Valencia.

Our conversation was so cordial that before I left he insisted that I see his little boy. He called one of the servants in his home to bring over the child, who was truly, like all healthy two-year-olds, a beautiful baby.

How far I was from imagining that this man had already made plans to betray the Republic and surrender the people to fascism!

Daniel Ortega, who worked in Casado's General Staff headquarters, told us of his doubts as to Casado's loyalty, stating that he had suspicious relations with foreigners, especially the British, who had recently paid him several long visits in his office. Other people from the CNT Defense Committees had also held lengthy conversations with him. But Ortega, who was later shot when Franco's troops entered Madrid, could offer no specific proof to substantiate his suspicions; therefore, we had no real basis on which to make any judgment of Casado's character.

We began our work in Madrid, not in preparation for the Fifth Party Congress, which obviously could not be held, but in something more pressing—supplying food, even though it was a minimal amount, to children and factory workers. We called upon the women of Madrid to help us and in less than a week more than 6,000 women had volunteered, providing an eloquent example of how in spite of the misery and shortages Republican sentiments were still very much alive in Madrid and, indeed, in the whole country.

But the plan of supplying food to the factories which I had previously discussed with Casado ran into a snag right from the start. The Socialist commissars in the factories did not allow the women to distribute the packages containing flour, bacon, preserves, powdered milk, sugar and soap. They insisted that the packages be given directly to them, alleging that if we distributed the food we would be "proselytizing." The women refused to entrust the precious packages to the likes of those commissars. Actually our volunteers were not Communists. Many were Socialists, and most of them had no party affiliation at all. The Communist Party had arranged this deliberately, to avoid any political conflicts.

After the loss of Barcelona the busy little rats of capitulation now left their holes, biting wherever they could.

For many of those advocating the surrender of the Republic, these defeatist moods were not an expression of despair before a dead-end street—which would have been more or less understandable. They were the culmination of anti-unity activities that had been carried on throughout the war. It was their revenge on the people, on all those who had defended the Republic with dignity and heroism.

Those advocating surrender were miserable moral pigmies, incapable of understanding self-sacrifice or greatness of soul in others. They agreed to the ignominious sale of Spain, the sale of tens of thousands of lives, in return for the safety of their own rotten skins. They broke the resistance of our proud and fiery people, reducing them into a suffering, hungry mass. The people of Spain would need long years of hard fighting and herculean efforts to recover their full strength.

The British government, which, from the start of the uprising, had been openly hostile to the people of Spain, was anxious to end the resistance, in the hope of making deals with the insurgents and protecting its position in the peninsula. There was no pawn on the political chessboard that they did not move nor any circumstance they failed to exploit to reach their objectives. "We do what England tells us to do," replied General Miaja to Comrade Montolíu, who visited him in General Staff headquarters after the formation of Casado's junta which was to betray the Republic.

The parliament meeting in Figueras and the publication of the three-point program hastened the culmination of the conspiracy.

In view of our defeat in Catalonia and in support of the three-point program, the Communist Party, then in Catalonia, published a declaration denouncing the weaknesses of the government, and the intrigues and treachery of the cowards who were in favor of surrender.

The proponents of capitulation used this declaration to paint the Communists as a war party, accusing them of plotting a coup to prevent the peace settlement that "honest and loyal military chiefs" were negotiating with "politicians of reason." As a result of this infamous propaganda, the Communist Party appeared before the masses as the obstacle to an "honorable peace."

Colonel Casado now began to reveal himself. The political sewers spilled over and bands of louse-ridden rats appeared on the scene. Casado ordered the arrest of the Communists in Madrid who had published the party's declaration on the three-point program.

I called him by telephone to ask for an explanation. He assured

me—while he was preparing to knife the Republic in the back—
that he had done this "because he considered our declarations
defeatist." I gave him a fitting answer, and he promised to suspend
the order of arrest.

Some days afterward I received an invitation from Casado to visit
him in General Staff headquarters. In that atmosphere of behind-
the-scenes maneuvers, the invitation appeared very suspicious. The
party hesitated to authorize my going to Casado's office, for they
believed him to be capable of any baseness. Nevertheless, they
decided that I should go.

Instead of finding an office reflecting the feverish life of a country
at war, I found the silence of a cemetery. Casado was inside his office,
thin, pale, preoccupied, nervous. His hands were cold as he took
mine and offered me a seat. After a brief silence, he said:

"Did my invitation surprise you?"

"Yes, it did, especially in view of your recent attitude toward the
Communists," I answered.

"You people are mistaken about me."

"It's possible, but our opinion is based on the facts."

"I'm going to talk with you as I've never talked to anyone, except
perhaps with the President of the Republic."

"Thank you for your confidence. Go ahead, I'm listening."

He began telling me what he thought of the war. In his opinion,
"the war, from beginning to end, was a mistake. The Republic, when
it found itself without an army, should have renounced the idea of
resistance and accepted the situation, until the political pendulum
once again swept back to a situation favorable to the Republic. Now
there was only one solution, to abandon Madrid—to send all the
armed forces to Cartagena, along with the leaders of the workers'
organizations and political parties, to make Cartagena a stronghold.
Its location was very desirable and there were many powers who
would like to control that strategic spot on the Mediterranean."

I thought for a moment that I was listening to the ramblings of a
mentally unbalanced person, like the people who had so often come
to see me to propose fantastic schemes to end the war quickly with
ingenious weapons of their own invention.

I let him finish and then I said:

"I don't think you've given sufficient thought to what you've just
told me, because almost three years of war prove that your opinion

about the resistance is wrong. If we analyze the situation from a narrow, academic viewpoint, a military viewpoint, then you could arrive at the conclusions you've just drawn. But there is a factor you haven't taken into account, a fundamental factor—the people. The people did not accept quick surrender to fascism; they organized militias. The people resisted the savage enemy attempts to besiege Madrid; they defended Madrid. They defeated the insurgents in the first days of the rising in Barcelona, in the Basque Country, in Asturias, Valencia, Madrid and in the principal cities and nerve centers of the country. And they have resisted until now. And if there were errors in waging the war they were not the fault of the people but of those who, underestimating them, failed to do their utmost to help them militarily and in all other aspects of the resistance. It's the fault of those who didn't know what to do with the Republic's victories and how to use these victories to break the enemy fronts.

"No, Señor Casado, you're wrong. As for abandoning Madrid and going to Cartagena, if the first action is stupid, the second is insane. How long could resistance last in a city without water (even though it is a seaport) surrounded completely by enemies on land, sea and in the air, with no possibility of receiving supplies? What country would negotiate to acquire a strategic base under those conditions and what Spaniard would stoop so low as to offer a Spanish base to a foreign power? I don't know anything about military matters, but I still have enough common sense to know that your proposal amounts to collective suicide."

"Then you disagree with my opinions, my good intentions to end a resistance which is becoming impossible?" Casado asked.

"Yes, I disagree with them, and anyone with full use of his reason would do the same."

Casado kept returning to the problem of the food shortage. I renewed my offer made weeks earlier to give him what we had received as a women's aid organization, a dependency of the Defense Ministry.

When we parted, he said: "Let this prove that I'm not an anticommunist, nor a tool of any committee!"

"We're not against you either. You can count on the same support in everything that relates to the defense of the Republic as you've had all along. But if you take another road, don't expect to find us walking with you."

Leaving Casado's office, I saw in the waiting room the CNT Defense Committee, including the persons who had formed Casado's junta of capitulation.

I returned to party headquarters, where everyone was uneasily waiting for my appearance, and told them of our conversation. Not even then did we come to the conclusion that Casado was plotting treachery—a prime example of our naiveté in assessing men.

The Republic was living through tragic days. The Republican Army in Catalonia was retreating because of lack of sufficient equipment to maintain the resistance. Hundreds of thousands of peasants and their families, with their few animals and belongings, were walking on the roads in an heartbroken exodus toward France, with the army in their wake.

Our resistance in Catalonia was broken. Our soldiers couldn't perform miracles. In front of them were some well-equipped units and in back of them was the French border. Our men stayed on, fighting to cover the retreat of Azaña, the members of the Central Government and the Generalitat into France. Then their turn came. Heartsick, defeated but not conquered, they crossed the border under the watchful eyes of the French police. They were later taken to special concentration camps in Argèles, Colliure and St. Cyprien.

My son Rubén was among them. He had received his baptism of fire in Catalonia. A member of the Ebro Army in the communications battalion, Rubén was one of a group of soldiers who were separated from the main body of troops during the retreat. They had managed to escape with their lives from a burning forest. The experience of the Spanish war, where he lived and fought together with the valiant commanders, Líster and Modesto, what he learned from them in the concentration camp in Argèles, taught him how to fight and later to die like a hero in the defense of Stalingrad.

Since before the fall of Barcelona, the party had been greatly concerned about the situation in our Central-South zone, as well as about problems relating to the unity of the working class, the Popular Front and the military situation in general. Nevertheless, our party leaders were not fully aware of all the changes that had taken place in Madrid, changes which were hardly in our favor.

The party informed Negrín of its concern over the situation and advised him to make some changes in the military commands, replacing General Miaja with a more dynamic chief and removing Colonel Casado, whose loyalty was in question, from his post. Negrín refused to do this, arguing that these were ill-advised actions that would lead to a break in the resistance.

Before the fall of Catalonia, the party strongly urged Negrín to move the largest possible amount of war equipment to the Central-South zone. Negrín agreed, but did absolutely nothing about it. The equipment that Negrín failed to send to the Central-South zone either fell into enemy hands or was transported to France, reducing the fighting capacity and morale of our troops in that zone.

During all this time, the party was preparing the army of the Central-South zone for the enemy offensive which, once Catalonia fell, was believed to be imminent. Before the arrival of the government in Madrid, after the defeat in Catalonia, the party held several provincial congresses where we discussed the problems of mobilization and the preparedness of the army, with the aim of reinforcing the resistance.

This was no easy task, however, because of the opposition of the authorities, the military commands and commissars, in whom the idea of capitulation had taken root. Our comrades continued to support the policy of resistance, hoping that with the arrival of the government in Madrid the situation would improve.

On January 19, 1939, Negrín officially declared a state of war in Spain—as if the country hadn't already been at war for three years—an act which made the continuation of the resistance even more difficult. Undoubtedly it was a maneuver by Negrín to put all the responsibility on military shoulders at a time when the resistance was on its deathbed. The military for its part did not hesitate to act under the new circumstances and joyfully assumed powers they had not enjoyed until then. The state-of-war proclamation was immediately used against the government, the resistance and the Communists.

Because we trusted Negrín's sincerity, we made a serious error when we approved his proclamation under the existing conditions. The declaration of the state of war meant in fact putting power in the hands of the military, who wanted to surrender; and in the hands of the enemy, who used the power delegated to them by the government to intensify their campaign of defeatism and to muzzle the party. The most rabid anticommunists in the country were in charge of censoring Communist Party publications. They tried to keep us from holding meetings and even told us what we should discuss when we met—"economic matters, nothing else."

The party in Madrid convened a provincial congress from February 8th to 11th in preparation for the Madrid National Convention that we were planning to hold in place of the Fifth Party Congress. The Provincial Congress uncovered the weakness of our work in Madrid at the time when the Socialists had increased their activities and were undermining the influence which we had acquired at the cost of so much effort and sacrifice. Every speaker told us something new about the activities of those advocating surrender. I denounced those activities and called upon the Communists and all the people to support the Negrín government.

We were much too honest, if there are degrees of honesty! Deep down within himself Negrín was hoping for a catastrophe that would free him of all state responsibility. This was fully demonstrated by his conduct. While Negrín has frequently been accused of being a tool of the Communists, in reality it was we who were *his* victims, because of our blind loyalty to our responsibilities and our unconditional support of the resistance policy, which was the only just one at the moment.

At the close of the congress we learned that the government had arrived in the Central zone. This brought a wave of enthusiasm from the delegates who thought, as we all did, that now the conspirators would be checked. Along with the government came the principal Communist military chiefs to strengthen the resistance in the Central-South zone and in the event that the tide might turn, to propose conditions to the rebels.

To a certain extent the arrival of the government and the military chiefs did put a stop to the rumors spread by our enemies that the Communists were about to take over the country. The larger the lie, the more it is believed, and in this situation the absurd rumors fabricated by fascist agents to undermine the popular resistance were accepted as truth even by the government itself.

Negrín, who was anxious to get rid of the governmental burden and find a justification for drastic measures, turned very surly and menacing toward the Communists in the first government session in Madrid, until our minister Uribe put the dots on the i's and brought him back to reason.

Who, if he were not an imbecile, could believe that the Communists were going to take power, when the cream of its ranks were prisoners in French concentration camps? And at a time when the Central army was riddled with treachery? How could the Communists be planning to seize power in 1939 and have refrained from doing so in 1937 when circumstances were favorable, when weariness had not yet dampened popular enthusiasm and when a major part of the combatants were party supporters?

We were not ignorant of our strength and influence among the popular masses. Neither were we oblivious of the fact that if the resistance had been maintained for three years it was thanks to the Popular Front, with all its shortcomings, and the enormous political and organizational work of all democratic forces, in particular the Communist Party. The party had borne the weight of the resistance all during the war, both politically and militarily, in the front and at home, becoming the enemy's prime target, since it was the only solid force of Republican resistance. The Communist Party was the driving force of the Republic, a constant pressure acting upon a sometimes negative, sometimes positive entity, but unfortunately it was not the determining factor in spite of its importance.

During my long years in exile, many comrades have frequently asked me: Could the Communist Party have seized power in Spain? And if it could have, then why didn't it?

To this I have only one answer: At no moment during the war did the Communist Party propose taking power in Spain. Those who like to compare the situation in Spain with that of Russia in October 1917, and who arrive at the conclusion that we could have made a revolution, are gravely mistaken. Russia was bleeding to death from an imperialist war which was hated by all its people. Spain was fighting a national revolutionary war against fascism with the participation of not only the working class, but also, preponderantly, the peasants, as well as the petty and big bourgeoisie.

If at a given moment of the war, for example, in 1937, when the Largo Caballero government was in crisis, certain conditions existed which would have permitted the seizure of power, the Communists did not do so (although many of our combatants desired it) for a basic reason: Neither the national nor international situation was favorable to such a change.

Communists do not play at revolution, because the lives of the workers and the fate of a country are too precious for them to be hurled into a revolutionary adventure without a good chance of succeeding. It would have been nothing but criminal adventurism had the Communist Party attempted to seize power in a Spain divided by a civil war of such a special nature, and in the midst of a capitalist world pandering to Hitler and preparing for World War II. We would have had to push aside all our allies in the Popular Front, thus clearing the way for the fascist powers and international reactionary circles to intervene openly in Spain.

It should also be remembered that the Spanish working class was divided and that neither the Socialist Party nor the Anarchists would have sat back peacefully before a change of this nature. During the war the only serious and open attempt to establish dictatorship by a political group was the Anarcho-Trotskyite putsch in May 1937, which failed, as any other similar attempt would have done.

The democratic bourgeois revolution in Spain was further developed and transformed by the war. With all the people in arms the bourgeois Republic of Spain became a Popular Republic, the first in the history of contemporary democratic revolutions. While the 1905 revolution in Russia left a positive balance in its wake— the workers' councils or Soviets—as the most democratic form of proletarian power, Spain's national revolutionary war against fascism gave birth to popular democracy, which, after World War II, became one of the forms of peaceful transition toward Socialism in some countries.

Why should the Communists have impetuously sought to grab power, forsaking all their allies, if truly revolutionary transformations were already taking place in the country during the course of the war? The Communist Party's main interest was the defeat of the rebels and into this task it put its heart and soul. Defeat of the insurgents was the key to the consolidation of popular victories and the development of a democratic revolution in Spain.

# 45

# Whither Negrín?

Negrín's inactivity, the tolerance with which he viewed the activities of the conspirators, led us to the conclusion that he wanted to let events take their own course and do nothing to channel them into a direction favorable to the Republic's interests.

In a meeting of the Politburo, it was decided that a committee composed of Comrades Checa, Delicado, Dieguéz and myself would visit Negrín to discuss our opinions and anxieties. Negrín saw us, and we explained the position of the Communist Party on the situation. "If the government were willing to continue the resistance, the Communist Party would support it. If, on the other hand, it was determined to negotiate peace terms, the Communist Party would not put any obstacles in its way."

We reminded him that the Communists had in 1938 retired one of their ministers, that the Communists had enthusiastically supported his thirteen-point program, as it was now supporting the three-point program, and that we were willing to make any concessions in order to save the Republic and spare the people further sacrifices.

Negrín told us that the only solution was to continue the resistance and that he wanted to hand in his resignation to Martinez Barrio, who was the President since Azaña had resigned,* but that he could not do so until Martinez decided to return to Madrid. He did not think it was possible to begin peace negotiations in the absence of the President.

"Then," we asked, "what is the solution?"

"Resistance," answered Negrín, "I plan to take a series of measures designed to reorganize and strengthen the situation on the home fronts."

* On February 28, 1939, Azaña, in Paris at the time, resigned, after news came that Britain and France had recognized Franco.—Ed.

335

When we arrived at the Prime Minister's residence we had met one of General Miaja's aides leaving Negrín's office. Curious as to what was going on, we asked Negrín if the aide had brought him good news.

"Good news? General Miaja has asked me to give him a million pesetas, the kind that Franco likes."

"What kind of peseta does Franco like?" we asked.

"No kind. That's just it; he wants a million pesetas in dollars. That's how honorable those people are. How can they continue to command the army?"

We left Negrín's office in low spirits, not so much because of what he said, but because of what he had not said, at what could be read in his gestures, his weariness and his tone of indifference. He appeared to be a man completely overcome by events, a man who had used up all his strength in a difficult battle against the conspirators and now was letting himself be pulled down stream by the current, trying to preserve a minimum of dignity as he went down.

The party decided to publish a document explaining the situation to the people and calling upon them once again to renew their efforts for the sake of the defense of the Republic and their own fate.

The document, which produced a deep impression and gave the lie to the propaganda of the anticommunists, declared that, "As bad as our situation is now, it would be sheer disaster if the leaders of our organizations and parties, if the government and the army commanders lose their presence of mind and confidence in the combative capacity and spirit of sacrifice of our soldiers and our people; if they now work not toward resistance but toward surrender." After pointing out that fascist victory in Spain would mean the end of all that the workers and peasants have won in dozens of years of work and bloody combat, the party expressed confidence that "resistance is possible and will permit us to save the lives and liberty of thousands and thousands of our brothers." Urging a swift and determined effort to correct the weaknesses uncovered by the defeat in Catalonia, the party insisted that "resistance can once again turn the tide, as it has done at moments like November 1936 and March and April 1938, when many thought all was lost. New events may take place in Spain or on the international scene which might well be in our favor and open the way for victory."

The Party reiterated its unconditional support of the three points announced by the President of the Council, and insisted that sufficient arms were on hand to resist and beat back any enemy attack, and that industry and resources could be mobilized—with "sacrifices equally shared by all"—to carry on to victory. It demanded "that the fight against the fifth column be intensified; that all increase their vigilance in the fronts and at home to crush mercilessly all enemy attempts." Again it emphasized the role of the Popular Front and of all the antifascist parties and unions, calling for antifascist unity and fraternalism. "The Popular Front not only must continue to exist and function, but it must multiply its activities and become the axis of popular resistance." It declared that "Communists will never abandon the line of unity of all parties, all leaders, all trade unions, all politicians and military men. This does not mean that we will not denounce and fight against vacillation, against deserters, cowards and other enemy agents. This means that we Communists make a distinction only between those who work for the unity of the people and those who sabotage this unity. The unity of the working class will guarantee the unity of all the people."

The party was placed in a permanent state of mobilization, its offices manned day and night, its leaders affected by military mobilization automatically replaced by men and women ineligible for military service.

This document, published on February 23, 1939, showed exactly where the Communists stood. Our chief concern was to maintain the unity of working-class and democratic forces in order to strengthen the resistance of our people.

Was resistance really feasible in the Central-South zone? Yes, it was. In a meeting held in Aguyana, Catalonia, on January 28, some military chiefs considered resistance impossible because of the lack of war equipment; however, in a meeting held in the middle of February in the Central-South zone, the commanders in charge of the fronts came to a different, although provisional, conclusion.

According to Metallana, "with the arms and the men at our disposal, we could resist for about four months." But he added: "Why resist if we'll be defeated just the same at the end?"

Menendez, chief of the Levante front, said: "We can maintain the resistance for four or five months. Then we'll just have to wait and see. If the enemy decides to begin an offensive on the Levante front, it will find itself up against a stone wall, because we're well prepared and morale is excellent."

Casado's opinion was: "Resistance is possible only in Cartagena and for this reason we should reinforce that city and move all war equipment, food and men there. Madrid won't last a week."

At the end of February, Negrín believed that if we had a pause of three or four weeks in the fighting, we could resist for seven or eight months, which would be a setback to the enemy army. Italo-German intervention was already becoming unpopular among the insurgents. Negrín also believed that we should take into account possible changes on the international scene which might be factors favorable for the Republic's situation.

Other military chiefs thought that while we could from a military point of view resist for five or six months, Spain needed a strong, united political leadership; a firm and loyal command and an implacable policy of purging the fronts and the rearguard of defeatists and saboteurs.

[46]

## The Great Crime

In opposition to our clear and definite position of defending the Republic, the conspirators continued to tighten their grip around the Republic. At the end of February a local CNT leader warned our comrades of a plan to assault our party offices. "I'm a revolutionary worker," he said, "and I can't go along with what certain people are plotting against you and the Republic."

He told us how the homes of Communists were being watched and when the assault would take place, giving us details that bolstered the truth of his information, which we quickly confirmed. As a precaution, we decided to organize the defense of the buildings occupied by the various party organizations and prepare the battle to guard against any breakthrough. Domingo Girón and I left Madrid and went to El Palmar, situated on the main road just outside Murcia.

The next day other comrades arrived, among them Palmiro Togliatti, who had participated in the entire Catalán campaign. With our comrades, he had come to Madrid to help us in spite of the constantly mounting risks, showing himself to be a great revolutionary leader.

In the last days of February, Negrín decided to move his residence and that of the government to Elda, located in a small, inaccessible valley. After the government and the leaders of the trade unions had left Madrid (the UGT moved to Elda with Negrin, while the CNT went to Murcia), the Politburo decided that the party would also move to El Palmar to prevent the possibility of an enemy offensive that could overwhelm the party leadership if it were divided.

The party moved to this point, halfway between the residence of the government in Elda and Madrid, so that we could get news of government decisions rapidly and be ready to act in the capital. Telephone and telegraph communications were already beginning to get difficult.

On March 1, the Council of Ministers met and agreed to make public Azaña's resignation as President of the Republic. In the meeting, the Anarchist Blanco, seconded by Peña, Paulino Gómez, Bilbao and Velao, bitterly attacked Negrín for allegedly planning to remove Casado from the Central Army command.

In view of the connections these persons had with Negrín, the attack could only be construed as a carefully staged attempt organized by Negrín himself to show the Communists that everyone else had confidence in Casado. In spite of that tragicomic defense of the Judas in our midst who already had the 30 pieces of silver in his possession, the Communists were right when they judged Casado to be a double-crosser who would surrender Spain to Franco.

On March 2, Martinez Barrio in Paris sent the government a statement accepting the Presidency of the Republic under the condition that Negrín immediately undertake negotiations for an "honorable peace" for all Spaniards, as had been agreed in a session of the Permanent Delegates of Parliament and all the political representatives, with the exception of the Communists, who had not attended the meeting because they had not been invited.

On the same day, the Official Gazette published news of new

military appointments and certain changes which apparently were intended to make the army more efficient.

Modesto and Cordón were made generals, while Líster, Galán and Márques were made colonels. Casado was made a general, and Matallana was namd Chief of Staff. Colonel Muedra became Under-Secretary of the Land Army and Colonel Garijo was put under the orders of Miaja, who was relieved of his functions as Supreme Chief of Armed Forces and named Inspector General of Land, Sea and Air Troops. Francisco Galán was appointed Chief of the Naval Base in Cartagena (he was arrested by the rebels when he arrived there to assume command). There were other changes of minor importance, among them the appointments of Etelvino Vega, Curto and Mendiola to the commands of Alicante, Murcia and Albacete.

Had these changes taken place earlier they could have improved the situation, but at that time, when capitulation was steadily gaining ground, they were, to say the least, aggravating it. Promotions in themselves were not the way to improve the situation; rather, we needed to place loyal men determined to defend the Republic at any cost at the head of the army whether they were officially named or not.

These appointments produced strong indignation among the conspirators, who felt that their plans would now fail. But an ally they never suspected came to their aid: Negrín himself inexplicably held back the newly appointed commanders from assuming their posts. By order of Negrín almost all the political and military leaders arriving from France were concentrating in Elda, waiting to assume responsibilities that never materialized.

On March 4, a rebel uprising took place in the base of Cartagena. We immediately communicated this to the government in Elda, and a division of the Peoples' Army under the command of Rodríguez and the commissar Llanos was sent to Cartagena. The rising was swiftly quelled, but the fleet set sail in the direction of Africa.

The Politburo decided to send Comrade Delicado and me to Elda on March 5 to inform the government in detail of the events in Cartagena.

As we were leaving Murcia, we were stopped by the Assault Guards. When they recognized us, they said: "Go ahead! You people are all right. You can go on!"

"What's happening?" I asked.

"We don't know, but we have orders not to let anyone leave Murcia."

The order had been given by the Socialist governor of Murcia, Eustasio Cañas. What the Assault Guards never imagined was that Cañas had done this precisely to prevent the Communists from leaving. The Murcia police knew where we were staying. The conspirators' plan was, in collusion with Cañas, to demonstrate that they were good anticommunists by making Franco a gift of the leaders of the Communist Party and the United Socialist Youth of the Central-South zone, as they had done with Domingo Girón, Ascanio, Cazorla, Mesón and many other unforgettable comrades.

Thanks to the unsuspecting Assault Guards, we arrived in Elda, where Vicente Uribe had set up the Ministry of Agriculture. We had to wait for the cabinet meeting, which was already in session for several hours, to end. Shortly after our arrival, Uribe came from Valencia to inform us and the government of the atmosphere of revolt being created in that region under the direction of Colonels Muedra and Garijo. We had repeatedly denounced these persons, and now they were appearing in their true roles as Franco agents. Líster and Modesto also arrived to await Negrín's orders.

On the afternoon of the 5th, the radio announced that Casado would make a speech that evening. He had succeeded in alienating a large number of professional military men from loyalty to the government by falsely informing them that they had been removed from their posts.

Cabrera, of the Málaga front, who was now military commander of Madrid, ordered that the members of the Politburo be kept under guard "to protect them, in view of the possibility of an attack by the fifth column." He was a hypocrite and a coward.

On the same afternoon, Casado, who had refused to accept his promotion to general, met with the Central Army command and put the finishing touches on his plan.

That evening, while the cabinet continued in session discussing the rising in Cartagena and the contents of the speech that Negrín would shortly give, the radio broadcast the news that Colonel Casado had rebelled.

Negrín called Casado in Madrid by telephone:

"What's going on there?" asked Negrin.

"We've rebelled!" answered Casado.

"Against whom?"

"Against you!"

"Against me? You're fired!"

"That's what I was expecting."

Casado cut off the conversation. Negrín attempted to continue with the meeting as if nothing had happened, but Uribe demanded that he take all necessary steps to put down the rebellion.

In the morning Negrín came to see us. We discussed with Negrín the need for informing the people and the army about the situation. At first he refused, but finally he agreed to prepare a brief speech. Benigno, secretary of the presidency, tried to put it on the air, but we discovered that the radio had been dismantled. Since the situation in Elda was getting more dangerous by the minute, the comrades decided that I should leave Spain. I refused, giving my reasons, but it was no use. The party had decided that I should go, and go I did.

We were defeated. The intrigues of those without conscience and the pressure of the great powers broke the resistance and prevailed over the will of the people to defend Spain, to keep our country in the camp of democracy and peace.

Our fight, however, had not been in vain. Refusing to fight would have been so ignominious that neither the people nor history ever would have forgiven us.

We had to leave Spain, go into exile, far from everything dear to us. But it didn't matter! We had done our duty and the people would understand.

In that moment Comrade Jean Catelas arrived. He was a French deputy who was organizing aid to the Central-South zone in behalf of sympathetic French organizations. Because of his later participation in the French resistance against nazism, he was beheaded by the Gestapo.

The time had come to say goodbye to the comrades who would remain behind. What to say to them? To Checa, Togliatti, dear friends? Would we ever see each other again?

What would happen to Irene, who had been sent to Albacete and who still hadn't returned? Was she safe? What would become of all our comrades, of Spain, of the people?

I gave all my things to the women who worked in the house— my new dress; new shoes, a gift from the comrades in Madrid; a silk kerchief, a remembrance from the women in Almadén. I had to burn a marvellous edition of *La Barraca* by Blasco Ibáñez, a gift from Julio Just with a personal dedication, because I didn't want it to fall into enemy hands and compromise the giver.

We arrived at the airport in Monovar. Hidalgo de Cisneros had reserved some small planes for use of the government and put one at our disposal. He remained in Spain until the departure of the government and the Communist military and political leaders.

A group of guerrillas came to say goodbye. "Good luck, Comrade Pasionaria! Until we see each other again!"

I embraced them all. They were my comrades, friends and sons. Many of them I knew I would never see again; and who knew when I would see the others?

With me went Catelas, Monzón, Moreno and a mechanic, a party member. The mechanic closed the doors of the plane. The propellers began to turn and the plane began to advance on the last strip of free Spanish territory.

The guerrillas stood in formation, then immediately broke ranks. That was the last glimpse of Spain I carried away—the guerrillas as they stood below with their rifles raised in salute.

Hours later, the government left Spain. Comrades Checa and Togliatti stayed behind to prevent the total disintegration of the army and to organize the departure through the port of Alicante of all those who were in danger because of their activities. Togliatti was arrested in Valencia with Checa; luckily the enemy didn't know him. Later they were joined by Claudín, Melchor, Gallego and other comrades from the United Socialist Youth, who lived the tragic hours of Casado's rising and fought to prevent the collapse of the fronts.

The formation of Casado's junta, with its purpose of surrendering the Republic, came as a surprise because of our misplaced confidence. As Marx wrote in *The 18th Brumaire:* "A nation and a woman are not forgiven the unguarded hour in which the first adventurer that came along could violate them."

We did know of the anticommunism of many professional military men whom the defeat of Catalonia had rendered completely useless for the rational exercise of their commands. We knew that they were capable of any crime against the Communist Party because it was a proletarian revolutionary organization. This was confirmed all during the war, as, for example, by the murders of Communists during the

THEY SHALL NOT PASS

horrible, short-lived terror reign in Madrid. Even though we knew this, and in spite of other evidence, we still thought of them in better terms than they deserved.

It was hard for us to believe them capable of treason to Spain and the people, although history had already shown, without a shadow of a doubt, that anticommunism in politics walks hand in hand with the most monstrous reaction; in the realm of justice, it bears false witness; in social life, it deals in defamation and spying; and in the national struggle, it leads to treason.

Obsessed as we were with the task of preventing a rebel victory, we failed to pay attention to daily incidents that were happening right under our very noses, incidents which should have warned us that treason was being hatched. This explains why our comrades were unprepared to face many of the exigencies of the home fronts and why we had no plans to cover the possibility of defeat. We lacked clandestine printing presses, paper, radios, money, safe hiding places or, indeed, any underground organization. We had prepared nothing and had to improvise to meet the most urgent needs of the fight under these new conditions.

In spite of the difficult situation and the lack of concrete guidance —the Communists had only the Central Committee's document published on February 23 to go by—our comrades in Madrid rapidly prepared to fight the junta, whose first orders were to arrest the Communists and attack their offices with the aid of the police, the carabineros and the Anarchist forces, directed by Mera. These had previously been withdrawn from the front, to the astonishment of all the combatants who had not opposed the move thinking that the Minister of Defense had ordered it.

The military forces in which the Communists had influence were on the fronts, and thus the way was clear in those first confused hours for the attack on party offices and the arrest of hundreds of Communists in the capital.

Many comrades, especially Ascanio, a capable military chief and a great political leader as well, organized resistance to the junta's violence and strove to prevent enemy infiltration into the fronts. Comrade Simón Sánchez Montero fought till the end in Ascanio's division. He was later taken prisoner by Franco's troops and condemned to long years of prison.

When some comrades objected to the defensive and offensive orders given by Ascanio, claiming that he had no instructions to issue them, he answered: "In dealing with treachery like Casado's, I don't need orders from anyone. Let every Communist fulfill his duty."

Ascanio captured Jaca, the former seat of Casado's General Staff, together with numerous prisoners. With the forces of Manuel Cortina and the carabineros who joined our units, we took the Museum of Natural History and began to prepare for an attack on the Ministry of the Interior, the junta's refuge.

A surprise insurgent attack obliged the Communists to establish a truce with the rebels of the junta in order to close the way for Franco's troops. The truce was used by Casado to reinforce his position, while the Communists once again shed their blood to prevent Franco from reaching Madrid. However, even with our victory over this new fascist attempt, we could not retrieve the situation. The morale of our troops had fallen to a new low.

In their efforts to prevent the collapse of the resistance in Madrid, our comrades were aided by the Communists in Valencia and in the North, especially Levante, both in the army and home fronts. Uribes, Palau and other leaders prepared the party and the army to cope with the situation and organize joint action of all the party's forces against the junta.

Meanwhile, the 47th Division of the 22nd Army, located on the Valencia-Ademuz road between Chelva and Casinos, commanded by Lieutenant Colonel Recalde, who had acted so bravely in the Estremadura campaign, and the commissars Gallego and Farré moved their troops in the direction of Madrid on March 10. They disarmed the troops in Etapas, cut the telegraph and telephone lines of the Levante Army and captured trucks and all the other vehicles they found in their march.

While they were trying to prevent the rupture of the fronts, the Communists had to fight as never before to keep from being mowed down by the enemy. Their decision and courage won them everyone's admiration, even that of military chiefs who were more or less involved in the junta. When Colonel La Iglesia learned of the activities of the 47th Division, he issued the following orders:

"(1) Comrade Recalde, in rebellion with his division against the junta, is named acting commander of the 22nd Army. (2) Other units of the Army, the Army of Levante, the Director of Etapas and the Army Transportation unit are ordered not to offer resistance to the comrades of the 22nd Army, under any circumstances whatsoever.

(3) For the purpose of supplying ammunition, sanitary and other services, artillery chiefs are ordered to maintain the normal supply line of the 22nd Army."

This was the swan song of Republican resistance. Now the most important thing was to save the largest possible number of combatants, military chiefs and well-known comrades who were most in danger of losing their lives in case of enemy victory. We were not able to bring all to safety because of the swiftness with which events moved.

At first the enemy refused the proposals of the junta and demanded unconditional surrender. When it began an offensive through Estremadura and Andalusia, the junta completely took off its disguise and accepted all of Franco's demands.

The enemy advance toward Levante and the Italian ring around the port of Alicante, where thousands of soldiers, women and children were seeking refuge, prevented our comrades from organizing the evacuation of our combatants and the best-known comrades, as we had planned.

After Casado's victory, when the Communist hunt was on, the comrades who by order of the party had remained in Spain now left. There was nothing more for them to do in Spain; any sacrifice now would be useless.

Dozens of Communists taken prisoner in the days of the junta were handed over to Franco by the junta's agents, in particular by Melchor Rodríguez, an Anarchist.

Courageous soldiers who had defended Madrid, among them Domingo Girón, Cazorla, Ascanio, Mesón and many others, were sent to Franco and later shot. They died as bravely as they had lived, showing their fascist executioners that Communists knew how to fight and die.

The British government, the instigator and patron of Casado's junta, as it was earlier of the nonintervention policy, sent a battleship to a Valencian port to pick up and save the traitors, who left Spain with the mark of Cain on their foreheads.

The valiant armed resistance of the Spanish people against fascist military aggression and foreign intervention had come to an end.

"Honorable peace," fascist peace, the peace of the jails and cemeteries, extended its sway over Spain, bringing mourning and sorrow to thousands of homes.

# A New Beginning

A glorious and tragic page of our history was drawing to a close. A new period of fighting was beginning.

Those who had fallen were invincible. A new generation of combatants was germinating quietly in the furrows that the war had plowed into the bleeding land of Spain.

Over a country in chains, over the Spain of prisons, of torture, of summary executions, had come the light of new faith and hope. The light that inspired the epic resistance of our people against perfidious aggression; the light that guides humanity toward the future; the light that radiates from the depths of suffering of a nation and breaks through the thick walls of prisons, saying to all the world with the ringing voice of an immortal people:

Spain lives! Spain fights! Spain is!

A new generation now exists in Spain. The generation of 1939. It is not a monolithic block; it is rather diverse, composed of workers, students, intellectuals and peasants. A single generation with various interests, various aspirations, but with a common bond: They are anti-Franco.

Of the bloody three years' war in Spain's cities and fields, a part of this new generation knows only the official version, the distorted and lying rationalization of Franco's great crime. Another part of this generation knows only its family's version—the painful, tragic and emotional side.

By different routes, from different and distant starting points, one and the other have arrived at the same resolution: "To fight to free the living from the burden of the dead. To continue the history of Spain that Franco stopped dead in its tracks."

For centuries, the Escorial's tombs cast their gloom over the country. The Monument to the Fallen Heroes cannot stand as a barrier to the further advance of our people. Let the dead bury the dead.

The new generation which grew up muzzled and trussed in the shadow of Franco's prisons rejects the Spain built by the Falange with the aid of foreign bayonets, the Spain built by the Franco dictatorship with blood and mud. The Franco dictatorship acts as a brake and a chain. Its disappearance is a historical necessity.

At the crossroads where the hopes and desires of the new generation meet, there is a signpost marked with a question: "Shall we return to the past?"

The reply can be found in life itself. The past can never be retrieved. Spain and the world around it are today different from the Spain and the world of 1930, or even of 1936.

Profound changes have taken place, changes that do not favor the old dominant castes. Today, the Socialist camp exists and grows stronger each day, spreading its influence even in countries under imperialist rule. This rule is still powerful and in its craving for more power it can still bring terrible suffering to the people. But it has lost its dominant position in the world. Today it cannot, as it had done in the past, control at its will the pace of industrial development in this or that country, nor the technological development of other nations, nor can it dominate the scientific world. It is rapidly being outdistanced by the rate of development of the Socialist countries, chiefly by the Soviet Union.

This is not a partisan boast, but the inescapable truth. We do indeed live in the era of the collapse of capitalism and the triumph of Socialism.

In Spain the people have experienced various forms of political bourgeois domination: monarchy, republic, fascist dictatorship. In the crucible of war, men, parties, doctrines, actions and systems have been put to a crucial test.

From this recent, living, tremendously instructive experience an irrefutable conclusion has emerged: Only the forces representing the true interests of the country, that express the currents of social development, and move forward with them can provide a base for the political rebirth, the economic and cultural rebirth of Spain.

Do I mean a Socialist solution? Yes, emphatically yes. Only a Socialist solution can stop the interminable procession of revolutions and counterrevolutions which have been the history of the Spanish state.

A Socialist solution in step with the needs and desires of the nation, with the participation of not only Marxists, Social-Democrats and Anarcho-Syndicalists, but of all groups and sectors who do not fear the historically inevitable changes in the economic and political structure of our country.

Only Socialism can release the immense stores of energy, vitality and capacity now lying dormant in Spain's people. Only Socialism can wipe out the centuries-old backwardness of our country.

Only Socialism can put an end to sterile centralism, regionalism and backward provincialism. Only Socialism can eliminate social inequalities and reorganize the structure of the Spanish state on new economic and political bases. Only Socialism can bring about a renaissance, inconceivable and impossible to achieve under the present system or any similar one.

And we are not dealing here with a situation that must be forced. If Socialism arises naturally as a stage in the development of society, then the road leading to it is not determined solely by the wills of men. It appears under specific conditions determined by historic causes.

In the past, when capitalism's reign over the world was absolute, the road to Socialism was conceived chiefly in terms of civil wars and violent revolution. But today, without entirely repudiating force, the use of which is determined by the degree of resistance offered by the dying classes, there is the possibility of a pacific route, of a democratic road toward Socialism; a road which may be long and subject to conflicts and collisions. This road is marked by the daily, constant, permanent struggle in both the political and economic spheres to take the next step forward, to make each structural change as the need arises.

The war in Spain offers many useful lessons to the new generations.

While we were fighting the war we were also making a democratic revolution with characteristics such as had never existed in previous bourgeois revolutions. This did not happen without violent resistance from the Republican camp itself, as these pages have shown.

Revolution is the motor of history. Entire peoples find themselves authors of marvelous feats during a revolution. But revolution as it moves forward also brings to the surface the sediment, the dregs of society. It uncovers ambitions and stimulates the appetites of politicians who try to harness the revolution in their service. These dangers must be fought against firmly, as the Communist Party fought against those who, all during the war, wanted to distort the character of the revolution to their own advantage.

While these destructive elements may be inevitable, it cannot serve as a reason to avoid the revolutionary struggle or of resorting to the cynical catchphrase, "they're all the same," coined by the revolution's enemies.

We are not all the same. The history of Spain in the last 30 years has shown the differences between the conscientious revolutionary and the occasional one; between those who work to better the lot of all the people and contribute to the development of the country, and those who play politics at the level of their own personal or group interests.

Resistance to fascist aggression was begun under the Popular Front headed by a petty-bourgeois Republican government. The resistance was mainly carried on by the workers and peasants, members of various organizations and subject to their respective disciplines and attitudes.

The unity of the Popular Front was not solid. It was not based on the unity of the working class. The Popular Front comprised different classes, different sectors, different interests and different political groups. For this reason, the Republic was beset by contradictions and conflicts with every step it took, all the more because the Basque Nationalists and the Anarchists who were in the anti-Franco camp were not members of the Popular Front.

This also gave rise to different criteria, different opinions, different manners of envisioning the war and its perspectives—all of which weighed heavily on the political and military life of the Spanish Republic.

At times we Communists failed to show the necessary flexibility in the face of positions which we considered harmful to the resistance; or we did not sufficiently criticize or evaluate defeatist attitudes and obscure maneuvers. Nevertheless, not for one moment either then or now have we underestimated the historic and revolutionary importance of the participation of the democratic bourgeoisie in the popular resistance to fascism.

The many negative factors in the Republican camp, both on the eve of the fascist uprising and afterwards during the war, do not testify against, but decidedly in favor of, the need for unity, understanding, compromise between different democratic groups and parties in our country; in favor of the need for a compromise even with those elements who, because of their composition, their interests, their way of seeing and understanding life, can accept only a minimal role in the realization of democratic changes in the political structure of the Spanish state.

Above all, what the Spanish war conclusively showed was that without the unity of the working class, the leadership of a democratic revolution will inevitably fall into the hands of the bourgeoisie, which will slow down the revolution, will stop it halfway and will even transform it into a weapon against the proletariat.

Franco's victory paralyzed Spain's democratic development. After three long decades of fascist dictatorship, the political and economic problems which have plagued Spain's historical development, and which during the war were just beginning to be solved by the Republican government, are still very much with us—only worse, far more in crying need of solution. The roots of the unity of democratic and working-class forces, of all national sectors desirous of bringing progress to Spain, are still very much alive.

It is the mission of Spain's youth to give impetus to this broad, Spanish unity; to wipe out the past of reaction and backwardness; to wipe out the present of jails and terrors and corruption.

The youth of Spain are our hope. I am confident that they will take, that they are now taking, the only way that makes heroes of simple men, that makes them builders of a new life, of a new world: the way of struggle for democracy, for peace and for socialism.